FITTED UP

FITTED UP

THE MITCHAM CO-OP MURDER AND THE FIGHT TO PROVE MY INNOCENCE

GEORGE THATCHER

First published 2014

The History Press
The Mill, Brimscombe Port
Stroud, Gloucestershire, GL5 2QG
www.thehistorypress.co.uk

British Library Cataloguing in Publication Data.
A catalogue record for this book is available from the British Library.

ISBN 978 0 7509 5965 0

Typesetting and origination by The History Press
Printed in Great Britain

Foreword by Anthony May

In 1972, the playwright David Halliwell replied to an advert in the back pages of the *New Statesman* which said: 'Lifer needs help. PO BOX 142.' The lifer was a man called George Thatcher who had been convicted of the capital murder of Dennis Hurden during a robbery at the Mitcham Co-op in 1963 and sentenced to death.

He was defended by the eminent lawyer, Christmas Humphreys, who has been credited with introducing Buddhism to the United Kingdom. He had been the senior counsel at the Old Bailey responsible for the successful prosecutions of Ruth Ellis, and Bentley and Craig. The summing up by Mr Justice Roskill lasted six hours and was clearly biased towards the prosecution. The jury was out for just four hours.

After four weeks in the condemned cell, George Thatcher was reprieved, but was to spend the next eighteen years in prison for a crime he did not commit. David, who wrote the 1960's hit play 'Little Malcolm and his struggle against the eunochs' built up a relationship with George, visiting him in prison and encouraging him to write firstly a document telling his side of the story and then two plays. David, myself and the actor Michael Elphick travelled to the Albany prison on the Isle of Wight to see George.

It was a high security jail and after passing through several barred gates we eventually were ushered into a small reception room where George was waiting for us. He seemed in total control as he gestured to the guard to leave us alone. I don't recall much of the conversation, but I do remember a guard bringing in a landscape painting. 'The gift for your friends,' he said to George.

As soon as the Isle of Wight ferry left the shore we went to the very windy upper deck and carefully pulled off the back of the painting and there was George's first play 'The Hundred Watt Bulb' which was put on at the 'Little Theatre' in St Martin's Lane. George wrote another play 'The Only Way Out' about his experience in the condemned cell which was put on at the Royal Court. Michael played him in the original production and Brian Croucher, who became a good friend to George, reprised the role in a later production. It received excellent reviews. *The Times* wrote 'George Frederick Thatcher has been awarded an Arts council grant of £50 for his play, but what he is likely to receive for it is a spell in the punishment block as his play was sent out of prison without permission.' George , eventually was given a pass out to see his play performed – but a week after the play finished !

After being interviewed about Michael Elphick for his The History Press biography, I decided to reread the document written by George about his case and his plight. Unfortunately, it had become damaged after forty years in a weather-beaten loft, but with the help of the actors Stephen Greif and Brian Croucher, I tracked George down to a small village in western Ireland where by an amazing coincidence he was living, with his wife Val, next door to some old friends of mine, Neil Johnston and Mark Long. We managed to get hold of, not only the original story, but an autobiography of George's life which you are now about to read. It is a riveting tale of poverty, injustice, incompetence, skullduggery, survival and ultimately freedom.

Stephen Greif and I have spent many hours going through the Metropolitan Police files and the trial transcript at the National Archives and we are both convinced that George did not shoot and kill Dennis Hurden, the Co-op worker who happened to be in the wrong place at the wrong time. The only evidence against George was police verbal evidence, which was clearly fabricated, and the dubious statements of Phillip Kelly, who on the last day of the trial and just after the Judge had put on the black cap, stood up and said 'I shot Dennis Hurden.'

To be sentenced to death and then imprisoned for eighteen years for a crime one didn't commit is the ultimate nightmare and hopefully in the near future he will be exonerated.

My thanks to Val Thatcher, for all her help; David Halliwell; Mark Beynon of The History Press; and above all to George for allowing his story to be told.

I was born on 27 August 1929, in a small country town called Farnham in the county of Surrey in southern England. A year behind my brother, Bill, and four years ahead of my sister, Mary (though I know not where they were born, as my parents tended to be a migrant family, who moved house every few years). My mother's maiden name was Lillian Kitchen. She was a warm and simple country girl to whom life wasn't over-generous. She had two brothers and a sister named Maud. Their father was a farm labourer who lived in an isolated country cottage on the outskirts of a village called Beckham, one mile from the town of Marlow in Buckinghamshire on the banks of the River Thames.

My mum's brothers emigrated in their teens, just after the First World War. One went to America to work on the railways in New York, and was last heard of living in Brooklyn, many years ago. The other brother went to Australia as a deckhand on a steam ship and was never heard of again. So there may be lots of distant cousins around the world that we know nothing of.

I am a believer that family are first in all things. That the first rule of life is survival and people born and raised in poverty do not owe allegiance to any establishment.

My mother's sister, Maud, married a local lad and lived in Beckham all her life. She ran the post office and sweet shop from the tiny front room of her cottage. They had one daughter who also married a local lad, who ran the village pub many years ago.

My father was a fine-looking man, who was born and grew up in Marlow. He had two brothers, George and Bill. All three went into the forces at the beginning of the First World War. My dad, Charley, went into the army with George, who was killed in France in 1917.

Bill joined the Royal Navy and served twenty-two years before losing an arm to gangrene and being pensioned out. He never married, and lived the remainder of this life in Marlow, never worked, spending most of his time in the local pubs, maintaining that beer was the substance your body needed for a good life. He was a happy, kind man who always had love and time for me, often telling me tales of the sea which I'm sure were mostly fantasies he would invent to entertain me. When I was about ten, he would come to the house at five in the morning and take me into the fields to find and collect wild mushrooms, which he sold or cooked for breakfast, before Bill and I went off to school. At one time I had no shoes and wore girls' slippers and felt so ashamed; we were always very poor.

After the war, my father soldiered in India for eleven years, before returning to Marlow and marrying my mother. Not a good match. He was proud of having been a military man, always acting like a soldier, stiff and upright. I don't remember him ever being cruel or unkind to Bill or I, though we saw little of him. He was either working at various seasonal jobs on the land or for the council, or in the various pubs in the town. He would try to teach us discipline and loyalty – keep your mouth shut and never tell tales or snitch on anyone – to be strong to survive in an underprivileged world that offered no charity of love for the meek, where those who had, had no time for those who hadn't, and it's only the strong who survive.

The first recollection I have, as a very young child was taking a neighbour's little girl into the middle of the ripening cornfields at the bottom of the small crescent of council houses where we lived, to play doctors and nurses – naughty maybe, but at four it was to play, curious and totally innocent. When my mother found us, she put me to bed for the rest of the day. Later, in the winter I would walk across those frost-covered fields, on my way to junior school, crying with the cold and the chilblains on my toes and the lobes of my ears.

Those early years I could have been an only child, as I have no recollection or images of my brother, Bill, as a playmate or companion – though we shared the same bed and I wore the old clothes he grew out of. We were dirt poor, and I remember my mother telling me how she would take the pram and walk us the long miles to the closing market on a Saturday afternoon, in Aldershot town, when the produce would be sold off very cheaply – she would have $1s$ $6d$ to do the week's shopping to feed three kids, and she would tell how she would take me into the fields to pick the potatoes in harvest time.

We lived in a little village called Ash, before moving into Station Road on the southern edge of Marlow. It was then 1937, and Bill and I attended the local church school where the pupils were graded at twin desks, according to their abilities. Bill and I sat together at the bottom of the class. Our teacher had a gold pocket watch which he kept in a velvet pouch in his waistcoat pocket, regularly taking it out for polishing.

We soon moved from Station Road to a smaller, cheaper semi-detached cottage near the town centre where the loo was 100 yards away at the end of a narrow lane. Next door to us lived the Prices, a family of seven – three young boys with two older sisters – all sharing the same bed in a house no bigger than a matchbox. We were separated by a thin lath and plaster wall that had a hole in the corner which we spoke through. Dickie, their eldest lad, was Bill's age and they soon became bosom pals and spent most of their time together, occasionally letting me tag along when they went off into the woods or fishing and swimming in the river.

I was a dyslexic, quiet child who spent lots of time exploring the fields with a small mongrel dog that a little girl had given me. My parents were constantly arguing, and I would leave the house to climb over the wall at the end of the lane into the playing fields of the nearby grammar school to get away from it, feeling outcast and alone. One day, my mother took Mary and left, leaving Bill and I with our dad, to run wild in the back streets, into the night to steal the lights from the bikes parked outside the picture house to play 'Dickie, show your light' in the unlit alleys around the town.

I was taken into care when I was eight, and put with foster parents some miles away where I stayed till the outbreak of war. My father re-entered the army and my mother and Mary returned, taking me back home. We only saw my father after that when he got his bit of leave.

With the war came rationing, both food and clothes, and we cooked what we had on an old stove in the corner of the room with dead wood we collected from where we could find it.

Before my dad re-joined the army he had worked on an estate as a game-keeper, where the manor house was surrounded by a forest of dying trees that I would often explore or play in. It was a few miles down the road from our home. Once, my father was back with the forces and we needed fuel for the fire as it was winter time and the house was bitterly cold, so I borrowed a builder's cart and went looking. I collected a pile of dead wood by the entrance to the estate, where my dad once worked, ready to freight away. The lord of the manor appeared and told me to leave it and to get off his land. I headed for home and watched him disappear, then went back and loaded the barrow. My young sister was at home crying with the cold and, to me, stealing firewood was not a big deal. Halfway home, a copper came along on his bike to arrest me and I got convicted for stealing. I was thirteen, and got my first conviction and enrolment on the official 's★★t list', which would grow in the years to come.

Mary, as I remember, was around without being obvious, and spent her time with my mother. Boys and girls were not encouraged to be equal in those days – boys went to boys' schools, girls went to girls', girls played with girls, boys played with boys – not just sexually and physically different, encouraged to be humanly different and think differently about relationships and behaviour towards each other. Girls were domestic and boys paid the rent. We knew we had a sister and that was about it.

Before school in the mornings, I got a paper round for 2s a week at a shop across the street. At the same time, an afternoon job and after school, running errands and putting up the shutters at a jeweller's shop. The jeweller would give me money to pay for the postage for his out-going mail and I would pocket the change – till one day he asked me for it, and gave me the sack.

At 5 p.m. on a Wednesday afternoon, I went to the manor house in the centre of town to polish the family silver for sixpence, and I joined the choir at the local church as a choir boy to get twopence for attending practice, and I joined the Protestant Chapel and the Salvation Army when their annual summer outing was due, and I dug a lady's garden for the cash to buy my first pair of long trousers.

I was growing into a big strong lad and was never bullied, while Bill often had fights at the back of the school yard, but I only remember one that he lost. Then one day the German bombers came to raid the town and missed completely, leaving massive craters in the fields by the river and when they filled with water, I would swim in them. I stole apples from the orchards, strawberries from the fields and pears from the cricket club.

A paedophile worked in the tailor's shop at the top of the high street, who to me was just a queer guy. I had nothing to tell them, and wouldn't have done, anyway. Most kids who lack attention are easy prey for paedophiles as they offer kids affection – a reality.

Shortly after this, I had my tonsils out with several other kids. We were bussed to a town 5 miles away to sit in a bare room to wait our turn. We were all terrified. A mask was put over our noses and ether dripped onto it. The smell of it was diabolical. Late in the afternoon, they bussed us home in various states of shock. A few weeks later, I developed a mastoid and was shipped to London for several operations.

When the saturation bombing of London they called 'the blitz' was over, life was reasonably normal and we moved to rooms on the top floor of a Victorian terrace in Tulse Hill, south London.

Then came the doodle bugs – the V2 flying bomb, one of the first generation of rockets, designed more as a terror weapon than anything else. These things made a loud popping noise as they flew low overhead and could be heard miles away. They were totally indiscriminate, launched from sites in France to destroy London, and kill and demoralise.

I left school at fourteen – academically a non-starter. I got a job in a local pet shop, delivering pet food in the area on a bicycle, six days a week for £1. Bill worked next door as the storeman for a local grocer. In those days, the shops shut for lunch – 1 p.m. to 2 p.m. – and we would ride our bikes home, a mile away. Some days, Bill would shut the warehouse and have lunch on the sacks of grain in the back with the ginger-headed counter girl from the grocer's shop, and tell mum he had to work over. He was more mature than me in many ways.

One Tuesday, as I remember it, we were at home having lunch – a lump of bread and a piece of cheese – and we heard the sound of the doodle bug coming over, and we all sat silently, holding our breath. When the engine stopped, the bomb came down – and it stopped right above us and cracked down in the street below. We were up and out in seconds, helping to find and rescue people from the debris of the house, and I lifted a three-year-old child with no face left, from beneath the rubble – that seems like only yesterday – and I never took the bike back to the pet shop or worked there again. Shortly after this we were bombed out ourselves and moved to Kennington Oval, further into central London.

Bill and I were growing fast – over 6ft and filling out. Both a little on the wild side – never staying in one job for long, and no concentrated interest in anything. Bill seemed to work more regularly than me and often worked as a prop-maker and stagehand in West End theatres, while I did more bumming around, as London became more vibrant with the fever of war and a brooding atmosphere of expectation for a Normandy invasion.

There were foreign soldiers everywhere and most of them were GIs, and many of them were living on nervous energy as they lived from day to day, waiting to invade Europe and die a hero's death – to leave their mothers in tears. They all seemed like glamorous guys in smart uniforms with pockets full of money, full of bravado and uncertainty and wanting a good time. They all seemed so wealthy and so eager to treat. We thought they were all millionaires who wanted to give it away. We were all too young to know that they didn't all come from Hollywood, and that half of them wouldn't live to see another Christmas.

All the young girls had a field day as they 'did their bit' for the morale of the troops. This was now 1943 and I was still fourteen, learning to live by the day, and the western world was rapidly revamping its Victorian attitudes. Sex before marriage was popping up everywhere. Divorce was only for the film stars, although being a virgin on the right way was a desirable achievement. The GIs opened many doors to new ways and everybody loved them, though some, of course, were straight out of the hills and as naive and 'the good life' as the rest of us. They opened the Rainbow Corner in Piccadilly – a massive PX store and leisure centre in the heart of London, like a honey pot in a land of flies. It became the place where things were happening.

Bill and I were working at a fruit and vegetable warehouse in Covent Garden – me as a porter, Bill as a delivery driver, taking fresh fruit and vegetables to the Ministry of Defence and various hotels in central London, on a horse and cart. Bill was sixteen. He would get up at 6 a.m. and take the underground train from the Oval to Leicester Square to clean and feed his horse at a stable in Soho – that poor old horse never saw a stream or walked a field, and Bill drove the cart round the streets as if it was a chariot. Then one day he had a row with the firm's salesman, who he punched on the chin and laid out in the gutter, and got the sack.

I stayed on a couple of weeks till I got the sack myself. I had been sent out with a young delivery driver who nicked a 28lb block of butter from the kitchen of a hotel we delivered to. He dropped the butter into an empty fruit box in the back of the van and took it to a friend's. He saved the fruit box in the back of the van with a lump of butter stuck on the side. We were nicked when we returned to the warehouse – me as an accomplice – and in the magistrates' court the next day I was fined two quid and got the sack. I was just fifteen.

We often nicked things to finance our lives. We all got into minor bits of trouble, though nothing of much account in those early days. There was so much temptation in a world of uncertainty that nobody really cared. There was challenge in the atmosphere, and a black market everywhere, and in the unconsciousness of the times, many things we got up to on a regular basis were a feature of the times and seem now much more bizarre than they really were.

The West End was then becoming the centre of the universe for the street kids I was growing up with. I was making new friends all the time, and doing all sorts of things, and gradually growing into the subculture in a quite natural way. We had no peer groups to imitate so we did whatever we wanted to do – and we were always looking for opportunities. We became known and identified as 'spivs' – guys who lived on their wits – sharp dressers, in suits we called 'drapes' with padded shoulders and long lapels, cut away just below the bum. They had to be tailor-made and very expensive, and it would take weeks to hoard enough money to pay for them. Our shoes we called 'creepers' – soft, silent soles to creep around on – moving around without making a sound, living one day at a time. Interested only in the moment – or what was on at the cinema – and more energy than you know what to do with. I worked when things got desperate, and gave my mother some money each week. Otherwise, it was anything goes.

I guess there were people around who considered our behaviour antisocial at times, but what can anyone expect from that sort of environment? We lived life to the full with what we had, and being young and without control, we took nothing seriously and most things for granted.

In those early war years, the London Opera House in Covent Garden was used as a dance hall, but by the time the Yanks came in '44, the dance had moved to the Lyceum just down the road at the corner of the Strand, and that soon became a rendezvous for the budding youth from in and around the Elephant and Castle, the Lambeth Walk, and the Old Kent Road. Bill and I soon found our own way in, which wasn't through the front door. We discovered we could open the rear exit doors from the outside with a thin iron rod with a hook on the end. We kept this rod on a ledge above the emergency doors of the Lyceum, and used it on all the cinemas and theatres in the West End to see the shows we couldn't otherwise afford.

Things were so much easier to do and get away with then, as long as you played the game and lived by the rules in your neighbourhood, you were accepted. Nobody seemed to care very much about anything, so long as you didn't give anyone any trouble – role models, for what they were, were Sinatra, Humphrey Bogart, Edward G., James Cagney, Robert Mitchum, Burt Lancaster and any other macho, smart, tough guys. It was more important to be smart than tough – and clever, rather than thick. None of my friends seemed to care about drugs or booze, although both were available even then. Cannabis and cocaine were in the jazz clubs and seemed to be restricted mainly to the music world.

My best friend at the time was a couple of months older than me. His name was Chick Jacobs, he lived by the underground station at Kennington Oval, just around the corner from the Oval cricket ground. His dad was a pickpocket who worked with a bunch of other 'dips' and was often away for weeks. He was also on the run from the army so didn't feel safe at home. We lived behind Kennington Park, and I would wander over to Chick's about 10 a.m. and chat with his mum and aunty Flo, who was living with them (her husband was away in the forces and she was in her early twenties). I can't remember the exact details, but I do remember her and me standing in a doorway opposite Chick's house, watching out for the military police because Chick's dad was at home. We acted like lovers, and she tried to seduce me but I didn't know what to do, and I was tall and she was short – and it was all very awkward – we didn't get beyond some heavy petting and she got really p★★★★d off with me.

It was about this time that my father died, after being wounded in France. I remember my mother having to go to Manchester where he was in hospital, and I had to collect my sister, who was ten years old and staying with an aunt, and take her on the train to visit him. He had a head wound and didn't live very long. We hadn't been much of a family really – nevertheless, I felt the loss and remember it vividly, although I cannot remember how supportive I was to my mother at that time, or how it was for her.

Our home in Kennington was very basic – camp beds in otherwise bare rooms. We didn't have much going for us, but neither did the rest of the neighbourhood – which consisted mainly of bombed and derelict houses – no wonder I was a bit wild and insensitive in many ways. I look back on that period with both wonder and regret. That was my world – lacking understanding and short of wisdom, with loyalty only to my friends – never giving a second thought – thought was somewhere in the back streets, hidden in the debris. My mother applied for a war widow's pension and discovered that she wasn't entitled – as my dad already had a wife in India with two children!

Chick and I met up in the mornings to plan our days to suit our moods. Sometimes we would wander off to meet friends outside Jane's Café in the Lambeth Walk, play dice with them on the pavement and get the local gossip, then maybe spend the rest of the day mooching around the West End to see what was going on – or look for earners and fool around. One day, Bill was with us and we picked up a wad of yesterday's unsold newspapers from the doorway of the Turkish baths at Charing Cross, then sold them in the rush hour outside the underground stations, when people were too busy to notice what they were getting – stupid stuff like that.

I was still only fifteen, and already 6ft when the war in Europe ended, and when it did, everything went wild for a few days – singing and dancing in the streets of central London, like nothing before.

People came from everywhere, by the millions it seemed, and it was often impossible to move around. This was the war in Europe, the one in the east with the Japanese was on its way to ending a few months later.

Both Chick and I began bumming around, getting bolder and a little more reckless. We often started the day by waiting at the traffic lights on the corner where we lived. Waiting for lorries going in the direction of the City or the West End. Lorries in those days were mostly flat-backs with canvas canopies. When one we fancied stopped for the traffic lights, we'd wait for the lights to change and as the lorry moved off we would jump on the back and go wherever it was going, then jump off when we wanted to. If there was anything sellable on the back, we'd lift it. We always got on or off these lorries when they were moving so the driver wouldn't notice any unusual movement.

It was on one of these excursions, a couple of months after the end of the war, that we landed up on Leadenhall Street in the City. The City of London is the business centre, and Leadenhall Street is where all the major shipping companies have their headquarters. I had romantic ideas of sailing the seven seas and going to exotic places. In one of those shipping offices I was given an application form to fill in so I could join the merchant navy. They had to be signed by my mother as I was just sixteen. A few weeks later, a letter arrived from the Seaman's Federation for me to report to a training ship on the Bristol Channel in January 1946. It was now October 1945.

Walking home late one night, Bill, Chick and I had been wandering around the West End. The buses had stopped as it was past midnight. On the way we decided to break into a large wine warehouse we had to pass. We certainly weren't thinking of emptying the place, as we had no transport. I don't know what we were thinking, if anything at all. Bill was pretty good at getting into places – he seemed to have a knack for it – and in no time at all we were inside doing our best to drink the place dry. We came out of there several hours later, hardly sober enough to stand and, within no time, we were nicked for being drunk and disorderly. By the time we had sobered up it had been discovered that the wine place had been raided, and we were nicked for breaking and entering; and I've never since acquired a flavour for booze.

We were sent for trial a couple of weeks later and Bill and Chick got thirty days. I would have got the same if I hadn't been due to leave London to go to sea. Instead I was given two years' probation, which was considered better than going to jail – though, like most things, it had its shortfalls. By the time Bill and Chick got out of jail I was gone.

I guess this was really the point in time when Bill and I drifted in separate directions and into separate lives, never living together again, though we would see each other when either of us were around. By the time I came back from my first trip away, he had taken up with a girl, got married and moved into his own place with a regular job making stage sets, before he was conscripted into the Royal Navy. So we never seemed to be in the same place at the same time very often. When he came out of the navy he had a four-year-old daughter called Christine, and discovered that his wife had been fooling around – so he quit and landed up in Australia.

I don't know what happened then, or if they were divorced, only that Bill signed on with the P&O shipping company who were then trucking families to Australia on the £10 emigration scheme. He had a nine month contract and signed off in Sydney, worked a while in the outback with a pal named Jeff; formed and performed in a travelling entertainment group; met and married a lovely Oz girl named Loll, in MacLean, Queensland, and had two kids. They spent fifty years together. Bill was deeply wounded by his life in England, and blanked it out completely when he settled in Oz and would never talk about it.

But before that, after the trial and the probation order, there were a few days before I had to leave and I was bumming around late one night with an older pal in Oxford Street, just around the corner from the PX. He introduced me to a girlfriend standing in the shadows of a doorway. Her name was Doris Peach, and she was every bit a peach. She was a very attractive twenty-five-year-old hooker with a regular pitch. My friend wanted me to get laid before I went away, and Doris liked the idea. She took me home to her flat in

Black Lion Yard in the East End. Black Lion Yard was a tiny narrow street of Jewish jewellery shops and she had a flat above one of them.

Doris was my first serious sexual experience, and all that went before was just fooling around. We liked each other, and over the next few years we would occasionally meet up and spend time together. There was never any commitment between us and never anything prearranged. I would call her up and go over, and we would spend a bit of time together; then I'd disappear until the next time. I don't remember why I stopped calling. I think I'd been away for a while, and we both lost interest. Other things were happening, and now I can't remember what she looked like, except she had blonde hair and beautiful legs; though I don't really remember them either, only that they were beautiful and that our relationship was totally undemanding and very laid-back.

2

In January 1946, I joined a training ship in the Bristol Channel on the West Coast. It was an old four rigged German schooner called the *Vindicatrix*. We slept in hammocks on the crowded lower decks, and washed at six in the morning in cold water on icy upper decks. It was so cold in January that we had to break the icicles from the rigging, and row the life boats across the Severn Estuary in bitter winds. We were there for two months to learn basic seamanship skills like compass reading and sailors' knots, and pass lifeboat exams, without which you weren't allowed in the union. Then you got your seaman's book to record the ships you sailed in.

As soon as the course was finished I signed on at the Seaman's Pool at London Docks. The Pool was then the job centre for seamen where you would sign a contract to sail on whatever ship you chose to go on. At the Pool they told you what ships were in port, what hands the ship needed and where it was going. I signed onto one of the newer motor vessels that were replacing the coal burners. It was called the *Pardo*, belonging to the Royal Mail Company and sailing to South America. It was a 5,000 ton cargo ship with a crew of twenty-five.

In those days there were no container ships, and all cargoes were loaded on and off by stevedores which could sometimes take a couple of weeks – which meant two weeks in port and time to see the sights and visit the bars. I can remember that first trip quite well – as we all remember the first time for most things.

All ships' contracts in those days were for two years, and you could sign off when the two years were up in any Commonwealth country in the world that the ship docked in. (At that time, over a quarter of the world was British Commonwealth.) If, in that period of two years, the ship returned to the original port of contract the whole crew would sign off and then sign a fresh contract if they wanted to. Most seamen are wanderers and all ships are different; so, new ships, new places, new crew, new friends, and new experiences, was the way of life for most seamen, who couldn't really cope with a 9–5 job. Going to the same place every day, the same routine of having to get up every morning at the same time, catch the same bus, and waste the time travelling to work. It all seemed such a waste to earn money to pay for a ride that was more a burden than a joy. I thought there must be better ways to live than that.

The *Pardo* was going to be in London Docks for a week, unloading corned beef from Argentina. I signed on as the galley boy, and put on 8lb in the week before sailing for Liverpool. I had never before had access to so much food, or even dreamt that I would peel so many potatoes or wash so many dishes. We were in Liverpool for ten days, taking on cargo for South Africa; including four race horses for Rio in horse boxes on the after deck. The night before we sailed I went to Lime Street, hoping to meet 'Maggie May' – the girl that every sailor told stories about, and who had broken a thousand hearts, including Rod Stewart's. 'They've taken her away,' they said, so I went to the movies and saw *Brief Encounter* and thought it was wonderful. In the morning, as the sun rose, we set off for the Canary Islands. For a wage of £2.50 a week we were going to Rio de Janeiro, and I was having a good time except for the endless sacks of potatoes I had to peel by hand. I would sit on a capstan by the ship's rail with two buckets of water and peel away, watching the sea for dolphins while getting a golden sun tan. We refuelled in the Canary Islands, where small boys actually sold canaries in bamboo cages on the dockside. Then headed south-west for the ten day trip across the South Atlantic to Rio. Watching shoals of flying fish, surrounded by the calm silence of the deep blue sea, and the circling horizon a straight line everywhere. The sun as wide as your open arms, gradually sinking out of sight – then Rio with the early dawn, its sky scrapers rising slowly through the haze like enchanting fingers, larger and larger as they filled the horizon ahead in a mystical, futuristic way, like no other.

There are many things I recall of those days, which mean more to me than they will to anyone else, and as time moved on, in years of solitude these memories lived with me. Sitting on the stern deck late into the evening, listening to old hands spinning yarns of places they had been, sights they had seen, the lovers they had in exotic places. All the stuff that captures the imagination, and leaves you wanting more; enchanting tales to fill your dreams, while sleeping in makeshift hammocks on the open decks, covered in the warm, South Atlantic breeze.

Rio was sunshine and samba, and my pay was gone on the first day. My free time I spent on Copacabana beach, daydreaming and watching the golden legs of the girls going by. Most of that Copacabana skyline was funded by ex-cons from Devil's Island who had prospected the jungles of Brazil.

From there, we shipped south to Santos, and from Montevideo to Buenos Aires, then back to Rio, to London and one day's leave for every week away. That gave me three weeks to bum around and catch up with my friends – and occasional nights with Doris, and freebies at the cinemas and dance halls.

Months later, I was working as a steward on the cross-Channel ferry, from Dover to Calais (part of the Golden Arrow link from London to Paris). Tuesday was my free day. The ferry docked in Dover at 5 p.m. on Monday, and I would catch the boat train to London at 6 p.m., and join up with my friends at the Hammersmith Palais at 8 p.m. for the regular Monday spot, where I met my first regular girlfriend.

Her name was Betty Webster, and she wore draped jackets with padded shoulders and wrap-around skirts. She lived in the Old Kent Road with her parents, and younger brother who suffered from smelly feet. Betty was two years older than me and worked as an accountant in the City in the day time, and was part of the regular crowd in the evenings.

The Hammersmith Palais dance hall was the place to be on a Monday night. Ted Heath's band was the big noise of the time, and his lead singer – Paul Carpenter – crooned like Sinatra. Our crowd were into jiving – which entailed a routine with a regular partner – and after the Palais closed that night, I met Betty. She gave me her office phone number so I could call her the following day, before returning to Dover. So began a regular Monday meeting until I quit the Golden Arrow.

New Year's Eve that year was on a Monday, and plans were made for partying, but on that morning I was told the company wanted to transfer me to their sister-ship in a place called Folkestone, which meant

I would lose my day off and I would miss the New Year activities. So I quit, and that night a crowd of us gate-crashed the Chelsea Arts Ball – the major event of the year, and the first since the end of the war.

A month passed before I joined another ship and sailed for America and, when I returned, the new meeting place was the Friday night dance, in a hall above Burton's tailor shop in Brixton. The dance was over, and I was going to spend the night with friends in the Walworth Road, so we caught the tramcar on the corner. The tramcars were like you see in San Francisco or Hong Kong – rattly iron boxes that rocked and rolled on narrow lines down the middle of the streets. We had been on the top deck, and were getting off at the next stop, on our feet heading for the stairs, when the tramcar swerved on a sharp bend and I lost my balance and fell between two bench seats. I raised my arm as I fell towards the window and the glass shattered, cutting through the ligaments of my left hand, putting me out of action for several weeks. It was almost a year before I could use my hand normally and I never went to sea again.

Out of money and out of luck. The union gave me two quid a week, not enough for an extravagant lifestyle or to put enough food into a hungry face. So, I looked for other ways, and I soon teamed up with some other guys who were in the salvage business. The oldest one was about twenty-seven, quite old by our standards. He had TB and so was physically unfit for the armed services. He also had a truck, and we would meet up in the morning at a local café in the Lambeth Walk for a breakfast of beans on toast, then cruise out to areas, still sparsely populated, where there were streets of large empty houses waiting to be renovated from the war damage.

You didn't have to break into these places, because most of them had no doors or any windows and we would work away like any normal working crew and remove the lead, which we took to various scrap merchants. Scrap lead fetched a high price, and in one day each of us would earn what most workers earned in a month. It was, of course, a short-lived opportunity. Despite the ravages of war, people were returning to London, and you couldn't go to the same street too often without being noticed. The scrap merchants never asked questions and were as keen to do a trade as we were, and there were quite a few of them about. Some even ordered items like sinks from us. They all seemed to have larceny in their hearts, like everyone else I knew. When the salvage business began to dry up as the empty streets began to fill, we would nick the lead from one merchant and sell it to another, and life would go on.

Betty and I were going steady, spending more evenings together, and late nights on the sofa when her parents had gone to bed. Nevertheless the rules were rigid. I would walk the 3 miles home in the small hours, as regular as clockwork, with a pain in the groin and 'no satisfaction', as the Rolling Stones would say. That's the way it was. While I became reluctant to sign on the Pool for another ship, and kept putting it off – I was doing all right so why bother.

Then Chick and I arranged to meet one evening to pick up a load of lead from a site near Buckingham Palace. It was, in effect, once too often and we were nicked. In court the next morning we were found guilty by the magistrate, and each given three months and then the realisation came with a jolt how suddenly and quickly life can turn around. One day you're a free bird, doing your own thing and the next you're in chains. I was nearly eighteen, and found it extremely difficult to cope with being caged. I hated every moment and I wanted out and back to sea. Of the three months I would serve two, and that seemed just about forever, an eternity, a space of time that would never end.

In retrospect, this was the start of my adult education, although I couldn't see it then. At that age and period I was growing, and not reflecting. I lacked the foresight to see where I was heading, and within me there was a stubbornness which caused me to resist the things I could not respect. So, in many ways I became, from then on, a product of the system. A system that is self-propelling and in the broad sense serves only its own interests.

One week into the second month and the clockwork frequency of the routine was beginning to wear me down, and the mindless brutality of a system going nowhere was starting to engulf me. I was no longer an individual, only a number in a chain of numbers that made up yet another chain of numbers, and there were so many numbers that when you got towards the top, the numbers changed. That's jumping ahead a bit, and I hope that my reference to numbers becomes clearer later.

We were only allowed two letters a month, and received the same number in reply – two small pages. If other letters came we were told that they would be thrown into the waste bin. A visit for twenty minutes, behind glass, after one month served. No newspapers, no radio, no contact with the outside world, locked alone in a tiny concrete cell in silence for twenty-three hours a day and the outside world, what we call the real world, became unreal, and all life out there became a fantasy.

We walked around a barren yard for one hour each day in circles, paired off with another young convict whose crime, in all probability was of no consequence and no threat to humanity. We were only allowed to talk on the exercise yard, then only to the person we were directed to walk with, not to the couple behind us or to the couple in front, and the pace we walked was controlled by one of the Home Office thugs standing around the circle. Those outstretched arms going up and down like a railway signal, spacing us out, equal distance apart. I hated every moment, and felt completely trapped. I made no friends on that exercise yard, at least none that I can remember, though some faces I would recognise in other prison yards in future years.

And there began for me the reality of what prison was all about, and it wasn't about compensating society as a whole for my sins, although that was the crap the law enforcers would have us believe. This style of internment was not about morality, as there wasn't any morality in sight. It was about control, the pecking order, with lots of revenge and plenty of stupidity.

I had completed three weeks of the eight that I was to serve on that three month sentence, when I was issued with a production warrant to appear back in court, for violation of the previous probation order that I had been given twenty-three months earlier. I hadn't seen much of the probation officer. I didn't inform him when I was home, as I saw it as aggro, so we didn't have anything going for us in terms of a relationship.

When I appeared in court a week later, I wasn't represented and, as far as I can remember, I didn't have a lot to say. I probably said I was sorry and I won't do it again, and of course I *was* sorry. I was sorry to be there as I knew I was going to get hurt. The vast majority of people live on double standards, and the politicians and law enforcement on treble, and we are only ever sorry for being caught. Everyone is sorry for the transgression when their luck runs out and the law lays its hand on your shoulder.

The court, in its wisdom, sent me to a borstal institution for three years. Borstal was a so-called correction system for young offenders aged between sixteen and twenty-one, and like other punitive ideas before and since was a complete failure and was subsequently abandoned. There were several of these institutions around the country. Some were open, some were closed. The open ones were ex-army camps or military hospitals, redundant after the war and now taken over by the prison service to house young people for a course of training.

After the sentence there was a three week assessment period in the borstal wing at Wormwood Scrubs, which was one of the major London prisons for men. A chief officer ran the wing. He was shortish, very thin, had a very loud sergeant major voice, wore a peaked uniform cap that looked too big for his head, and spent most of his time shouting at boys to get their hair cut.

Chick was let out on my eighteenth birthday, the same day I got off the bus with a bunch of other unfortunates to begin this course of training. The place was called Northsea Camp and that is what it was, a group of army sheds turned into dormitories, each shed given a name and called a 'house'. Within the hour we were fed, located to a house, dressed in prison shorts and in the gym working out under the instruction of a gym master. We were informed that the object of the exercise was discipline and fitness. Purity of the body leads to purity of the mind, or so they say, but, after two months in Wormwood Scrubs with one hour a day shuffling around a yard, just thirty minutes in the gym and you're ready to drop dead. The emphasis was on fitness and hard work. Up and out in the mornings at 6 a.m. for twenty minutes of physical jerks, breakfast of porridge and beans, then out to the mud flats beside the camp to reclaim land from the sea.

The camp was located in that part of the Norfolk Broads known as 'The Wash'. Miles of mud flats which needed protecting from the incoming tides that swept in from the North Sea and flooded the land. We had to create barriers on the shore line when the tide was low – built from the mud, shovelled into open containers on narrow tracks, then pushed up the ramps to empty on the top. Soulless, destructive labour, advocated by those who wanted to teach their wayward youth a lesson, and the harshness of the task compounded by the high tide of the cruel sea, washing the mud back from where it came. And those cold winter days, some shrouded in a hazy kind of mist that closed the world. Bone-chilling, icy east winds that swept across the mud flats, piercing to the core, blistering your hands and making your balls look and feel like walnuts. So physically demanding that it compounded a hatred for everyone and every-thing associated with it.

Mindless. That kind of hatred is not a good emotion. Fitness and intensive hard labour won't control the mind either. Of course, dis-regard sex, desire, hunger, humour and daydreams, it may raise the spirit to something noble. Who knows?

After a few months of shovelling mud and many days of con-templation, questioning my own logic, should I stay or should I go? I had no feelings of obligation to that place, and anything I felt I owed was to myself. But to take off would mean going on the 'wanted list', living each day looking over my shoulder. It might be never-ending and could destabilise my life in the future. The odds in the long term weren't in my favour; I lacked the temperament to be a fugitive. I was still a naive optimist in many ways, living in an atmosphere of detention, and with nothing positive to offer. From shovelling mud, I was relocated to shovelling earth on the camp gardens, with a small bunch of other misfits. The labour was easy but the boredom no less.

In theory, there was no fixed rule as to how much a boy would serve of his three year period. It all depended on the opinions given in the governor's recommendations, and he in turn, would mainly form his opinions from the reports of the borstal staff, some of whom were pure aliens lost in space, and would copy most of what they wrote in reports from what others had written before them. Some, who didn't like you because you wouldn't play the game by their rules, would write a lot of s**t, germinated in their weird imaginations and total lack of understanding of anyone different from themselves. Prison officers need no qualifications to become prison officers. All that is required of them is the ability to obey orders, regardless.

The average stay was fifteen months, and as all inmates were of military age they were transferred straight to the army to do their two years' conscription after their stint in borstal which, to me, seemed over-the-top and unacceptable.

The governor's name was Bennett. He was a slight man, aged about forty, with small squinty eyes that looked bunged up, and he always had this old, smelly golden-haired retriever hound with him. Everyone hated this hound for some reason, and would fantasise about the things they wanted to do to it.

The girlfriend, Betty Webster, would write to me almost daily. We could still only write two letters a month out, but had no limits on the amount coming in, and she and her mum, or my mum, would come and see me every month, even though it was a long train journey from London. I think this lasted about eighteen months, till Betty wrote to me one day to say she was going to marry a painter and decorator, and we should go our separate ways. I think I felt I was losing a friend rather than a lover, which in any case we had never quite been.

The average age of the guys was about eighteen. There wasn't a black face anywhere, because there were very few black families in England then, although Jamaican families were beginning to migrate by the boatload to work on the buses and fill the needs of the London labour market. There were a few Londoners, but none from my area that I can remember, and the rest came from all over. Different backgrounds, from different parts of the country, different outlooks and different humour and all, in the main, more interested in getting through than making life more difficult.

Friends were made, as a rule, within the various huts, and the huts were encouraged to compete with each other in sport and other activities. I was involved in this as much as any of the others, but I was never turned on to competitive sport although, being tall and comparatively strong, I could get by, even without being a star. There was, of course, the usual macho crap with some guys as you would expect to find in any group of young law-breakers, but I never had a problem with this because you learn that it's easier to create an

impression of toughness than to prove it, and if you don't challenge
and don't threaten, you save yourself a lot of grief from both the
young and the old.

I made friends with a guy named Derek Gold, a west Londoner a
year older than me. I don't remember what dirty deeds had landed
him in the joint with the rest of us, and it doesn't matter anyway. He
was into larceny just as I was, and always looking for opportunities,
so we had a lot in common. He was due out a month before me, and
although he should have gone into the army, he wasn't having any
of it and we arranged to meet up when my date came up. We used
to have a couple of free hours in the evenings, and would sit around
the iron stove in the middle of the hut on winter nights and chat
about this and that, things to do, where to look, how to take a car
and change the plates, where to get them, what they cost and how
to open locks with master keys. There was never any talk of normal
work or steady jobs, not from the inmates or any of the borstal staff.

It was, from the very beginning, a 'them and us' situation. You had
no chance or desire to be constructive, but as long as you kept your
eyes open and your mouth shut you got by.

We were always hungry and would plot to get more food. Always
for breakfast there was porridge, and this was made in a large steam
boiler in the kitchen and left overnight to simmer. The huts weren't
locked at night, there was no point as all the windows opened.
There was a night patrol which checked the huts every hour to see
if anyone had taken off. Four of us from my hut would take turns
dodging them to raid the kitchen for a basin of this, often half-
cooked, porridge. We were always hungry, and anything tastes good
when you're hungry. However, that didn't last long because word
got around and other huts joined in till someone got careless and
left a trail of porridge across the kitchen floor to their hut.

Another time I had a friend working in the kitchen, and he would
make a couple of bread and potato sandwiches and plant them outside the kitchen while the rest of us were in the dining room, and
when we set off out for work we'd pick them up and find a spot in
one of the ditches to sit and eat them before the day shift came on.
Sitting in a wet ditch on a freezing winter morning with a warm
potato sandwich was magic.

Each month a board meeting in the governor's office, chaired by Bennett, and made up of a small group of local JPs (Justices of the Peace), would review the cases of all boys who had been in the camp for twelve months or more and decide whether or not to release them in the following days. During this period, each boy would register for his military service and undertake the required medical examinations, before being drafted into the army. I wasn't very popular with the establishment, and it was eighteen months before it was decided I couldn't justifiably be held any longer, and was told by Bennett that I must do National Service.

'I don't want to go in the army,' I told him. 'I'm a registered seaman, I'm exempt.'

'You will go into the army like everyone else, and your seaman's identity will be cancelled.' Take it or leave it, do as you're told.

The thought of being a soldier, standing to attention to say 'Sir' to anyone, fostered an unnatural resentment in me. I was so out of tune with the regular life, in the real world, that I had no thoughts of conforming. I had lost any, if I ever had any, respect for authority. Fear was the only emotion I had and, in many ways, I understood that my fear of authority was as natural as its corruption. I saw Bennett's world only in terms of control, ruled by attitudes, geared to its own interests and 'Joe Bloggs' public didn't really give a s★★t as long as I didn't intrude into their space. Of course, I was still very naive in many ways, and believed – like most youths believe – that I knew it all. The world's a jungle, after all, some parts at peace, others at war.

A few weeks later, with several others, I was taken by prison bus to a makeshift medical centre where a group of eight doctors were assembled to examine the next month's intake of conscripts. We stripped off and followed in line through the cubicles of doctors. The fourth doctor was the ear, nose and throat man, who, on learning I'd had a mastoid operation when I was young followed by a bout of meningitis, took particular interest in my hearing. I was lying on the couch while he examined me, and he went to the screen behind me and told me to get up in a soft voice, which I ignored. After a moment he came back and told me to get up and dress. He was only a young doctor, and I doubt he was looking for fakers or whatever.

He had a word with the supervisor, and I was drummed out as unfit to be slaughtered on some far distant foreign land.

This really made my day. It meant I wouldn't need to go 'on my toes' (on the run) when I left borstal to avoid the army and I would be out of their control, and in fact, out of control. Back at the borstal everyone expressed surprise at the medical board's decision, and I doubt I was completely able to suppress my delight. I asked Bennett, the borstal governor, what I should do now about recovering my seaman's registration and all I got from him was, 'you can sort that out when you're discharged'. Sure I could, with a criminal record and a medical rejection!

At seven o'clock one morning, dressed in my own clothes, I was driven the 7 miles to the nearest railway station, given a ticket to London and £5, and my days of borstal training were over.

I don't know what the past twenty-one months had cost Joe Bloggs, or what had been achieved of any merit. It hadn't enriched my life in any way, or given me a sense of any type of responsibility. All I felt was that it had taken something from me which it had no right to. Had Bennett not taken my seaman's registration book away, I could have gone and seen my mum, then gone to the docks and signed on the first ship that needed a crew and been on my way, anywhere. With no rent to pay, no food to buy, and a few quid to throw away on late nights in exotic joints, at twenty that's all you need.

My mother had quit the Kennington Park place and moved, with my sister, to upmarket Chelsea to housekeep for someone or other, so I could only stay there for a couple of nights. Bill had got married, got a daughter, got a flat in Kennington and was away in the navy doing his conscription stint. His wife spent most of her time with her parents and I could use their place occasionally. I was back in the West End on the second night and met up with Doris, who was still working her regular pitch. She hadn't changed a bit and welcomed me with open arms, and things were as they always were between us – except I was probably fitter and more active!

3

Lots of things had changed over the couple of years I had been away. Many of my friends had found work that suited them and weren't hustling anymore. They were marrying and raising families and settling down. Nevertheless, there was plenty going on. The dice games outside Jane's Café in the Lambeth Walk were still going, though most of the players were different. My age group was on the move, and mostly looking prosperous. There were some good jobs on offer in the wholesale markets, the print in Fleet Street and the London Docks. However all of these were 'closed shops', the money was very good and sought after, but the jobs only went to family or close friends, and anyway, I'd lost interest for a regular commitment. I preferred to drift and get by on my wits. Borstal, in terms, had done me no good, or maybe it helped f**k my head up even more than it was already. I felt the loss of time and not growing up in the ways my old friends had, and I had a real contemptuous attitude towards most things and life itself, without being aggressive or obnoxious.

I met up with Derek, who had been my friend in the training camp, and together we began playing the field. My old pal Chick was dodging the army, and was 'on his toes' with his brother Jimmy. We met occasionally and would do whatever was on offer to earn a few quid. Everyone I knew, both men and women, bent the law occasionally. Even those who had regular jobs seemed to have something on the side or be playing the black market. The fact that I had been away doing time meant nothing to anyone. The fact that I was known in the area meant everything, and I was accepted without question or criticism.

I had been back in the old territory a few weeks and was cutting across the goods yard at the side of Waterloo Station one day with Chick, nosing around as we always did and taking an interest in everything. We watched the men at work unloading the containers, and began speculating about their contents and wondering where they were going and if they had anything of interest for us in them.

There were six or so main railway stations in London, each serving various sections of the country. All rail goods traffic between the north and the south had to cross London by road. The system for this involved freight containers that were easy to off-load onto trailers towed by a three-wheeled vehicle called a 'mechanical horse'. These mechanical horses spent their lives going back and forth between stations taking containers with them. Those going north, those going south. Nosing around, we discovered that they could all be opened with the same type of simple common 'tee' key – unbelievably simple.

Waterloo was the station in my area of London –in what we called our 'manor' (tribal territory) – and there was always a heavy flow of containers crossing the city from there. There was also always a shortage of drivers and a shortage of workers. To be a driver all you needed was a driving licence and a set of National Insurance cards. There were a lot of illegal people around, dodging the armed services, who had family to support and needed money. Driving licences and insurance cards were obtainable, and quite often people I knew had two sets.

Later that day, Derek, Chick, Jimmy and I sat drinking tea in a local cafe, discussing topics of interest.

I didn't have a driving licence of my own. I couldn't be bothered to fill in the forms and go through the test, and the only transport I had at the time belonged to someone else, as did the licence I carried when I did any driving. I had learned a little bit about cars while in borstal and I'd learned the basics of driving previously with Bill when, one Sunday, we nicked a lorry from the City Corporation maintenance yard to drive to Marlow on a day trip. Traffic was a lot different in those days. There were no traffic cops, as such, and 'cop cars' were a joke – never seen. This lorry was loaded with school desks, and we drove the round trip of 80-odd miles in one gear as we didn't know how to change – amazing. But we were full of energy, complete confidence, and didn't give a s**t. We taught ourselves to drive and; I was fifty before taking a driving test for my own licence, and I failed the first time.

Of course, back then it was a different world. 95 per cent of all cars on the road had an ignition key with serial numbers ranging between MRN1 and 50 – and these keys were obtainable at all car accessory shops. I bought the whole set across the counter for a few shillings. To make life easier, most cars had the ignition number stamped on the boot lock which anyone could read while walking past. Stealing cars was so simple in those days, it was part of everyday life, and car registration plates were obtainable over the phones – a one hour service. If we wanted to keep a car, we would call in the number of an identical car we'd look for on the streets, and transfer the new plates onto the stolen car. That way it wasn't listed at stolen. But we would only do that when a car was needed for a special reason. Most of the time it was – take to use, then abandon. I can't remember ever nicking a car just for a joy ride, there was always a reason, with or without merit.

Anyway, talking about the containers in the Waterloo goods yard with the other guys, it was agreed that Jimmy, Chick's brother, would try and get a job as a driver at the depot. I can't remember what name he used – not his own. Then we nicked a London County Council van from their transport depot, which was half a mile from Waterloo. We 'rang' the number plates in for those of an identical van in the yard, then parked it up in a spot where it didn't look out of place. I think we got a bit of a buzz out of having two lookalike vans on the road with the same number. It would have been ever weirder if the two vans had met up.

Jimmy was in the second day of his new job when he parked his mechanical horse and container in a side street. Derek, Chick and I were already in there with the van and we unlocked the container with a tee key that you could buy in any hardware shop and we unloaded everything we could trade on (mostly from that first load was bed linen), then we locked the container and sent it on its way. We never knew if the things we took were reported as taken or simply written off as lost in transit. When Jim unloaded the container in whatever depot, he would remove the labels.

We weren't grossly ambitious or devoted to becoming millionaires. We would spend whatever we earned, and then try to earn more when we needed to. There were rows of empty lock-up sheds under the railway viaducts that carried the railway lines into the city, and we put our own lock on one of them and used it to store stock. Then we spent most of our time selling it off – often to people we knew, for peanuts.

Jim liked his driving job because they were running a scam at his goods yard, whereby he could sign on for work without turning up and half his pay went to the yard's timekeeper. We were doing all right for quite a while, till the guy doing the job scam got tumbled and Jim pulled out. But, other things were beginning to happen and people were beginning to put things to us. Quite often it was speculation on their part, hoping we would follow it through and we would give them a share, but most information was useless, though not always – that's just the way it was.

Derek and I got a 'bedsit' in Earls Court – that's a 'bedsit-land' not too far from the West End. Streets of four storey Victorian terraced houses, originally built as town and family homes for the wealthy, were now converted into single bedroom apartments with a single or double bed, a gas ring, a wash bowl and a bathroom down the hall. A place to stay with the bare necessities, that didn't require any loyalty or cause difficulty in moving on, and great for occasional friends. We spent most of every night in the West End, the only place in London where the night clubs were, and where a skeleton of life existed in the small hours, where a cafe was open in the 'Corner House' on the corner of Warren Street, Lyons, Piccadilly at 4 a.m. The hustlers would come in from the shadows of doorways for refreshments after business hours, often looking for friendly familiar faces to complete the night with in their bedsits, or simply plain company, and the 'mysteries' would wander in, looking tired and anxious, lonely with nowhere to go and desperate for a friend.

These homeless girls we called 'mysteries', because that's what they were, in all senses, ranging from as young as fourteen and averaged out at sixteen, with an occasional exception. Runaways, escaping the old life and looking for a new one, a place to stay, someone to stay with. Many times Derek and I would pick them up and spend time with them – often several days – before the landlord told us to leave when there were too many sharing the room. Then I would ring Doris and spend some time with her.

Then, early one morning Derek and I met a couple in the Corner House. His name was George and his girlfriend was called Ann. They were a nice couple. George was in his early twenties, 5ft 10in, and Ann was about the same age. During the following days we became friends. George told us he had recently escaped from Oxford Prison and was looking for back-up to rob Lady Brooke, the Ranee of Sarawak, who lived alone in a mews flat near Marble Arch and was mega-rich.

George needed money to move on, and was becoming desperate, so Derek and I agreed to join him. He told us that he was armed and wanted the weapon as a frightener, which we thought was a good idea at the time. (In the late forties, guns were considered taboo with the majority of active crooks. Good only for avoiding violence rather than anything else.) George had been told that the Ranee would be home alone after midnight, and that she carried a fortune in jewellery.

We met at Marble Arch shortly before midnight and sat on the grass in Hyde Park discussing the event. We would ring the doorbell and if she opened the door, we'd go for it. George would mind the Ranee, keeping her quiet, while Derek and I searched the place. Home alarms were a thing of the future at this time.

'Hello – who is it'?

'Friends of your daughter, Cynthia,' said George.

She opened the door and we walked in. George showed her the gun and explained the situation. She wasn't a bit intimidated, just looked at us, wide-eyed and spoke in low tones as if she didn't want to disturb the neighbours. The mews flat was in a cul-de-sac, small and fashionable, and the four of us filled the entrance hall. We squeezed up together to close the entrance door and the Ranee showed us into her small sitting room. She was a smallish woman in her sixties, alone in the house. George had been told she spent her evening in various drinking clubs and was invariably legless by midnight. She wasn't sober when we got there and she offered us a drink when we went into her living room.

She was a nice lady who was treating the event as an experience – she obviously knew she was in no danger. Derek and I left her there with George while we searched her bedroom for jewellery. She owned a diamond ring given to her by King George VI on her wedding day. We searched her bedroom as carefully as we could and found several pieces of small value, but not what we were looking for. We didn't search any other part of the house, having been told it would be nowhere else, so we had drawn a blank. None of us wanted to pressurise the lady, so we left, asking her not to call the police for the next five minutes. We walked out of the door and into the night, little better off than when we started. We hadn't found what we were looking for, or what we thought we should have found. It hadn't been a good experience, and I hadn't felt at ease with that type of confrontation. It posed too many risks, as anything could happen.

George was arrested a week later for escaping from Oxford Prison and the following week, Derek and I were picked up coming out of the Corner House at 4 a.m. The following day we were identified by the Ranee and charged with armed robbery. George had been charged a few days earlier and we landed up at Number One court at the Old Bailey. Six weeks later, we were offered a deal: take a plea and three years, or go for trial and get five years.

There are many courts at the Old Bailey and Number One is where the major offences are tried, mainly murder. There was a murder trial going on when the three of us were taken to the corridor to wait by the stair leading to the dock, commonly referred to in jail slang as 'Up the Steps'. We were there for sentencing, which would take up little time and could be fitted in while the jury were out in the murder trial. When we reached the stair to the dock, our escort was told to hang on, as the jury in the murder case had reached a verdict and the defendant was about to return.

A young army woman in her early twenties was accused of killing her lover in Berlin where they were both part of the occupation forces. Berlin was divided into four sections then, each section controlled by one of the winning sides in the war, Britain, US, France and Russia. Any crime committed in the UK section would come under UK law and that brought the young woman to the Old Bailey. We knew nothing of this trial, having never heard of it. Moments later, a plain looking young woman in an army shirt came into the corridor, escorted by two female screws. We were told to stand aside, as we watched this pale, nervous creature being taken up the stairs between her guards.

The screw with us whispered, 'Be very quiet and listen. The sounds from the court will tell you the verdict,' and we listened to the silence.

Five minutes later the young woman was helped down the stairs by her twin escorts in floods of tears, sobbing like a child. She had been convicted and sentenced to death, twenty years before capital punishment was abolished. I didn't know her name or what it was all about, or even learned what happened to her later. Hopefully she got reprieved and released after a few years. Whatever, she would always have to live with that part of her life – if the system gave it back to her.

We had our own problems, though minor in comparison. Nevertheless, it was impossible not to feel sympathy for her – a victim of fate, caught up on the dark side of a system that needed to kill in cold blood to achieve nothing of value.

We faced the same judge ten minutes later and fortunately, the Ranee had no malice towards us. She had told the court that we had treated her with respect, and we each got three years. George had his added to the term he was already doing. Derek was sent to an adult prison, while I was a few months short of twenty-one and got sent to a young person's prison – which was the same as an adult prison, just marginally easier.

I applied for a job in the prison kitchen on the strength of once being a galley boy and that's where I spent my time, washing dishes for a few weeks before taking on other kitchen tasks, till I became a storekeeper in charge of all food supplies. Food was still on ration and the prison officer chef was a blockhead who would stand to attention when he answered the phone. Most of the time he spent at his desk reading the comic books that cons would get for him from the library. The menus were set on a weekly rota and never changed. Each week I'd cut off a large family joint from the prisoners' meat ration for the chief officer to take home, and every day take a pint of cream from the top of the milk churns for the chief engineer in charge of prison maintenance. Other things were left out in the storeroom overnight, and disappeared. That was the system and you either went with it or you didn't work in the kitchen, and the kitchen was the only place you got enough to eat.

Derek was sent to a prison in another part of the country but we both got out on the same day and knew where to meet up. We were both back to square one, out of home and out of money. We weren't interested in getting regular jobs and were feeling out of sync with the mainstream. We looked up what old friends were still around and the new friends we'd met in the boob who were out and about. Doris had sent me a letter saying she was packing up and going home to the Midlands. I hope she found a good life – she'll be eighty now if she's still around.

4

Things hadn't worked out between Bill and his wife when he came out of the navy and it wasn't going to, so he signed a nine month contract to work for the P&O shipping line on one of their passenger liners sailing backwards and forwards to Australia. This had happened while I was away. He completed his contract with the P&O in Sydney, and signed off there with a friend he had partnered up with, a guy named Jeff. They worked the outback together for several years. It was twenty-nine years before I saw Bill again. He had his own cabinet-making business then, a nice home, a nice wife and two grown-up kids. Jeff owned a mountain in a place called Maclean in New South Wales, where they both lived for several years and where Bill met Loll.

Jeff bought the 300 acre mountain from the government when they were selling land to new settlers. The price was $300 – that would be about £75, or $250 US – which he didn't have. He still signed a contract to buy it though, and went off prawn-fishing to earn the money. And the boat sank. He returned to Maclean stony broke, but found that road building ballast had been discovered on the mountain and so the royalties paid off what he owed the government. He's lived there on top of his mountain ever since. Bill says Jeff gets up in the mornings, makes tea and discusses the day. Then it's time to go to bed. I spoke to Bill yesterday, 30 May 1999, and he'll be seeing Jeff in a couple of weeks. One of Australia's original hippies.

Anyway, that's jumping ahead a bit. Back to the early fifties …

My mother had moved on with my sister, and was housekeeping for an admiral and his family, just outside of London. There was nothing there for me, but they were OK.

For the next year I got up to all sorts of things in the 'underworld' of central London, a lot of it with Derek who was then living with an old girlfriend, until one day we were down on the south coast doing something or other and he got nicked. All I can remember now is being chased around the town by a police car for half an hour at 4 a.m., till we ran out of juice. Then we took to our heels down the narrow side streets and split up. I caught a bus out of town three hours later, but Derek was nicked. He got nine months – and we never met again. The last I heard of him he was running a drinking club in west London.

We used to spend a lot of time in the West End drinking clubs and 'spielers', where guys of a similar nature to us would meet and gossip. There were licensed drinking clubs all over the place that only catered to members, and were run by people who were grafters of one kind or another. Leaving one of these clubs early one morning to wander around looking for 'mysteries', I met a really attractive girl called Molly.

We first met at the high counter of a kerbside tea and sandwich stall in the Kings Road, Chelsea, at two o'clock early one morning. She was with a friend called Sue, and I soon gathered they were both runaways from a care centre where they had been placed by a court order for being 'out of control'. So they were both on the wanted list and were surviving by sleeping around. The stall was on the corner of a street that led down to the river. It stood beneath the branches of a tree which set everything in shadow from the inadequate street light. There were just the three of us, the streets were deserted, and the silence was embracing. London thoroughfares produce a strange, hollow atmosphere in the small hours which I loved.

I had a bedsit at the back of Olympia stadium, a short bus ride away from the Kings Road, and I had stopped there at the stall to wait for the hourly bus, going my way, which ran through the night. When the double decker rolled along, the three of us climbed aboard and we went for the upper deck, Sue, Molly, with me in the rear, and as Molly climbed the stair I could see the curve of her perfect legs and rose to the occasion.

She was just seventeen and completely wild, real fun to be with as she really didn't give a s★★t for anything. She thought her father was a currently notorious spieler (illegal gambling joint) owner who her mother had had a brief affair with years earlier. Molly and I lived together for several months, often falling out and getting back together. She always wanted to work with me, but that couldn't happen. I would always feel too inhibited with her around, and we would fall out.

Molly plucked her eyebrows and wore red lipstick. I was always telling her she was too attractive to wear make-up, which to me, she was. But try telling that to a seventeen-year-old delinquent nymph. I was very fond of her without any illusions. Whenever we were together we had no ambitions except for the moment and we often did crazy things. She once wanted me to screw her as we waited in a cinema queue without anyone noticing.

With Derek gone, I needed to adjust. The landlord at the bedsit at Olympia asked me to move, as the room wasn't intended for three. So Molly and I moved to Ebury Street, Victoria, where the landlady was the caretaker, not the owner, and easy going as long as you paid the rent of £3 a week.

I think the bedsit days have more or less gone now, most converted to self-contained flats and costing a fortune.

I left Molly in bed late one morning and walked out across Hyde Park towards Park Lane. We were skint and the prospects didn't look promising. I crossed over onto Curzon Street, wondering what to do with myself and how to earn a living. Looking for a regular job wasn't a serious option. I needed that sense of freedom only money can give you, and that for me couldn't be found in a nine to five. This rather limited the field, and previous wartime experiences, a reckless youth, the lack of peers and my cynical view of mankind made life what it was.

I had these thoughts as I walked along Curzon Street to the famous Curzon Street Cinema, then crossed over to the exclusive restaurant on the opposite side of the road. It was lunchtime, and parked at the kerb was a shiny black Austin Seven – a popular car of that period. Walking past, I saw a suitcase on the back seat with a mink coat over it. The ignition key number was stamped on the trunk lock. I'm not certain, but I've a feeling it was MRN 27, the day of my birthday. I always associated one number with another number as it helped me remember. Anyway, I always carried a full set of keys.

The bedsit that Molly and I shared was about 2 miles away in Ebury Street and I drove the Austin there to unload. This was the first time that I had ever taken a private car off an upmarket busy street in the middle of the day for its content. I dumped the car in a residential side street a mile away as soon as I'd removed the case and coat, then returned to the bedsit to see what the score was. I couldn't believe my luck – inside the case was some very expensive lingerie and dresses, and a fair-sized satin lined vanity box with sparklers (diamonds) in, like nothing I'd ever seen – even with the Ranee of Sarawak, who said 'Diamonds are a girl's best friend' (or was that Marilyn Monroe? That blonde girl with the famous legs, an intimate friend of the Kennedy boys).

I hope I didn't break that lady's heart that day, but there again, if she got a buzz from wearing a $5,000 coat on her shoulders made from the slaughtered skins of animals, then I won't lose any sleep. She probably upped its value on insurance anyway.

I can't remember exactly what I got for this stuff. Most of it traded off to hookers I knew, the coat went for £50 and the jewellery for about the same. Most of that went to the clubs and living it up, having what was then a good time. The woman who bought the coat a few hours after I stole it asked me if the one case was all I had, and I realised I hadn't searched the boot, so I got a cab over to where the Austin was still parked and retrieved two more, which I sold to the landlady for a month's rent. I was never greedy when selling off various things that I came to acquire. I was interested in taking the money I was offered rather than actual values, then moving on. Everything I did in this period was speculation.

This event started a new trend and improved my lifestyle. For some obscure reason this became known as the 'jump up', the taking of commercial loads which were left unoccupied for a few minutes. I worked alone and worked frequently, sometimes stealing a car in the morning and then going to a factory or warehouse and waiting for a delivery van to come out, tailing it off till an opportunity arose to take it, leaving the stolen car behind. The adrenaline was high and the rewards often good, anything from chocolate bars to raincoats, though not every day was a winner, some days I'd drive around the whole time for nothing.

I would use the various drinking clubs almost daily – not to drink especially but to meet people who were interested in doing a trade on whatever I had going. As I got to know more and more people I could sell to, I guess more and more people began to know me. Looking at it logically now, with a certain amount of wonder, I realise my whole lifestyle was outrageous, spending every day living on the edge and not really caring about anything.

Because I always had money and things to part with, I must have been becoming known to the local crime squad. One way or other, working as a grafter meant they would be interested in me for all sorts of reasons, money being one of them – I would know who they were. Already there had grown a hard contempt in me for the London CID (Criminal Investigation Department). I was learning, from tales I was told and things I had seen, that they were more corrupt and unprincipled than anything I had imagined. Everyone needs something to respect and consider moral, and when you realise through experience how dishonest the English institutions are and how unscrupulous the whole judicial system is, you can't take any of them seriously. All you can do is try and avoid them.

Because I was in the commodity business, I needed to know people, and the drinking clubs were good for this; but they were no good if you wanted to be invisible, because they were full of gossip and hidden dangers. Guys looking for ways to score, with rumours to spread. There was always 'iffy' business going on and 'iffy' characters lurking and always a lot of macho crap surrounding the ones I used, odd characters who seemed only interested in being tough guys, which I suppose in their own way they were. Lots of gossip and disagreements, someone 'taking a liberty' resulting in them being cut across the face with a razor, then money changing hands to sweeten the vanity of the injured, and girls fighting each other for having it off with their boyfriends. Funny times, strange world.

Often I would walk back in the early hours of the morning to wherever I was living. I loved the streets of London in the small hours, all lit up with street lights and totally deserted. For me it had a magical charm that I could never get enough of or find anywhere else.

The rave period with Molly was becoming more on than off. Often great, sometimes brilliant, at other times she would do my head in. She wasn't interested in money beyond her needs, no interest in drugs or booze or fancy clothes. But she was really into sex, like some people are into popcorn and pipe dreams, and I guess when you're good at what you're into, it becomes addictive. Sex was that way with Molly. She was addicted and wanted to addict both the male and female population. A bit of a tall order, but she was only seventeen, and like me very strong-willed. She had the ingredients of a vixen, the looks to go with it and a temperament both cool and intolerant that made her so different and magnetic to me. In a way, our relationship was similar to my affair with Doris, not quite the same but with many parallels.

Sometimes Molly and I were together, sometimes we weren't. We would disagree over something or other and she would take off and sleep around, and I would go 'mystery' hunting for someone to spend time with. Then we'd meet up again in the Corner House in the small hours and go through it all again. Neither of us were really interested in a proper commitment but both attracted to each other.

It was that way when one day I went over to a luxury flat in Knightsbridge – one of the upmarket districts in central London – I had been invited over by a guy named Hyman who wanted to have a chat. He was with a small group of Oz (Australian) hoisters (shoplifters), who were working their way around the world. They had rented this mews flat for three months as a base to work from. We'd met the night before in The Pigalle Night Club in Piccadilly. There were five of them, two Oz couples and Hyman. They were all in their mid-twenties. The Oz couples had come to London from Paris, and were then going on to Chicago. One of the girls had taken a job as a housemaid with a wealthy family and then taken off with their goodies – which financed the mews flat. Hyman was their London guide.

We sat around for a while chatting about stuff I can't recall and then I left. Hyman came out with me. He was very Jewish and looked like a young executive. He was dressed in an obviously expensive grey conservative suit and looked very prosperous, but what you saw was what you got – he travelled light and only had the one suit. His image was very different from mine – in my 'birds eye' padded shoulder drape, with a single split where the forked tail would be.

Hyman said he'd asked me over because he was looking for a car and driver to do some work with him. He wanted to do a 'run-out' and the Oz guys weren't interested. They had talked about it, that's all. Hyman's idea was to rip off a jeweller's shop in Leicester Square which he had already staked out. He would go into the shop and get the salesman to put a whole tray of diamond rings on the counter for him to select from, then pick the lot up and run out, hence the term 'run-out'. He needed a car and driver at the kerb to get him out of there, quick and dependable. He'd split it down the middle.

There was no way I could do what he had in mind in any jeweller's shop, or any other kind of shop, because I would never deliberately have my photo taken (show my face), which Hyman would be doing with a salesperson. However, as a driver I wouldn't have that problem, so we agreed to meet on the following afternoon and give it a go.

By that time I must have known just about everywhere in London where cars were available, and I'd nicked so many I knew what to go for. I picked up a Ford Pilot with a V8 engine. A solid, stubby (sedan) type of car which I'd always found reliable. Hyman was waiting as arranged, and we set off for Leicester Square. When we got there, I immediately turned his idea down due to risk. The nearest I could park was 100 yards away on a very busy street. I'd be locked in traffic in minutes. However, I did know an expensive jeweller's shop on the corner of Black Lion Yard where Doris used to live.

We parked on the corner a few yards from the front door. I thought Hyman might have a little trouble getting into the pilot's side door when he came charging out, as it could slow down his progress. I suggested he came head first through the window.

When he disappeared into the shop I had to guess, more or less, when he'd be coming out because we were on a busy main street with plenty of traffic. I sat looking in the rear view mirror at the traffic lights 200 yards behind me. There were buses and cabs queued up there waiting for the lights to change, and I knew I'd be blocked in when they moved and got to me. When the lights changed I waited till they were approaching then pulled across the road, blocking the street. Hyman came out of the shop shouting for me to go, with the salesman behind him. As I pulled away he came through the window tossing a tray of rings before him, then caught a bus out of the district.

I didn't really know much about diamonds. It all looked like glass to me, and it has always amazed me the amount of money people spend on them. All the rings on the tray Hyman had taken had a small label on giving the retail value, adding up to several thousand. Hyman and I got a quarter of the face value of the rings from a man we discovered was fencing (selling stolen goods), who I then knew till he died many years later. He was a gentle and good old boy, occasionally mentioning the type of pieces he was interested in when we took stuff to him.

This was supposed to be a one-off event, but it had been so easy that we both wanted to do it again. The 'jump-up' for me was being played out – but I was going to the same streets too often, and nothing lasts for ever.

A week before I met up with Hyman, I was in Bill Hill's club in Gerrard Street, early one evening, doing the rounds. I met up with two old friends from south London who were now professional hoisters. They wanted me to nick these three very expensive Leica cameras that were in the window of a camera shop in Bond Street. But neither of them were tall enough to reach over the back of the display cabinet to lift them off their plinth. The shop was L-shaped and the shop manager could be manoeuvred down the 'L' so that he couldn't see the front, or anyone entering. When he was out of sight from the front door, I would step in, reach over the wooden screen and lift the cameras. Unfortunately I wasn't tall enough, I had to jump up, hook myself up with the top of the screen under one arm and reach the cameras. One-handed, I could only take one and left. I waited on the corner for the two guys to catch up. They said the shop manager hadn't noticed, so we did it again and he still didn't notice. For us, at least, 'two out of three ain't bad'. The second time I hooked myself up, I stared into the face of a sailor and his girlfriend who were looking at the cameras, but in a moment, both me and the second camera were gone.

Over the next few weeks Hyman and I did a whole string of jewellers all over London. We knew it couldn't last as jewellers became more cautious, so we decided to take a break and go to the coast for a week. Brighton was the obvious place, and we stayed at the Marine Hotel on the front (the same hotel I would stay at a few years later). After Brighton we were going north to try some of the major cities there, as we felt London was played out and was becoming too difficult for this kind of stunt.

After a few days in Brighton I rang a friend in London who I needed to see before going north. He told me he'd rung my flat and got an inquisitive guy on the other end who he reckoned was Old Bill and I should give the place a miss.

Hyman and I left Brighton a week later, and I wanted to pick up several new shirts I'd left at the flat. I thought whoever had been in there must have left by then. No one answered the phone. I parked outside. It had been snowing overnight and the streets were covered. I figured if there was anyone inside I could get out in time to drive off. Neither of them heard me enter but saw me immediately I came into the main room and, before I made the door, they collared me and arrested me for assaulting them.

I was taken to Paddington Green Police Station, and into one of the CID offices where all anyone seemed interested in was the alleged 'assault'. They were full of indignant rage that someone had whacked one of their comrades, and physically expressed their outrage by taking it in turns to whack me. There were at least six of them in that room the whole time, and others would come and go, each taking a swipe. You could never accuse them of not sticking together – the whole station would tell you this never happened.

I was recovering in one of the cells several hours later when a Detective Fuller came in. A very amiable and friendly guy, showing all the signs of sympathy and being on the same wavelength as me. They say it takes a thief to catch a thief, and I was looking at one. The difference of course – Fuller had the establishment on his side and a licence to break all the rules.

Apparently the police had heard rumours that I was being very active and they wanted to question me about it. Nothing positive, but enough to give them an interest and, as I seemed to be a reasonable person, he'd have a chat with the DI (detective in charge of his area) and see what the score was. He came again later that night and told me that he had been put in charge of the case, and we could probably come to an agreement as long as nothing else turned up in the next seven days; but there wasn't much he could do about the assault because it had already been recorded and one of the detectives had gone off sick. However, he could probably get them to play it down so that it wouldn't come too heavy. I would have to do the customary seven days on remand, though, because that's the way these things worked. He would come and see me during the week and talk about bail etc.

We're now in the early fifties – and just as there are two sides to every coin so there are two sides to the established forces of law. The one you're shown, that creates the image of integrity, and the other, which is the everyday real one.

I wanted out of there. I wanted to be on the loose. I wanted bail. I wanted to be free and I wanted to take off, be anywhere but where I was.

The way the system worked, I'd be lucky to see the streets again for a least a week. I was charged with assault and would be in a magistrates' court the next day, where I'd plead 'not guilty'. The police, that is Detective Fuller, would ask for a lay down (remand for seven days). The magistrate would ask if there was any objection to bail and Fuller would say, 'Yes, we are making further enquiries which may lead to more serious charges, therefore we oppose bail'. And that was it, I would be remanded in custody for seven days regardless of anything I could say or do.

Magistrates were laymen, not professionally trained or qualified in legal matters. They were appointed after being recommended for the job by someone already part of the system. The 'one-of-us' syndrome. They relied on the clerk of the court – a qualified lawyer – for advice and guidance, and the police were riding high in those days, seen as being totally up front, unquestionably honest. Magistrates relied on them to be straight and wouldn't have it any other way.

Fuller came to see me in Brixton remand prison during the following week. He said that for two hundred quid they wouldn't oppose bail on my next appearance in court, and we could meet up when I was out and about and we'd sort something out. Trouble was, I didn't have two hundred quid. I was just back from the coast and needed to earn. This didn't seem to be a problem with Fuller. He said I could pay him the next week, and without saying, he knew as well as I did that I'd have to nick it from somewhere. Well, that's what I did, sure, but for me – not the Metropolitan Police force! It went against the grain to steal for a copper, because it wouldn't stop there. They would be into me forever, and they wouldn't always just want money. They would feed me information on where to score, and look to me for information in return – bad news, as that was a no-win situation.

I had absolutely no intention of giving Fuller, or any of them, a penny. F★★k 'em, and who did I see about the beating in Paddington Green? However, while I was in custody I couldn't say that. So I got bail on a promise to pay Fuller two hundred quid. I had no intention of honouring any kind of arrangement with a 'mob' – which in reality was the most stupid thing I have ever done or am ever likely to do – but I just couldn't do it.

The friend who had warned me that the police had been in my flat was Tommy Brennan, an occasional cat burglar. We'd been friends for quite a while, though we had never done anything crooked together. He lived in a bedsit in the same house where I had once lived. That's how we met and, in the room below his, lived a delicious looking petite blonde who never seemed to wear any clothes when she was at home. Very teasing, and she played music the whole time on her small turntable – Ella Fitzgerald, Billie Holliday, Sarah Vaughan, and Nat King Cole. Can you imagine this? Knocking on her door (which I did frequently), this beautiful lady, this very naked beautiful lady, opening her door in all her glory, standing there looking at you with soft moist eyes and Nat King Cole singing softly in the background, 'When I fall in love'. It was enough to turn the head of any innocent. Then Ella singing 'Every Time we say Goodbye' as you leave. Tommy spent more time in her room than he did in his own. We called her 'Moonlight Melody' because she never went out before midnight.

Tommy arranged the securities for my bail, knowing that it would be forfeit when I went on the missing list, but that wasn't a problem because no money changed hands at this point. No money was required unless I absconded, and then the full amount of the bail still wouldn't be required because the amount of forfeit would be decided by the magistrates' court after listening to the final status and pleas of disbelief from the person giving the guarantee.

Tommy left the magistrates' court with me after I had arranged to meet Fuller the following week.

Tommy occasionally grafted with a guy named Raymond Jones, a Welshman in his mid-thirties who lived in the West End, with a middle-aged hooker, and their teenage daughter who Tommy was having a thing with. Raymond Jones was, in his own way, quite talented. He had the ability to silently climb drainpipes and open bedroom windows while the occupants were asleep, take their goods and leave without disturbing anyone. Already he was acquiring a reputation within the 'underworld' for being one of the best cat burglars of the period. Of course, he didn't have the state-of-the-art technologies to worry about; alarms and other securities came in the sixties as a result of the things he got up to in the late forties and fifties, along with a few others, like George Cheatham who, to me, was a very gentle, smashing person.

Lots of stories go with George. He was a totally addicted gambler, and I suppose had to steal to support his addiction like a lot of young people do today to support theirs. He drove to the races one day in a brand new Bentley and had to borrow the bus fare home. And he stole Wellington's sword from the National Museum just for the diamonds in the handle – priceless. All he did was smash a window, then climbed in and lifted it from its stand. He was never caught for this, and I rang the museum a few years ago after he died but they refused to discuss the subject.

However, then as now, the very wealthy always kept their tiaras and bracelets and stuff in bank vaults and would only get them out on special occasions, such as weddings and balls held in stately country homes, when guests would spend the weekend. These were the places and events targeted by the Raymond Jones fraternity, and they had some sensational scores.

Raymond Jones needed transport to freight some artwork he wanted to nick, and I was invited along. So, the very evening I was out on bail I was out again trying to earn some money – but like all things, it doesn't always work out that way. After getting into the place while the people were out, we discovered that the things we were after weren't there and we left empty-handed. On the following day there were banner headlines in the dailies about this outrageous burglary and the fortune that was stolen – though who stole it, we'll never know, since it wasn't us.

I met up again with Hyman, and we found an easy jeweller's shop in South Kensington which gave me the stake I needed to get lost for a while. A few days later, I left London in a car I'd acquired for the occasion. The idea was to be self-indulgent and do something I'd always fancied, drive all around the south coast, staying at each sea-side town for a day or a month and looking for opportunities to earn. I knew no one would be looking for me. A few questions would be asked around and about, but that was it. The police had other things to do and would rely on the chance that sooner or later I'd get nicked and then they would take care of it. I wasn't anticipating anything too heavy, but I knew I'd be going down, unless I was really lucky. All I was doing was delaying the inevitable – hopefully forever.

I must have been crazy, though, to think I could outrun the 'long arm of the law'. I had more contempt for them than was healthy, and a reckless disregard for just about everything, though subconsciously I suppose I respected the things the law professes to represent, like integrity, fair play, and straightforward honesty. There again, if they were an honest lot they wouldn't catch anyone. So I guess you 'can't have your cake and eat it' (as me mum would say). Of course, I really wanted the police force to be completely honest and the judiciary to be totally pure, so that I could do what I liked and get away with it – in an ideal world.

Eight o'clock one Saturday evening some weeks later, I booked into a small hotel in Bournemouth. The hotel's evening meals were finished, and there was only a single café open in the centre of the town doing light meals so I went there to eat. Later, when I was leaving, I saw a guy at one of the tables whose face seemed familiar, but I didn't place it. The next morning, as I was leaving my hotel room, I walked into two detectives who immediately arrested me. Apparently the guy in the café had recognised me and knew I was on the wanted list. He informed the local police who spent the night on the phone to London, getting a warrant for my arrest and checking the local hotels.

The next day I was back in the cells at Paddington Green Police Station, and my old friend Fuller was delighted to see me. The next thing I knew I was charged with the armed robbery of a well-known actress called Beckman, who lived in Maida Vale and meant nothing to me. A few days later, Tommy Brennan was nicked and charged with me. Neither of us knew anything about this robbery, but we soon realised it was payback, me for ripping off Fuller over the bail and promises, and Tommy for being my friend and helping me out.

At the magistrates' court a case was made out which sent us both for trial at the Old Bailey. During this 'case to answer' process we learnt some details of the case against us, consisting entirely of incriminating remarks (verbal) that we were alleged to have made in the police station – a load of b*****ks. However, we discovered we both had alibis.

Tommy's was sound, with plenty of back-up from witnesses; and he was smart enough not to let Fuller's crowd know, for fear of them intimidating these people. Most of our friends and the people we mixed with had some sort of 'form' and were very vulnerable to pressure from the police, and characters like Fuller were masters of dirty tricks. It's surprising the number of suspects in criminal cases, where there really is no evidence, saying, 'you'll have to prove it, governor', and crap like that.

My alibi however, was a problem. The robbery was happening while Hyman and I were at the jeweller's shop in another part of London, 5 miles away – which meant I was caught between the devil and the deep blue sea!

By the time we came for trial I wasn't confident of my chances, not with the options I had. So I decided to go up-front and challenge the police, which my lawyer warned me was dangerous. However, I had little confidence in lawyers because most of them have their feet in both camps and know each other well enough for the 'old pals' act to come into play, and deals get done which aren't always in your favour. I felt that if I was going down, at least I wanted it to be for my own misdeeds and not those of someone else. I was very p****d off.

Awaiting trial in Brixton prison, I met up again with Hyman who was himself awaiting trial for the stunt at the South Kensington jeweller's shop. No one knew I had been his driver and he wasn't saying. We talked it over, and came to the conclusion that he should name me as his accomplice. He had been offered a deal if he gave his driver up, so at least he could gain something; and I really didn't want another armed robbery conviction after the one with George Stower. As I couldn't be in two places at once, my confession to the jeweller's shop venture established where I was at that particular time, but the robbery charge had already been made and they had to follow through with it.

Lawyers at that time were of the general opinion that juries should not be made aware of a defendant's criminal record during the course of a trial because juries could then be biased and very reluctant to accept anything a defendant had to say – especially against hardworking detectives in armed robbery cases.
I was going to challenge the police in court which meant challenging their character, which would risk the wrath of the judge, because police officers were his troops and had his full support. They didn't like criminals challenging the integrity of their chaps, and when you did they introduced your record. Calling a police officer a liar was a mortal sin in those days. I knew all that, but it made no difference because I was steaming and angry enough to be self-destructive.

It has taken me a long time to come to understand, and accept the reality, that guys like Fuller and the rest like him were victims of their own culture. Their success was gauged by their advancement, achieved by their criminal conviction rate; their ability to find the evidence to convict whoever they considered could be, or anyone who 'would do' to be, the right suspect; who they could claim had incriminated themselves verbally under questioning, knowing that 'verbal' was accepted by the courts when there was nothing else. Nobody seemed to care that police corruption of this kind destroyed the fabric of democracy and weakened the quality of everyone's life.

At the trial for this armed robbery, a Detective Ellis gave a verbal time for when the robbery took place, which was seven minutes after Hyman and I left the jeweller's shop. He said in evidence that he believed when I left the jeweller's shop, I dropped off Hyman, picked up Tommy Brennan and *then* we did the armed robbery. Two detectives were instructed to check out the drive, and they said the trip from Kensington to Maida Vale could easily be done in seven minutes – a complete and utter impossibility. Tommy's alibi was sound and he was acquitted, but I was convicted on all charges – assault, the jeweller's shop robbery *and* the armed robbery at Maida Vale, and I was sentenced to eight years.

Several years later, on the prison yard in Dartmoor I met the two guys who *did* do this robbery. They hadn't instigated my convictions or been responsible for my problems so there was no animosity between us, only goodwill. They told me, as we talked about this business, that in fact the robbery had occurred earlier than was stated in court, and the whole thing had been engineered by the actress's husband as an insurance gimmick. All they did was put on a show and nick a few pieces of junk for good measure. They said I should try and get a copy of the recorded time it was reported to Scotland Yard, where all emergency crime calls went before being sent out to local stations. I did this, and after a lot of petitions and correspondence and much lobbying by my sister, Mary, I finally got a copy of the recorded time at Scotland Yard and sure enough, the time given in court was later by ten minutes. Mary took this information to her member of parliament, a minister in government who, incidentally, was gay and seemed to be getting a buzz from me – which was fine as long as it fired his interest. He finally came to see me shortly before my release and told me that he believed me. But there was nothing he could do. He invited me to visit him, but I wasn't interested, it wasn't my scene, though I'm sure he was in fact a nice person – a politician nevertheless, caught in the world of image and jealously guarded empires where you only survive in yours as long as you help protect the others' by looking the other way.

Tommy was gutted by my conviction and the length of the sentence. We were able to speak together for a few minutes before he went one way and I went the other. He had trouble keeping his eyes dry, just like the sentimental young Irishman that he was. I never saw him again, though I heard from him and of him occasionally over the years. The last I heard, he had an antique shop in a small town called Cirencester in the West Country which I never quite got round to exploring.

It was late in the afternoon when the court wagon came to the Old Bailey to collect whoever had been convicted that day and take us to the various prisons according to status. First offenders – Wormwood Scrubs, second offenders – Wandsworth. Wandsworth is in south-west London and, on the day after I arrived there, I went through the standing procedure of applying for leave to appeal against both conviction and sentence. That's the way the system worked then. You had to apply for leave to appeal, and the odds were never in your favour.

The lawyer who represented me was Cyril Sammonds, whose dad was a judge. Talking with Raymond Jones one day after I was convicted he told me that he had tied the judge up and nicked some heirlooms, and that young Cyril was ambitious and a member of the 'hang 'em and flog 'em' brigade. I was learning about the legal profession, and like all subcultures, they have their own rules and play their own games. Cyril Sammonds was paid to represent me at the Old Bailey, but that was it. So I filled in the forms and stated my case and waited the standard six weeks for the result. People were discouraged from applying to appeal because the sentence was suspended during the application period – it was like doing time in purgatory, neither in nor out.

In Wandsworth I made several friends while walking around the exercise yard, most of them were on their way to the Moor (Dartmoor) and we shared common interests. Many came from different areas of London and were doing time for various things. Most talked freely of their experiences and things they had done, or hoped to do, and often overstated events they had been involved in – but that's the way it was. Most thieves like to gossip and be known to other thieves and feel accepted in the subculture they are in. I was beginning to learn that pubs and clubs and spielers were not the places to frequent if you were living on the edge and wanted to pass by unnoticed, because people talk too much and their talk can make life difficult. I was becoming more widely known, with a reputation of being a grafter, and that wasn't what I wanted. A reputation, to me, meant exposure and being more vulnerable to ambitious abuse.

Then, just before going to the Moor, I met a guy named Bob Macanless who had just been sentenced to six years for grievous bodily harm. He was twenty-four, had been a boxer and he had a row with a bus conductor and whacked him. Because he had been a professional boxer, his hands, in law, were weapons – hence the six years. We would meet up again later on the Moor. In Wandsworth all long-termers were located in D wing, so most of the guys in D wing exercise yards were there for serious offences, and came from various backgrounds, but mostly from the poor and often toughest areas. Although exercise was restricted to one hour a day and you weren't always able to walk round with who you wanted, you got to know a lot of guys and heard loads of gossip.

5

Then came the day, with twenty other long-termers, chained together in one line, I was sent by train to Dartmoor Prison. Located in the heart of Devon's desolate moorlands, the bleakest place in England; constantly hidden in low clouds and mist, with everything covered in a fine wet film – bleak and bitterly cold in winter, bleak and bitterly cold in summer.

Dartmoor Prison was originally built in 1812 by, and for, French prisoners of war and the American privateers who supplied the French with merchandise. It held 600 long term prisoners, and once a month a new batch arrived to replace last month's discharges.

Today, there are over forty prisons for long-termers, which kind of suggests that prisons are a growth industry with perhaps a whole new set of jealously guarded empires.

The prison was contained by a round high dry stone wall, built in the style of the ancient ring forts, with just one entrance through a cobbled courtyard, and massive great wooden doors. The story goes that the French and American prisoners would make small objects and trinkets to sell in the market place, which was the cobbled courtyard. Of course, that was before I got there.

The nearest town to the 'Moor', as the prison was called by everyone, was a small place called Yeovil, 7 miles away. This was where the trains stopped, and all I ever saw of Yeovil was the station when I arrived with the other cons – and again when I left. We were bussed from the station on an old rickety bus, over a narrow bumpy road through a landscape of chilled emptiness, torn and ragged granite rocks everywhere – like traveling across the moon – with the occasional glimpse of wild ponies through rolling mist. A weird atmosphere of *Wuthering Heights* – 'you're not welcome here, you're not wanted, you don't belong, and time will stop at this point, and only come on again when you leave, and a lump of your life will have gone'.

There's a small village beside the prison called Princetown, one street of a few stone-built houses where the local people lived, some of whom worked on maintenance within the prison and would occasionally be seen about the place. They were the only civilian people I would see in the next four years.

The prison itself was behind that circular wall, three large separate stone-built cell blocks, four storeys high, 100 yards long, each pointing inwards towards the open central area of the walled circle, where stood a wooden sheltered platform for the chief screw and a couple of his subordinates to shelter in while they did the four daily head counts of the cons marching silently by. Wet, snow or dry, they spent most of their working lives counting heads, and they didn't always get it right.

Only those living on the 'fours' could see over the perimeter wall, and then there was only a cloudy layer of mist through which, if you were lucky, you might see the sky a couple of times a year – or if you set your mind free you could float in the atmosphere. I never made the 'fours', though quite often my mind was free and I travelled the world in my head with some marvellous writers, and had love affairs in make-believe places and got away with lots of daring deeds.

Each cell block was known by its letter, 'A', 'B', and 'D' – 'C' was derelict. Each block had 200 cells, fifty on each of the four storeys, called 'landings', which looked from the inside like railed narrow balconies behind which were rows of heavy wooden doors. Everything, including the air, was silent, broken only by the heavy tread of the screws' boots on the slate landings. Each landing was known by its number, the 'ones' on the ground floor, then the 'twos', 'threes' and 'fours', and each cell was numbered in order 1–50.

There were other stone-built units about the place. An administration block, various workshops, a hospital, a kitchen, a boiler-house and a large isolation block for the rule-breakers (like farting in line or laughing). Everyone in the place got there sooner or later, it was known as the prison within the prison. It was that tight. For instance, I was on a special watch for a period when I first got to the Moor, as a result of attempting to escape in central London while being taken to court on this rap. This meant I wore yellow stripes on my clothing, and my clothes had to be left outside my cell from 7 p.m. to 6.30 a.m. every day.

The cells were very cold, and often very damp with condensation on the walls, and all I had at night was my underwear, a low plank bed with a coir mattress, a pair of sheets and three well-used blankets. On the floor was a small rush mat which I would pull on top to add a little warmth during the nights. The rule was, you had to be up and out of bed when the day shift came on at 6.30 a.m. 'Special watch' were not allowed any clothing at night, and it was too f*****g cold to get out of bed before you had clothes to put on, so I stayed in bed till the day shift came on, which was OK most of the time when the regular landing screw was on duty – but when he wasn't, anything could happen. Most often the screw would just give you some verbal abuse, which was better than freezing to death, but if you did it again on the following day and the same a***hole was on, it would be trouble. Three times I was put in solitary for not getting out of bed, and each time I lost three days, and the prison governor who dished the punishment was as big an a***hole as the screw who booked me.

There was no special reception ceremony for newcomers. We were led to the isolation block, issued with a set of prison gear which was stamped with our numbers. Mine was '141' – a number someone else had once had. My own clothing, which I had worn on the journey, was put in a cardboard box stamped with my number, then taken away for storage. Strange how vulnerable you begin to feel when you're told to take your clothes off, then given other things to wear, most of which had already been worn by others, because the things you choose to wear are part of your image and when you're stripped of that you feel exposed. You fold your things up with extra care, touch them almost with affection as you lay them carefully in the cardboard box. Many moons will have passed and your body will have changed a little before you wear them again. Maybe even your taste will have changed.

With the departure of our clothes we were given a pale orange-coloured set of rule cards and informed they were a personal issue for careful study. We were then locked in cells to wait for food, which was handed through the hatch in the door a while later. The food came in the 'top-and-bottom' tin, which all midday meals were served in (a round tin made from an aluminium alloy, a tiny bit bigger than a one litre container, the top separated from the bottom, and the bottom was twice the size of the top). These tins contained whatever the midday meal was, according to the day of the week. The menu was regulated to set pieces – like fish on Fridays. All the cons got one of these gourmet tins about noon each day, when they were locked away for the two hour period while the whole place closed down for lunch. The main course was all-in-one in the bottom tin, perhaps pie and two veg, maybe a drop of gravy. The top tin, sponge, and custard made with water. It was food and you ate it, even though it had been prepared several hours earlier and was often cold.

I remember one Christmas Day I was in the 'Block' (punishment unit) and on a three day bread-and-water stint for an offence of no consequence. As it was Christmas Day the diet punishment was suspended for the day. I could hear the rattle of keys and the sound of food being issued at noon. I'd had nothing but 10oz of bread for twenty-four hours, and hoped for something more exciting. I lifted the top tin and for a moment thought I was in luck, because looking at me was a golden drum stick – whooo man it's Christmas! I pulled it out with a watering mouth, and the bloody thing was a parsnip.

So what do you do? You develop a sense of humour that is offbeat to all things, these are hard times and your mind needs to be in low gear because you cannot be invisible in a confined world like this. You must ride the storm of discontent within you and stay reasonably sane.

I had taken on a way of life and couldn't see myself taking on a different way, because crime was the world I knew and where my friends were. It offered a degree of excitement, like the taste of forbidden fruit; temptation that the recklessness in me could not resist; rewards, and threats of danger. Money can be the substance of all things – freedom in a dogsbody world – whether we approve of it or not, it's the magic wand, and more to those who haven't any.

I hated being in prison, it hurt my pride, and the long confined days and nights of inactivity were soul destroying. The meaningless post mortems as to cause and effect were fairly regular companions of the mind – what had been the mistakes? What did I do wrong? Had I been too flash, too arrogant, too careless, too stubborn? I really didn't want to be in jail when I was full of go, and wanted to go. I wanted to drive fancy cars, sleep with love and Betty Grable, wear expensive clothes and throw money around in overrated night clubs and, through it all, stay forever young and reasonably sane, but there again …

As I sat on the wooden stool with the orange-coloured rule book on the small rough wooden table before me, I knew there was a long way to go, and I wasn't doing so good.

The rules on the Moor were rigid – no newspapers, no radios, lots of enforced silence and just a weekly link with the outside world on a Sunday morning when the chaplain read out the football results from the pulpit. We were not allowed to speak – as silence was the golden rule – so you learned to speak with your eyes and the movement of your head. Talk was restricted to the exercise yards and the working places.

The whole prison was packed into the church at 11 a.m. every Sunday morning for the compulsory Sunday service – we were pressed together on long wooden benches where it was possible to pass notes and send messages unobserved by the eyes of the ever-watching screws. The church was above the isolation block and the chaplain's name was Gordon Reece, a Welshman who spoke with a singsong voice, and like all good followers of the faith he loved a sinner. At some time in the future he would become the commander of the religious section of the whole prison service.

While on the Moor, he would occasionally organise a film show for a Sunday afternoon in the church and, twice a year, a variety show made up of people from surrounding villages, who would sing country songs or recite monologues or do silly sketches – always with more enthusiasm and goodwill than ability. I remember one winter afternoon, there was a group of middle-aged, real country couples of odd shapes and sizes doing silly things, and their finale had them all standing on the low platform before the altar singing 'Old Macdonald had a farm, ee-i-ee-i-oh'. Each, in turn, doing a line and then the rest doing the chorus and it was so f*****g awful – it was hilarious – and everyone started joining in and shouting and clapping for more.

Us 'receptions' were kept in the block overnight, and on that first morning seen by the local doctor. The cell door opened about 10 a.m. and the doctor stood in the doorway and asked, 'Are you all right?'. That's the standard regulation medical question used by all practitioners in the prison service, and you reply 'Yes' and you're passed fit. Shortly after that, it was the governor's turn. He told you how long you were serving and how he wouldn't tolerate any

misdemeanours or cheek to his staff, and that he believed his officers
would never misuse their authority or tell a lie, and if they said they
saw you riding around the landing on a bike, then you were riding
around on the landing on a bike, and everything an officer put in a
report would be correct – understood? He then located me in 'A'
wing and told me I would work in the blacksmith's shop.

And there began a daily routine that was so clockwork it was
often difficult to know what day of the week it was …

A bell rang at six every morning to get you up and out of bed. The
day shift came on at 6.30 a.m. Most of the time it was the same screw
on each landing, and because the place was so silent you knew by the
sound each screw made what was going on. After a while you could
recognise their tread on the slate landing or concrete floors and know
who it was, as they counted the numbers and checked the cells to
see you were still there and that your bed was made up and propped
against the wall. This was when my cell would open for me to retrieve
my clothes from the back of the chair that I had to put out overnight.

Then you would hear each landing screw call out to the screw
in charge of the block, 'all present and correct, Sir!' and, when each
landing officer had called in his numbers and the tally been taken,
the screw in charge would shout 'unlock!' and the cell doors would
be unlocked, three at a time, for slopping out. You had one trip to
the recess (toilets) to empty your slops, a chamber pot in one hand, a
jug for water in the other. There were two recesses on each landing
and the whole block would be done in twenty minutes.

Breakfast was served at 7 a.m., brought to your door by the three
landing orderlies, one with a bucket of tea, which he ladled into
your mug, the next, a ladle of watery porridge and the third, a lump
of bread the size of a brick. The job of the landing orderlies was
much sought after, because it meant leftovers and a little extra.

Then after breakfast (it was then 7.30 a.m.), leaving one behind in
charge of the block, all the doors would be opened and we would
be marched out to the exercise yard for the first of the statutory
thirty minutes' exercise. Each block had its own yard and when
the weather was foul, which it often was, we would walk around
the narrow landings in pairs for half an hour, always on the landing
where your cell was, which limited your choice of walking partner.

Nevertheless, there was always someone to talk with, and something to talk about and, as the days went by, you got to know who was who and where they were coming from.

At 9 a.m. a whistle was blown and everyone formed up in small groups of two lines. These were the groups for the different working parties. A carpenter's shop, a blacksmith's shop and a stone quarry party. This mob broke granite rocks with sledge hammers in a quarry a couple of hundred yards outside the prison, except when the weather was really bad, rather than just bad. They were locked up while the rest of us were marched off past the central check point, where the chief officer, with the governor beside him, would take the third head count of the day, numbering the parties in his notebook as we filed past.

The first count was when the shift came on at 6.30 a.m., then again after their breakfast break, at 8.10 a.m. and the third at 9 a.m. They were so paranoid about getting the numbers right that someone would go around the workshop ten minutes later to check again. This was where I first met Wally Probyn who became known as 'Angelface Probyn'. He had already escaped four times from various prisons by the time he was twenty-two, and he was in his fifties before he actually finished a sentence and got out of prison through the front gate. He escaped fifteen times over the next thirty years. He was instrumental in getting the law changed, so that if you escaped, your sentence stopped and carried on when you were caught, plus a lump on the top for escaping. Wally, a slender, average-sized person with a great sense of humour, was in no way macho or arrogant. He just wanted to be invisible, like a deer in a forest, free to roam and be left in peace, and the crimes he committed after his escapes were survival and never amounted to much – sad.

We would get to the blacksmith's just after 9 a.m., and I was told by the old blacksmith who ran the shop to work on the bellows with another con called Fred 'Yocker' Robinson. There were six anvils lined up in front of the blacksmith's fires. Each fire had a hand-pumped bellows, which pumped the air into the heart of the blacksmith's fire. 'You work with him' the old chap said. His name was Bill and he was sixty. He'd been the village blacksmith all his life, and worked with his father when he was a lad, making wheels and horse shoes. He was a civilian employed by the prison to run the blacksmith's. He was in charge and the screw who remained in the shop to keep order sat in a raised box watching.

Bill was a good old boy, enjoying a joke and free with advice and would always ask if you wanted to change the job he'd given you. You were free to walk around and chat, provided you looked like you were doing something he wouldn't mind. I worked there for four years and he showed me how to make tongs, and what each one was for, and how to weld metal with heat from the fire and make horseshoes and fancy iron gates. We were paid 1s 9d a week, then you could go to his office and ask for a rise, which you wouldn't always get and would be no more than two pence anyway. The thing I remember most about him is the old light blue boiler suit he always wore, and when he bent over a piece of hot metal on the anvil you could see the large blackhead he had on top of his bald head, he must still have that, wherever he is, and he'd be at least 106 now. 'You work with Fred,' he said to me.

I'd heard of the 'Yocker' brothers before we met. He was known as 'Yocker' to his friends, 5ft 11in, in his early thirties, thick set and crop-headed. There were in fact two hair styles, short back and sides or crop'd. He had two years to go for – I can't remember what exactly, a robbery of some kind – and he was liked and respected amongst the 'chaps'. He was born and lived in west London, and was married to an attractive brunette who he had grown up with; he always referred to her as 'The Princess' and held her in great affection. She never missed a monthly visit. She couldn't have children for some reason, and was a dedicated family girl, if you know what I mean. Mums and dads and brothers and sisters were her world, and that was one of the reasons I guess she was always so loyal to Yocker. Yocker was a bit of a player – I remember the story he told me one day of him going to Roedean to watch the girls playing hockey. Roedean is a very exclusive school that teaches rich young girls to become rich young ladies with all the proper graces, in their white knickers and mini-skirts running around the playing field. In those days, a 'glimpse of stocking was something shocking', so it became a joke and I would often ask him if he was going to Roedean at the weekend. Yocker had a brother also known as 'Yocker', a little older, and both grafters and respected. 'One of our own' as the reference goes.

Yocker Fred went to Harrow in his mid-teens to further his education. Harrow is the most upmarket school in west London, and exclusively teaches the bright, wealthy and often pampered privileged. Many ex-pupils became politicians, bankers etc. – various types of suspects. Yocker was from the back streets, and got to Harrow on their boxing team because he was a gifted boxer. I don't think he did any serious studying – he was very streetwise, but not academic even though he was very intelligent.

We hit it off at once and became good friends, and over the next two years we formed a relationship that lasted till he died of a heart attack some years later. We never met again after he got out, because our paths didn't cross, but we were often in touch. He used to lecture me on behaviour, manners and self-respect, and what values in life were worth pursuing, and when turning the other cheek is a virtue. In many ways he treated me like a brother, and taught me many things. We had endless hours of conversation while heating lumps of iron in the old blacksmith's fire, many laughs and shared moments that warm the memory. He once said to me, 'there's nothing wrong with you, Georgie boy, that a few years of life won't cure' (and that applies to us all), and, 'never do anything with your eyes closed'. According to what I've heard, he had a heart attack after screwing the young wife of 'Jack the Hat' and that was just after Jack the Hat was killed by the Kray twins.

Yocker showed me how to pump the bellows, which took no time at all, and then I knew all I needed to know about pumping bellows. Our first task of the day was lighting the fire, we'd clean it from yesterday and put a burning coal, from the fire Blacksmith Bill had going, into the cleaned spot, cover with coal and pump. On a cold morning the fires were lit with enthusiasm, as you can imagine. As the side of each fire was an open water tank to dip the hot metal in and, if you threw water on the fire and pumped hard, great clouds of dark grey smoke would bellow out and when all six fires pumped smoke together the place was like being in a thick fog, you couldn't see a thing. There was an occasion when we had a particularly sadistic screw sitting in the observation box watching over us and all six forges pumped smoke till nothing in the shop could be seen, everyone knew where his box was and lumps of iron went flying around the place …

At ten to twelve, work stopped and we would put red-hot irons into buckets of cold water to heat it and wash our hands. There was no hot water on the wings so you used what opportunities there were to wash in hot water. Then we lined up in twos, inside or out, according to the weather, counted by the screw in charge and then marched off to the centre for the 'chief' to count as we filed past his sheltered hut. That was the eighth count of the day, and there would be that many again before the 5 o'clock lock-up. After a while the whole thing is so mechanical, you just function.

There were three incidents that I can remember in connection with these head counts. The weather was reasonable on all three occasions, strangely enough.

Our party was marching across the yard towards the 'chief's' check point for the midday bang-up, when the screw in charge said something to one of our group and referred to him by his number, then proceeded to boast how he knew everyone by their number and could identify them. This triggered off a reaction from the guy, which kept the rest of us suppressing our laughter. (Although the screw's remarks probably weren't the cause, just the trigger.) Anyway, this guy started to b****ck the screw, then stopped for a moment as he realised the screw would nick him, and then, realising he was going to be nicked for abuse anyway, he began mouthing the screw all the way to the check point with invectives of increasing richness. There were always at least six screws waiting to escort guys straight down to the block as the parties marched by. Every day someone made the block for something or other – verbal abuse being the most regular, because there are times when you say, 'enough!' We didn't see the guy again for a week.

There was never any heavy physical violence in the punishment block. There are plenty of ways to be sadistic without using violence, and there was a strange sense of unity among the cons in those days that was recognised by the screws. A few screws were as *macho de luxe* as they could be, in constant danger of crossing the line and everyone tried to avoid them and when you couldn't, you bit your tongue. But any rumour of violence in the block would have caused an explosion. They aren't all heroes, and their total lack of communication leads more to fear and mythology than wisdom.

The rule was, never talk to a prisoner and the thinking behind that was, that some prisoners were very devious and might corrupt some of them – they may have been right.

The second incident, I remember, took everyone by surprise. Our party was behind another at the tail end of the count and most of the other parties were already away. There were about twenty guys in the party ahead, when out stepped one of them to face the group of screws waiting to count them. All in one movement this guy floored one of the screws and, for a moment, everything was confusion, then all of the screws tried to grab this guy at once. The chief stopped his count, and the party who the guy had been with all cheered. The next thing, the whole party of cheerers were led down the block and all lost three days remission. The guy who whacked the screw got three months on top of his sentence, and the maximum punishment diet of bread and water. This con had a genuine grudge against the screw for constant harassment but he had no redress. The rules were – it was an offence to make false allegations against an officer ... and, of course, all allegations were false!

The third incident concerned an African guy, the only black man in the prison. He had an air of threat about him. He never spoke to anyone, and if you got close and bumped into him he would lash out without a word. Everyone kept their distance. He was a couple of cells down from me on the same landing, and I would say 'hello' to him whenever I got a chance, but never got a response. I always thought he'd had a bad deal. He was doing fourteen years for killing a police dog. Apparently, according to the grapevine, he'd come to the UK for political reasons and he was a tribal leader of some sort. He looked like a black version of a compressed Schwarzenegger, muscles coming out of his ears, solid as a rock.

He had been living in a room in Notting Hill and his neighbours had complained, probably because he was black and ugly – racial prejudice was everywhere at that time. The police came, and he told them to piss off, so they battered his door down and sent a police dog into his room, and he killed it. Anyway, he was a bit odd, and I'd hate to know what kind of treatment he got when they got him to the station. A group of screws were trying to take him down the block for some reason as our party got to the count, and he produced a blade of some sort and the screws backed off. The last our party saw of him, he was walking up the main drive surrounded by the governor and a bunch of screws. In the end a screw got his hand cut and the black man was sent to the nut house.

The midday meal, in the top-and-bottom tins, was waiting on trays in the cell blocks as we marched back in. They had been sent up from the kitchen at 11.30 a.m. and we would pick one up and take it to our cell, then be locked up as the whole prison closed down at 12.30 p.m. for the shift to go off. They came back at 1.30 p.m. and counted us again to make sure the numbers were the same, before slopping us out, three at a time, then exercise, then back to work. The afternoon was identical to the morning, except the time had changed. When we filed back in the wings at 5 p.m., that was it – a lump of bread, a pat of marge (margarine), and a cup of tea, goodnight.

I would feel the emptiness of the silent hours before me, a cold clawing in the stomach and would tell myself, this is not forever, because nothing ever is. Just be more careful in the future, don't get caught again, think about what you do.

Saturdays were slightly different. We only worked half a day, so there was no exercise in the mornings, just work. Then in the afternoon, from 2–3.30 p.m., a football match would be organised on the makeshift pitch behind D wing, and the whole prison was allowed to wander around the field for ninety minutes to intermingle and meet new people. This is where I picked up again with Bob Macanless.

We only met at weekends, until I was taken off special watch and moved to the wing he was in. Bob loved fast cars and fast women, which would be our downfall eventually, but that's the way it goes. We made friends with guys from all over and for a while we even made a 'book'. Taking bets wasn't a serious business, it just gave us something to do. Till we were set up one day by a screw who had a pocket radio and fed the results to a con he was pally with. We didn't lose any money, because this guy was owing us more than he could ever pay, and we tumbled. It was only prison currency anyway, so we quit. That reminds me – Jack the Hat owed us money on a bet …

Bob worked in the Dartmoor Prison quarry, and became friends with a guy named Fred Baker who was doing time for safe-breaking. Fred was from Yorkshire, that's northern England, and was now in his forties. He'd once been a miner in a coal pit in a place called Chapeltown just outside of Sheffield. One of his jobs was shot-blasting and he knew a lot about explosives – the various types for different tasks and different materials – and we spent many a Saturday afternoon talking about metals, laminations and the structure of safes, because Bob and I were hooked on the idea we should make a business of safe-breaking. We would be going out of prison with nothing and had a lot of catching up to do. Bob was getting out a few weeks before me, and we would meet up again. We spent a lot of time discussing ways of life and putting theories into practice. As the weeks and the months and the years went by, Fred told us where to look to find explosives, and gave us a target of a social club in Chapeltown where they kept their money in a safe.

My mother had moved to a flat in Fulham and was waiting for me to get out of jail. She always said she wanted a home for me to come out to, and would never leave while I was away. Bill and Mary were both in Australia and doing good, but my mother wouldn't join them, although we all wanted her to. She would never leave if I lived at home, and I couldn't live with her for long anyway, because the local CID would be knocking on the door occasionally and that would create problems which I needed to avoid. Nevertheless, I understood my mother's feelings and I would go and stay with her for a while and explain to her I couldn't stand the aggravation of those knocks on the door, and the life I was going to live for a while could create even more problems. My mother's loyalty was so natural. She never criticised or passed a cross word, and when the local CID did call, pretending they were looking for Bill, she just said she hadn't seen him and didn't know where he was, but I dropped in every week.

Shortly after Bob left the Moor it was my turn to leave, and I was escorted from the isolation unit where everyone spent their last twenty-four hours to the main gate where the old French marketplace was. Maybe it was just the difference the feeling of a softer material gave against the hardness of the prison garb, but all my senses seemed to come alive. I carried the small prison-issue holdall, the bag made in prison – same shape, same colour, all looking alike – given to all discharge prisoners to carry the change of underwear supplied by the Ministry of Defence, the 'quartermaster' of all things. At the gate I had to give my name and number to the gatekeeper of the day, just to check it was me they were letting out. The fact that we all knew each other meant nothing and no one was giving smiles away. The prison van was there waiting to take me to the station and that was it – six years of my life wasted, down the drain. But I couldn't feel that kind of sorrow now as I'd waited so long for this, and there had been times when I'd wondered if it would ever happen. Then it had – and I felt exposed.

The moors looked misty in the morning light, not threatening anymore, and the whispering wind was somehow bidding its own farewell. We drove in silence – nothing to say. I'd lost the knack of chatting with strangers, and I'd learnt to live with myself in a way that silence is golden. The moors seemed no different, just as bleak, just as lonely, and for a moment I felt their desolation. Then the prison van dropped me off at the railway station and suddenly I was alone in a public place without any confines to control the way I turned or what steps I took. Had I paid my debt, or do you owe me one?

I felt as if the spotlight was on me. Everyone was looking at me as if I'd come from outer space, and both heads of the crowd of two turned away. This feeling of people staring hung around for several days, because I'd lost the ability to feel at ease near people in an ordinary situation. I felt that people looked at me with eyes and said nothing – catch them, and they turned away. I had that feeling of being a 'nobody', as the train arrived at Waterloo and I got the underground for Fulham. Maybe I was a little crazy after all those years.

6

I was twenty-eight years old, with a mindset completely submerged in the criminal culture that I had lived in for the last six years. Prisons aren't designed to correct antisocial behaviour like mine. They may pretend they are, to appease 'Joe Bloggs' who foots the bill but, in reality, their policies inflict deprivation and crush the spirit into submission. Their victims are humiliated, isolated and brutalised. There is no moral high ground to distinguish the good guys from the bad guys.

The years in Wandsworth and Dartmoor, part of which were for a crime I knew nothing about, had shaped my mind beyond normal reason. I was not a macho person. I avoided conflict and gave violence a miss. I left the Moor with the clothes I stood in, £5 in my pocket and an underlying anger at the way I had been humiliatingly treated, as if I were some sort of freak to be held in contempt. If it weren't for my mother, I would have nowhere to stay or a place to go. The prison system had convinced me that any help you needed, you helped yourself. The benefits of the 'straight-and-narrow' for me were bulls**t, part of the blanket of ignorance.

You can see your family once a month, for twenty minutes, in a visiting room with a man in blue watching over you. And you can write a small letter to your family and your children every two weeks. And most of the time we will keep you isolated in a damp and cold concrete box so you can ponder our humanity and our contempt for you. And we will keep you safely in the wilderness, hundreds of miles from nowhere, where your family can only afford to visit you twice a year. We are the good guys. We make the rules, scumbags. A million decent people make a good living in the crime industry, many with mortgages and they don't want to be unemployed. They go to church on Sundays.

I hadn't expected to be housed in the Hilton, but I also hadn't expected to be further outcast or further alienated.

My mother welcomed me with open arms. She had a sparse, though comfortable, two bedroom flat that she had made into a home for me and she was the only person in the world I could let down. I knew I would not be able to live there for very long as the local CID would frequently harass me as a regular suspect whenever they were investigating a difficult crime, and this would frustrate and anger me and I was already full of resentment. I would do nothing at a local level to give anyone cause to harass me, but that would make no difference.

The day after my release Bob and I met up. He had been out and about for about a month, living with his sister in Ruislip, and he now needed to move on. We headed for Sheffield as planned.

We got to Sheffield early in the afternoon and followed the directions we'd been given for Chapeltown, and from Chapeltown to the coal mine. We walked down the narrow road that crossed flat, open fields and sheltered in the shadows. We watched the shifts changing at 10 p.m. under the lights at the pit head. In the shadows we were part of the bunker and they couldn't see us, and we knew the bunker wouldn't be used by this shift.

Three feet in front of the bunker door there was a blast wall backed by a mound of earth, from a distance the bunker was just a shadow at the side of an open field. It wasn't a totally dark night and there was enough light from the stars to make objects fairly visible. We could see the pit head beneath a spotlight, and the outline of several buildings as we made our way from the road to the bunker, following a ditch between two fields. Bob carried a small bag of tools we thought we'd need, that we'd purchased for the occasion.

When we reached the bunker we rested in the shadows for a while as we looked all around us for any signs of movement. Then, with the aid of a shielded torch we looked into the entrance and saw the heavy metal door confronting us and we knew immediately this wasn't going to be easy. The only heavy tools we had were a hammer and a 2ft crowbar. However, the hinges of the door were cemented into the brickwork and we went for them. We were tired and tried not to notice as we worked as quietly as we could, chipping away a little at a time, till finally after two hours and a lot of sweat, the door fell open and we were in.

There was a small chamber with hardly enough room to turn around. A few shelves on the left held a few packets of detonators, 100 in each pack. One pack was all we wanted. Facing us now was a second ordinary domestic-type door with a padlock on it, much easier to open than the first. Inside was another small chamber and we could see by torchlight the various boxes of explosives. It took us several minutes to locate the type we had been recommended, called 'Saninite'. They were wrapped in a greasy kind of paper, cartridge shaped, about 4in long and 2in diameter. Inside the wrappers the explosive had the texture and smell of fresh marzipan on a Christmas cake. Each cartridge weighed 4oz, and I guess the miners bored 2in holes to poke them down. We weren't interested in other varieties, just the one, and we quickly stuffed about forty in the holdall. We knew this stuff wasn't dangerous without detonators and could be bumped and tossed around.

We had what we came for and left, following the ditch back to the road. I took the bag from Bob and walked ahead, he stayed a bit behind so we could warn each other of anything approaching.

In Chapeltown we went to the lock-up garages and got an old Austin Seven that had seen better days. There wasn't a great selection and time was running out. Already it was 5 a.m. and would soon be getting light. We parked behind the social club, scaled the back wall and went into the club through a skylight. The manager's office was easy to find, his door was unlocked and the 4ft safe stood against the wall.

If my memory serves me right, it was a 'Ratner'. A Midlands company that had recently linked up with another safe manufacturer called 'Milner', and together they were getting a good reputation along with 'Chubb', but I wasn't concerned with all that and at that stage didn't care who made it, as long as it would blow open.

Bob removed the front locking plate and set about inserting half a stick of Saninite into the locking box, while I looked over the place. We'd had lots of discussion and lots of practical advice on how to open a box with just enough explosives to open the door without wrecking the building or waking up the neighbourhood. Two ounces was considered the right amount, and as this was our first, and we'd been up for almost three days, we disagreed on the amount and Bob went for 2oz and ran the twin wire from the detonator he'd inserted into the keyhole to the outside of the office door. Then we packed everything we could over the safe – carpet, cushion, chair – anything to muffle the sound.

There was nothing happening outside the club, no sound or sight of anything so there wasn't anything to offset the thud we were about to set off. Bob made the connection and it came like a body blow of deep thunder. I gave it a second, and went into the office which was dense with acrid fumes and difficult to see with just the aid of a torch light. The safe door was bellied out like it was pregnant, but it wasn't open. I could see inside a ½in bolt holding the inner plate of the door to the outer, which I could reach and cut with a junior hacksaw to get the door open. It would take half an hour and now someone was banging and shouting at the front door of the club. We had to leave, going out through the back door and driving off towards Sheffield in the old Austin Seven.

Then, a few miles down the road a foot patrol policeman saw us heading his way and signed for us to stop and I realised I hadn't put the lights on. We drove past him, and decided to head for the station and get a train back to London. We had just enough money to get us home. We stopped for directions from a milkman doing his morning rounds and then parked near the station a few minutes later. There was a train within the hour and we were back in London by about midday.

Bob took the bag at the station as he had a spot to stash it in overnight and we would meet again tomorrow. I went to mum's, who greeted me as always, glad to see me. She asked me where I'd been in her usual casual way, and I said 'Nowhere special – just looking up friends and seeing what's going on in the world' and she made me a cup of tea.

My mother used to say that I would always do things my own way so she never criticised or questioned me, and I was caught between wanting to stay with her where she would wash my shirts, cook my meals and let me bring a girlfriend home, and knowing that I couldn't. There were so many things I knew I should have done and somehow was unable to. We talked of joining Bill and Mary in Australia, and agreed that was what we'd do. When I felt ready. First, I had some catching up to do and needed the space in which to be a little crazy and take my form of payback and work out some of the bogeymen that were my own inner feelings of past outrages. I was twenety-seven years old and back to square one – or was square one the only place I'd ever been?

Bob and I met the following afternoon, and decided we needed a decent car. London, now in the late fifties, had moved into a faster gear. The place felt more prosperous and lots more seemed to be going on – more traffic, more people hurrying around. The Lyceum was no longer the dance hall it had been, and Covent Garden fruit market where I had worked for a few weeks during the tail end of the war was turning into a trendy place of stylish shops and jewellery stalls, with buskers entertaining on the cobbled streets; and Jones' Café, in the alleyway behind the Bird in Hand pub, where I would buy a slice of bread and jam for one and a half pence when I worked in Long Acre, was gone. But the streets and building were the same and I remembered them well. I knew where to go looking for what we needed, and found a one-year-old Mark Two Jaguar saloon in a row of open garages beneath a row of mews flats in a cul-de-sac near Hyde Park Corner.

In those few weeks Bob had been out and about looking for work. He discovered from a girlfriend, who had once been a cashier in a cinema that the ABC chain of cinemas kept their takings in the manager's office and only banked them once a week. There were three major cinema chains, Odeon, ABC and Gaumont, and there were lots of cinemas about. Bob had chosen one in a busy suburb on the outskirts of London. We were both down to odd coins in our pockets – no money, no eat – and neither of us had the temperament for that. I drove the car over to Bob's sister in Ruislip as he wanted to test-run the Jaguar on a new stretch of highway nearby. His sister was in her mid-twenties with two young boys. We sat chatting while Bob was out breaking the speed limit. He had a passion for fast cars and fast driving and would soon do most of the chauffeuring.

Early in the evening we went over to where Bob had left the holdall – a disused garden shed beside a railway line – and we put the few things we needed into a carrier bag and left the rest for later. We parked the car in a back street behind the cinema, just before the last person left and locked the place up. Then we walked around to the rear double-door exit and popped them open, just as we used to in earlier days when we were 'bunking in'.

The manager's office was easy to find and the Yale lock offered no resistance. We followed the same routine as before, only the safe was slightly smaller and we covered it with cushions. We had only been in the place for thirty minutes and were ready to blow the safe. It was getting close to midnight and the streets were empty. We didn't want to be driving along deserted streets in a stolen car at this time of night, so we decided to wait till the morning before setting the charge when the buses were running. We spent most of the night lounging on the sofas in the upstairs foyer, looking at the police station across the street, eating ice cream and munching chocolate bars from the kiosk.

The wires from the detonator ran to the side of the large foyer windows where Bob stood with the 9v battery ready to make the connection. We waited till the first signs of movement in the street outside and a truck was passing, before the charge went off with a deep thud. We both stood for a moment looking into the street to see if anyone had noticed. It was only our second attempt, and we had a lot to learn. I went into the manager's office that was now thick with acrid smoke and held my breath as I looked for the safe, and the door was open wide. I scooped everything that looked like money into the carrier bag and made for the door. I was keen now to get out of the place. Going out the same way as we entered, Bob counted the money from the carrier bag as we drove away, separating the tools and explosives. We had taken 8oz with us and had only used two. The tools and explosives were now surplus and we'd dump them along the way.

This was the beginning of a routine we would follow in the future, taking only the things we thought we would need, then dumping everything including, in time, the clothes we had worn. The favourite place for the explosives was down a drain in the street where it would break down and wash away.

By the time we stopped for breakfast at an early morning working-man's café we were carrying nothing but money. We each had two hundred and thirty quid. The average wage then was about twenty quid a week so we weren't wealthy, but we could afford breakfast and this was my first sausage, bacon and egg for a long time and absolute magic.

There were still things to do before we could go home. We got the number of a car plate firm in Paddington from a call box and ordered plates for the Jaguar that would take it off the missing list. This wasn't much of a problem anyway, because stolen cars were not registered as stolen for three days, they were treated as 'taking and driving away' by joy riders. Bob had taken a fancy to this car and wanted to keep it for a while so we picked up the plates and changed them in a derelict warehouse in dockland. Bob dropped me off at the underground and I caught the train home.

We met again the following day and read the story of the break-in on the inside pages of one of the newspapers. More money appeared to be missing than we had taken, and we speculated whether that was the manager of the cinema 'cooking the books' or the police playing games. Whatever, it goes to show you can't believe everything you read in the newspapers.

We did some shopping and went to the safe deposit building, which was then in Piccadilly, and each opened a deposit box, putting the detonators in one and the Saninite in the other. The keys were easy to hide and the boxes perfectly safe unless someone robbed the place. By the end of the day we'd spent most of our money and agreed to meet again the following week.

I loafed around at home for a few days playing LPs of Sarah Vaughan, Ella, Nancy Wilson, Tony Bennett, Frank Sinatra and the new guy, Elvis. I bought a record player with the LPs from an attractive girl with large breasts in a small music shop nearby. I looked at the bulges in her soft white sweater till I went red in the face. I was sexually frustrated and had become reserved and unsure of myself. A lot of my early cockiness and confidence had been stripped away, although I felt eager to make the changeover from no sex to lots of sex. I knew nothing was going to happen, because I was too embarrassed by my own nervousness and uncertainty to take the lead. She smiled at me and I could say nothing and left. I went back to the shop a couple of times, more to see her than to buy LPs but I never quite had the courage to ask her out. Months later, we drove past her on the street in Bob's two-seater AC Bristol prototype racing car. She waved to me and I knew I should have dated her and gone beneath the sweater. Except, having lived in the wholly male world for so long without even seeing a woman, they had become sexual objects of fantasy for me without any need of dialogue. That is not the real world or the way things work. I needed to learn some social graces and how to talk without being self-conscious.

The next decade – the sixties – was just around the corner and a new way of life would blossom with free love, flower-power, rock and roll; and girls would start taking the initiative. But we were still at the stage when most girls liked a little encouragement to take their knickers down, and I no longer felt at ease with them. What I thought I needed was a little romance without any need for fore-play – and it wasn't going to happen. I was in Hyde Park late in the afternoon a couple of days later when I saw this lovely looking hustler. She took me to a room she had, and it didn't work.

When Bob and I met up again the following week we talked a lot about survival and the pros and cons of the dangers we faced. We both knew we were sticking our necks out and things could go wrong if we weren't very careful, but both of us had a certain stubborn reck-lessness about us and a weird inner sense of anger. We knew we were putting ourselves on the line – we had no qualms about that, and we had no plans other than our immediate need of money.

The safe deposit building was closed over the weekends, so we would have to collect anything we needed on a Friday afternoon. We stuck to the cinemas for a few weeks because they were easy and we had lots to learn. We always thought they were a limited venture anyway, because sooner or later they would stop leaving their money on the premises – but it took them a long time. As we became more efficient we became more organised and began going out to work less often.

We rented a lock-up garage in west London from an old couple and locked the Jaguar away. We would only use it for working. Bob bought himself a white two-seater MGA sports car, which I rode in often but didn't particularly like. It caught people's attention and he loved it for pulling the birds, whom he would take out for long rides, sighting-up jobs and going further and further afield.

I had been out (of prison) about a month and was beginning to feel more at ease. I spent most of my money on tailor-made suits, expensive shirts and the rest of the gear so that I felt more prosperous and more confident. I never used the pubs and didn't know the clubs. The dance halls were different now and I knew no one. I turned around in the street to ogle at a nice pair of legs, but still wasn't having any luck.

I came home to my mother's one morning after being away for a couple of days visiting an old Dartmoor pal who lived up north. He had rumours of some work that a couple of local guys wanted to do, but didn't know how to go about it. He would meet up with these guys and tell me more. In the meantime there was other stuff to think about. My mother told me that two local detectives had been to the flat 'looking for Billy' they said and she told them she hadn't seen him in years. I don't think she really believed they were looking for Billy. He had been in Australia for ten years, and they were around the flat to check me out as a matter of routine. I'd made no waves in their district so they had no cause to harass me. Nevertheless, I guessed it was time to move on. My mother understood this and I avoided the tears in her eyes. She knew I had to work life out for myself, like we all do.

Bob had left his sister's home and was living in a hotel where he was keen I should join him. He picked me up, and we took off for Hastings, a seaside resort fifty-odd miles from London where we could be extravagant as tourists and not noticed as anything else, and most of the girls were on holiday and out to enjoy themselves.

We moved around and only worked a long way from home, and over the months we did quite a lot of cinemas, most of them I can't remember. The reason we did so many was because only Bob and I knew about it and they kept our extravagant lifestyle going till the 'big one' came along – the 'rainbow's end' dream of many.

There is only one job I can remember that had spin-offs for other people. We tried to organise our workload and minimise the risks. We had parked the Jaguar in a street in Guildford, near the cinema that we would start the night with. The manager went out the front as we were preparing to go in at the back. There was a flat roof with a window in the side wall. The window was over a stair, inside the cinema. I covered the window with my body and broke it, then let Bob in through one of the exits. Most cinemas were putting chains over the exits now, which took about five minutes to release and another five minutes to break into the manager's office. We left just before midnight with about five hundred quid, and headed for a place called Aldershot some twenty-odd miles away. Aldershot is a military town, and we hoped they all went to the movies on a Sunday night. The town was deserted when we got there. The streets were well lit and everything was asleep. The cinema was on a main street, and the obvious way in was through an open toilet window halfway up the front of the building. This meant I would be completely exposed for several minutes as I climbed up the 4in waste pipe to ease through the small window.

For some reason, we had problems with the office door and wasted time, and the night began to pass. We had a third cinema in mind that night but it would have to wait for another time. We blew the safe at 6 a.m. and were driving out of the town ten minutes later, with three times more money than we'd expected.

When Bob and I left Aldershot, we drove over to the third cinema we had been going to do but it was too late, so we dumped the tools and surplus explosives and headed for London. We were both tired, and I was driving merrily along the almost deserted road towards Chiswick, when a car some distance ahead of me pulled up at a traffic light. I braked, but not enough, and ran into the back of him causing no damage, but we both got out, made excuses and swapped addresses. I offered him twenty quid to cover any cost. However, he was on his way to work with a passenger, who interfered and told him to claim on insurance. I drove off to dump the Jaguar in an old spot I had used years earlier. It was still parked there six weeks later.

Bob upgraded his sports car and we rented a new garage and acquired a new Mark Two Triumph sports car. I bought a soft top Ford Consul and called on my mum every week.

We seemed to be pulling lots of money and spending it as if it had no meaning. We started hitting the main post offices and Woolworths, who favoured combination safes. We travelled north to visit guys we'd met in jail who were of similar minds, to learn of other things – like government-run egg marketing boards. They bought the eggs from the farmers, and paid them out in cash once a month from their local area offices. A couple of times we ran the gauntlet of near-misses, when we had to drop the money and our gear and abandon the ringer (stolen car), then hide in funny places till it was safe to move.

So we thought we'd try Brighton. It is a largish resort on the south coast with a population of ¼ million, 50 miles from London and with a lot going on. It had a bit of a reputation as the favourite spot for dirty weekends, and the town seemed to have a shifting population. It had the character of a London suburb, which gave the town a comfortable feel to stay in. We booked into the Marine Hotel on the sea front overlooking the pier. I'd stayed there some years before with Molly, the raver for all seasons. (Incidentally, at my mother's one day she told me that Molly had called around one evening looking for me, drunk, my mother said and she had told her nothing. I don't know how she even got my address, and I'll never know. I think if I had gone to the West End looking, I would have found her, but she wouldn't have been the same Molly. I don't know.)

We ate most of our meals in hotels, as they were as good as restaurants and you didn't have to do the washing up and you were treated well. The Marine Hotel had two waitresses, one with dark hair and one with light. They were both in their early twenties, a year apart – sisters. Bob and I debated a bit over the next couple of days, which one do you fancy? So we asked them out and I paired with Maria and Bob took Kazia. The days were our own so we had plenty of time to do things. We would go to London a couple of times a week for a concert or show, and to the car racing circuits, or whatever we fancied. For the concerts, we'd go to the Kilburn Empire on a Sunday night as that was *the* place. The first time we took Maria and Kazia we got them home at two in the morning, and their mum wasn't very pleased. She's been that way ever since. We planned to go out the following week, but Bob was distracted for some reason so Maria and I went to the concert alone, then afterwards to the Pigalle night club in Piccadilly where Sammy Davis Junior was performing.

Reflecting now for a moment, I must have created an image of prosperity, and Maria must have seen me as an everyday Father Christmas, and each in our own way became spellbound. Maria was different to other girls I'd known. She lacked the insight of city girls and believed men were in every way providers. I fell in love with her, much more than I should have done (to be fair to both of us). I should have walked away before it went too far. That would have been the right thing to do, but by then I wanted a relationship more natural than a casual affair.

Maria told me of her family plight, that they were Polish refugees from the early part of the war. First in Africa then England, where they were spending the six years required to emigrate to America. America was their goal. They spoke of it as the 'Eldorado' of all things, which to them it was.

Bob and I found a flat, as we had decided to make Brighton our main base, and I began dating Maria whenever we were there. Bob and I often went away for days at a time as we had met up with some guys in the north who kept talking about this Co-op collection of money, from all the twenty-three Co-op shops in the town, and we needed to check it out. I used to write to Maria when we were on those trips, and things moved along. Maria would tell me of her parents' reaction because they never invited me into their place or approved of me. They saw me as a threat to the unity of the family and the word was that none of the family would go to America unless they all went, and that I was a gypsy.

The Co-op in the north was, in many ways, a gift with a sting in the tail. A 'piece of cake' was the going term. Twice a week, a slightly-built accountant from the Co-op headquarters in the town would be chauffeured round the twenty-three shops by an old guy from a taxi firm, in order to collect the takings in a large holdall. Bob and I really wanted to do this on our own because there was a lot of money involved and we didn't need any help, but the two guys didn't just want a share, they wanted to be involved, which was OK by us, even though it would be overdone. The best time would have been Christmas, when two holdalls were needed, but that was too far away.

Bob and I nicked two cars in Birmingham, a long way from Brighton and a long way from Derby where the Co-ops were. They would be abandoned after the 'blag' ('blag' was the rough description for this type of event), and tracked back to Birmingham, giving the plods something to think about.

I wrote to Maria a couple of times in the week that we were away, as I was beginning to wonder about the future and I was getting the first feelings of doubt about our lifestyle. I wanted a break from the pressure and the growing periods of uncertainty when we actually went to work. I wanted to stabilise and think of less dangerous ways of getting a living, and if this Co-op thing worked out as good as hoped, it would make a difference.

There was a bus stop by the T-junction around the corner from the last Co-op shop, and Bob and one of the guys stood there waiting for the cashier to drive by. I was parked facing them a few yards up the road and, when the taxi was close enough, I pulled out in front of it like a stupid driver and they had to brake in front of the bus stop. Bob stepped off the kerb as if to see if the taxi passenger was OK, and lifted the holdall. The second car was across the street with the second guy at the wheel. We piled into it and drove away.

We abandoned the second car about a mile away, where one of the guys had left his own car, and we drove to an empty garage and split the money. Less than we'd hoped, though still quite a lot, we each had about £3,000. Bob and I were dropped off in another town, and we booked into a hotel that catered for travelling salesmen, and the following morning took the train for London.

I wanted to give my mother money towards Australia, and Bob wanted to pick his car up, so we met up again early in the evening and set off for Brighton. Maria had left her job at the Marine and was waiting tables in a new diner that had just opened. We got there about 10 p.m., found one of Maria's tables and I got the cold shoulder – heavy. After a few minutes I got up and took her arm and lead her into a corridor and asked what the problem was. She said that I'd been away and not been in touch with her, and then just turned up. I'd written those letters to her, so what was going on? She said she had to go home and we could talk tomorrow.

Apparently the family had been invited to the American embassy for medicals and their visas were then to be issued, so Maria's mother had hidden my letters hoping that I would disappear and not divide the family. A few days later, her mum, dad, and young Toshu, Maria's brother, went to London overnight and Maria and Kazia would join them the next day. Maria and I slept together in her mum's bed. I remember taking my music centre with a bunch of LPs to their basement flat in Devonshire Place in Kemptown, so we could listen to the sounds and get in the mood, but Kemptown was on a DC current and the music centre was AC so we had to do without.

Over the next couple of months I began to look around for a different source of income. Maria wanted me to go to America with them, but there was no way I could get a green card and my feelings were towards Australia. Maria didn't want that, so we compromised. Maria would go to America with the family and when she returned we would get married and, I hoped before long, give Australia a try.

The family sailed from Southampton on the *Ile de France* for New York late on a Friday afternoon. I forget now how the family travelled to Southampton. Maria and I were to meet them there. I drove her in my car, listening to the music on the radio. Both of us were a bit naive I guess – I wanted us to live together, but Maria would have none of that, and that's really what we should have done. She knew about my background, I made no secret of that to her, and in turn I knew she was flirtatious, though the mixture of love and sex can be both persuasive and blind, and my recklessness still lingered. We drove towards Southampton with the warm sun and light breeze on our faces, listening to the music on the radio which caught our imagination. 'I saw the Harbour Lights' was on the airways as we drove into Southampton Docks.

Then, as I left alone, driving silently back to Brighton, deep in those inner feelings of uncertainty that sometimes in our lives we all go through, there I was, footloose and fancy free – except, I was in love with her and she was pregnant.

Ten days later, I booked a flight from New York to London for Maria to fly back. I met her at the airport and we disappeared for three days and I was in trouble with the family for not telling anyone. We stayed at the Compleat Angler hotel in Marlow, Buckinghamshire, on the banks of the River Thames, at the side of the ornate suspension bridge leading into the town and beside a lock gate with a weir. My mother had worked in the kitchen of this hotel when Billy and I were young kids, and we had spent many happy days there playing on the river bank and jumping in the water. Maria and I rowed up the river and I showed her all the magic places of our youth and the cottage where we once lived, and we met Dickie Price, a playmate from next door.

In a house opposite the basement flat of Maria's parents in Devonshire Place, lived Victor and Helena Lenkiewicz. Victor was the brother of Maria's dad and they had fled Poland at the same time. Victor and Helena and two young boys, Richard and Andrew, Maria's cousins, were all part of the family who weren't interested in emigrating to America. Maria would stay with them while arrangements were made for our wedding, and we looked around for our own place.

We were married a few weeks later by the family's Polish priest, in the local Catholic Church, and then took off for a few days to Devon, where I showed Maria the outside of Dartmoor Prison. Don't ask me why – it was something I wanted to do, see the place from the outside when the sun was shining and with no sound of howling wind and bitter storms.

Bob and I hadn't done anything in several weeks to earn any money, and soon the wolf would be at the door. We had emptied the safe deposit boxes and dumped the surplus gear. Bob was living most of the time with a girlfriend, who incidentally, was the wife of a local wide-boy who seemed to be getting by without doing anything except pulling the birds. He was in fact, sleeping occasionally with his landlady, and I don't know if he was paying any rent.

The circle of local friends Bob and I had made met in the after-hours drinking clubs that were scattered around Brighton. Bob was a heavyish drinker and me hardly at all, but we would arrange to meet in them, and recognised the regular faces, the usual stuff. We got friendly with a couple of guys who had a club on the seafront, along with their wives and various friends. Bob and I would chat and laugh about who was cheating on who this week, because they all seemed to me to be cheating on each other. They were both called Ronnie. One was Ronnie Freeman, and I've forgotten the other. They used to lend Maria and me their flat keys when we wanted somewhere to go.

Bob wasn't ready to change his lifestyle or do anything else. He loved his sports cars and the image that went with them. He had bought a second-hand prototype AC Bristol from Graham Hill at his garage, The Chequered Flag. There were only two ever made and it roared like a lion. Graham Hill went on to be world champion, and I wanted to dump the AC Bristol over the cliffs into the sea but Bob would never settle for a Ford.

I was searching around for other ways to earn a living, something that would keep the show on the road and minimise the pitfalls. There was a shop and flat vacant in the town centre that was ideal for a sandwich bar, but the flat above was let before I got there. I was invited to buy a licensed drinking club but that was not for me. Then I was introduced to a couple of gay guys who had just opened a jeans shop called 'Silks'. They were making their own designer jeans, with Australia as one of their hopeful markets. They had recently returned from Sydney and needed capital to expand and someone to take over the shop end of the business. They needed money for materials, and I was very interested.

Bob had found a main post office in Stratford-upon-Avon, the home of Shakespeare, while joy-riding the girl of the moment, and he wanted to do it. The front windows of the place were smoked glass and from the outside no one could see the interior except where one of the windows had a clear circle in it the size of an old penny, one inch in diameter. If you put your eye to it, all you could see was the post office safe.

Maria and I had been married for two weeks. I told her I had to go away for a couple of days with Bob to sort out some business. Maria was never inquisitive and never pried. She preferred not to know the details.

We needed a new lot of explosives, which we would have to go out and find. We chose the Rhondda Valley in South Wales for this, because the valley was where the coal mines were and we could check it out. We'd go in my car and be just tourists nosing around. We could collect the ringer from the garage in London when we needed to. This was our fourth ringer, the first three were abandoned, the last one in a place called Raynes Park shortly after leaving a cinema in a town nearby at 5 a.m. one morning with the cash and gear on board.

As we passed through the junction at Raynes Park we noticed there were several squads of police hanging about. We were curious, so we stopped in a street nearby, left the car and hid in a group of shrubs in someone's front garden, overlooking the junction. Moments later, a squad car came by and stopped by our car to check it out. As soon as they had left we went to the car and found they had taken the keys which we had left in the ignition. We always carried a set of keys each for moments like this, but, before we could get into the car, another squad car came round the corner and we had no choice but to leave on foot. We scaled a garage wall and went through back gardens and down the sides of houses. We separated, with all sorts of noise going on behind us. I took a chance and crossed a major road into the countryside, where I stayed for a while before venturing out and catching a bus into London, then a train to Brighton. Bob turned up the following day. He had gone into an unlocked house and hid behind the sofa for most of the day till he could leave unnoticed.

Anyway, we got a new ringer a few days later and that's a story for another time.

We needed more explosives if we were going to do this post office, and hopefully we'd score enough to give the whole scene a break and go on to something else more civilised. We left Brighton early one morning, and filled up with petrol again in Wales later in the afternoon. We asked the pump-man where the coal mines were as we hadn't seen any. He pointed away off into the hills, and soon we passed one almost at the side of the road, with steep banks of trees behind it. We found a concealed spot to park a short distance away. We thought the bunker would be somewhere in the trees to the side of the mine. We found it without any problems and checked it out. It was seven o'clock in the evening, and this bunker was almost falling apart. All we needed was a crowbar and to be out of the trees before we got lost in the dark.

The road we had been travelling on towards the mine ran beside a railway line, so we got the car and followed it, looking for the line's maintenance hut which we hoped would be somewhere along the track. It was. We found inside a 6ft crowbar, almost too big to fit across the seats in the car. We had to let the top down for the bar to stick out the side. Then we had to stop a mile down the road, because there was this brilliantly patterned black and white snake crossing it. We got out to look and as we got close it hissed at us. We stood back and watched it disappear in the undergrowth.

Back at the bunker it was nine o'clock and the light was good. We could just see an outline of the mine through the foliage of the trees. The bar was almost too big to manoeuvre between the bunker door and the blast wall, and it took me several minutes to jam it into the door frame. When I pulled the bar, the whole lot came away, like peeling an orange. Then we had more difficulty getting the bar to the inner door than opening it. Inside, there were several boxes of the stuff we needed, so we were out of there and back in the car heading for Brighton by 10 p.m., just as it began to get dark.

The dawn was breaking and Bob was asleep as I drove towards the final bend in the road before our turn-off and home. I must have been dozing. We had been trucking for almost a full day and I was eager to get home and was driving too fast. The car began to spin as we went into the bend, then did a full somersault across the road, landing upright on the other side. The car was a mess and wouldn't go. I had hurt my chest and Bob had hurt his hip. We were both awake and knew that we couldn't just sit there, not under the street lights on the main road into the town – it was 5.30 in the morning and we had a bag of explosives in the back. We got out of the car, and managed to open the back and conceal the bag in a hedge-row opposite before anyone came along. Bob limped off to struggle home, while I waited for the police and the ambulance to take me to hospital. They let me go home a couple of hours later.

The next day Bob and I picked up the bag from the hedgerow and put the contents in the safe deposit in London, and the following day I returned to the hospital as my chest was hurting. The centre bone of my ribcage was broken.

One morning, there was a knock at the door. A friend had dropped by to show us a story in one of the daily tabloids. It was about these two guys travelling around in a sports car who the police would like to locate and interview. My first reaction was to get Bob to get rid of his car then Maria and I, Bob and his girlfriend would go away for a few days. Bob swapped his car with the ringer in London, came back to Brighton with the ringer and we set out for the West Country, where we stayed in a small hotel with four-poster beds, a few miles outside the city of Bath.

My mother had booked her passage to Australia when Maria and I married, and now was the time to join her – or was it too late already? Money was running out and there was a cinema in Bath doing good business. There was several hundred pounds in the safe and two guns. Bob wanted one of them, so he took one and left one behind.

Later in the day we all left the hotel and set off for Brighton. We were going to collect the things from our flat that we didn't want to leave behind and Bob and I would go our separate ways. Maybe one day we'd meet again – well, that was the fantasy anyway.

We were passing through a newly developed town called Corsham, quite near to Brighton. There was a garage there that specialised in sports cars, which Bob had previously been to and seen a car he was interested in. We needed to stop somewhere to eat, so we stopped at Corsham. Then Bob wanted to pop down the road to see what cars they had on offer and said he would only be five minutes. Five minutes was forever – we had waited that long, it seemed, and I was getting fed up, this was not the time for this. I left Maria at the table while I went in search of Bob. I asked the guy in the showroom if he had seen my friend. He said 'yes', he was out test driving a car and would be back in a few minutes. He started to show me the cars they had and the large sliding doors of the showroom began to close. He told me it was closing time, as three guys walked into the showroom and told me I was under arrest.

What for? They were arresting me on a warrant issued in Derbyshire. They would notify Derby who would come and collect me. They had no axe to grind, so didn't want to create problems. They were holding Bob. Where did we leave our car? They asked. The car, of course, was a ringer. Our clothing was inside, and the surplus explosives we hadn't dumped and the gun from the safe. Neither of us would acknowledge having a car, which they weren't concerned about. As they said, when the town emptied they would find it.

Always this danger lurked of being arrested and I always hoped if it had to happen, it would happen when I was clean.

None of the police in Corsham were unpleasant in any way. To them, Bob and I were traffic passing through and not their problem. They were mainly interested in spending their time and budget on local crime, and this kind of arrest was work they didn't want because there was no merit in it for them. When Maria turned up at the police station after looking for me at the car showrooms, they gave us time together and let me give her all the money I had.

Several hours later, an escort of six coppers in a transit van took Bob and I to Derby, handcuffed to the inside framework of the van – a long and uncomfortable ride. I can't describe the heartache or stress Maria must have gone through. None of this was a world she had ever known, though the world she had known had its own horror stories. But now, after all this time, the wounds should have healed.

The following day, Bob and I met the detective sergeant in charge of the case, who turned out to be a nice guy. He was fascinated by the whole business of this robbery, as nothing like it had ever happened in Derby before, and now the Co-op collected their money in a security van.

The arrest warrant had been issued for Bob and me in relation to the Co-op robbery which I mentioned earlier. The police had arrested one of the local guys who had stuck it up, and he had confessed and named Bob and me as the prime movers, writing a statement to that effect. Bob and I knew that this wasn't evidence against us unless the guy took the stand for the prosecution in return for a light (or no) sentence – and that's what the guy wanted to do. The sergeant didn't like this guy and made no secret of that. We were put on an identity parade before the two witnesses from the bus stop, and not identified. The only evidence against us was the whistle-blower.

Our real problem was the car at Corsham with our gear in it. It could be positively linked to us. It was a stolen car, containing both explosives and the gun taken from the safe in Bath, tying us to the break-in there. If we denied all knowledge it would result in a bunch of charges from various places spread over different constabularies, and take at least a year to sort out, giving everyone the hump for eating up their time and budget and getting us the maximum sentences for not cooperating. No one was interested in giving us a hard time. They just wanted it sorted out to their credit and within their budget.

The Met (Metropolitan police) were keen to interview Bob and I, but none of the various police forces had any time for the Met, the 'Mafia of the police services', so we got offered a deal – plead guilty to the Co-op robbery, which would be dealt with very quickly, and there would be no further charges and the whistle-blower would get no favours.

We were remanded for a week in police custody which meant being locked up in the police station for a week. Two months later the guy was given ten years and Bob and I got seven, with everything else taken into consideration and no further charges. We were taken to Lincoln Prison where we would have to spend at least a year before being shipped to Dartmoor, full circle!

7

Lincoln was a small prison in a small town, many, many miles from Brighton. One visit of twenty minutes once a month wasn't going to be easy. I was mortified as the full realisation of my responsibility to Maria became apparent, and my total inability to do anything to make it any easier.

I had made this situation, I had to live with that, but for her I felt she might not be able to cope with the four and a half years of waiting, the hardship and the loneliness and the uncertainties of the future. The pressure would all change her in some way, and seeing other people's lives around her progressing while hers stood still was a heavy burden. Were our links strong enough, or were our commitments just another bunch of words? Did our relationship really mean anything? Was it profound enough to survive in the poor as well as in the riches? Because without the full embrace you lose it all.

It's always easy in retrospect to be glib about these things and mention them in passing, though living them is where it's at. We were allowed two small letters a month, by the system designed to destroy any form of close outside relationships. Bob lived in the next cell to me on the same landing and was growing restless as the weeks went by. He wanted to escape, and I was growing bitter with frustration.

Then Antony, my son, was born and I began to feel differently again. Something special, a child of your own. Someone, a part of me, one of those mysteries that spins your life around, and I was still caught between rebellion and the desire to do the right thing – whatever that is!

Bob had acquired a master key that would open any gate in the prison, and there was a gate in the recess of the landing below us that opened onto an exercise yard, with a low gate in one corner leading into the prison maintenance yard where there were ladders. In those days, all of the gates inside the prison were on a single lock when the prison was on full shift. When the prison closed down, all the gates leading out of the blocks were put on a double lock which only the chief officer or duty officer carried keys for. This meant that we could go through the recess gate with Bob's key and double lock it on the outside, so that the screws on duty in the cell blocks couldn't get out immediately.

Education was becoming a feature of prison life. Two evening classes in basic subjects between 6 p.m. and 8 p.m. – eight guys on each class. The classes were held when the prison was, in effect, locked-up. Two screws were detailed to let out the students, who would go down to the centre and form a line. Bob and I were in the English class and would go past the recess. We tried the key, and it worked – but there was more to it than that – I was reluctant to create more problems than we already had, and certainly for Maria. Escapes into unknown territory are seldom successful without a little help from your friends. That takes a little time to sort out, and we had friends.

Antony was six weeks old when Maria brought him to see me for the first time, and I remember it well. A few weeks later Maria's mother wrote to me, in Polish, which took me a couple of weeks to get translated by a con who knew a little Polish (he was Hungarian). She asked me to let Maria and Antony live with them in America while I was away, and told me that they would care for them. I still have the letter.

As Antony's father, I had to give consent for Antony to leave England, and Maria, by marriage to me, could claim UK citizenship and then get a residence visa for the States without any trouble or waiting lists. The mechanics of Maria and Antony's going to America was no problem. The problem was, what was *I* doing? Maria and Antony were living in one room on next to nothing, obviously growing more vulnerable by the day and her mother's offer was one I really couldn't refuse.

I knew that America, to Maria, was the 'Promised Land', the 'El Dorado' of all things but, no matter what she said to me, we both knew that America would end our marriage unless her parents supported it. I held no confidence in that, but Antony needed a different environment from Brighton to grow up in, and I didn't want either of them separated, alone from their family.

Bob was pressing me for a decision. He wanted to leave while the chances were there, and I said I wasn't interested while Maria was in England. It would cause trouble for her. I was dragging my feet with uncertainty, and was tired of a life going nowhere. I felt that if I escaped it would need to be permanent, and not just another merry-go-round of 'cops and robbers'. To be permanent meant cutting ties completely and disappearing permanently, to break out of the system – almost an impossible dream. Where would the money come from? Because without it, it really was an impossible dream.

We had a post office in mind, which we had staked out but never got around to, and a friend wanted to lay on transport when we wanted it, but that would be looking for even more trouble. Did I want to run the risk and become a fugitive for ever? This was all too serious to be so simple.

Lincoln was a local country prison, run less rigidly than the bigger prisons. All the landings were unlocked at the same time for meals, which you filed down to collect on the ground floor. I was writing to Maria one morning when the cells were opened for breakfast, and I left the paper and pen on my cell table to go and collect mine. On the way back, I thought I saw a con come out of my cell and cross the landing to his. When I got to my cell I saw my pen was missing. I put my tray down and went across the landing to the guy's cell. He had shut his door, so I banged on it and told him I wanted to see him next time his door opened.

It was almost time to unlock the cell doors again after the staff came back from their breakfast, when my door opened and three screws came in. One told me to collect my personal things (a couple of photographs and a few letters) because I was being transferred – a process known as 'ghosted' – here one minute and gone the next. This process of moving cons from prison to prison without warning, and often in the middle of the night, was originally designed to get rid of potentially difficult cons, troublemakers – you know the type. They call them 'dissidents' in the real world. Like all bright ideas in the prison system it quickly became abused by the prison staff, as it was a very good source of highly paid overtime.

Within the hour, I was in a van heading for Birmingham Prison, 40-odd miles away. Apparently my comments through the door to the guy I thought had nicked my pen had been overheard, and I was being moved to avoid trouble.

Birmingham is a much larger prison than Lincoln, and my arrival there was viewed with suspicion by the staff, who saw me as a problem. On the exercise yard later that day I met up with Frankie Fraser, the most notorious prisoner in the system at that time and hated by the establishment for constantly challenging stupid rules. I had known him for years, both inside and out, as we were both from the same area in south London where he was a member of the notorious 'Richardson gang'. Fraser was never in the same prison for long, constantly being ghosted for causing disruption, and I knew that I wouldn't be in Birmingham long with him there. He spent most of his time bruised, and in confinement. I liked and admired his courage and whacky sense of humour – but only from a distance.

However, being transferred to Birmingham solved the dilemma of escaping from Lincoln. I had a family to consider and hopefully a future with them once this was over. Time was passing, Antony had been born and things were tough. I agonised over Maria's plight – how she lived, her isolation, her loneliness – and didn't want Antony living and growing in that environment. Maria was on her own without support. She was given a flat over a shop by a bookmaker named Georgie Holmes, an old friend who, incidentally, was the uncle of 'Raver Molly' of earlier years. We had been friends since then, and he and his wife were good people. Nevertheless, I felt it was inevitable that Maria would take up with someone sooner or later if left there. Anything could happen.

I wanted our relationship to survive into something of real value, and that wasn't going to happen as things were. As the days went by my confidence in Maria's ability to stay loyal to me was crumbling. I could understand the temptations she faced, and the growing doubts about our future. She had to go to her parents in America, where she and Antony would have a home and be cared for, and life would take its course. I gave consent for her to take Antony out of the UK and accepted her promise that we would sort ourselves out when the time came.

Two weeks after arriving in Birmingham, I was called to the governor's office and was informed that he had a request from the police to interview me, which they could only do with my consent as the law stood. They had to wait till a prisoner had served whatever sentence he was doing before interviewing him further, unless he consented. I wasn't anxious, just curious, so I consented. A few days later, a screw took me to a room in the administration block where two guys in their thirties were waiting. They introduced themselves as detectives investigating a safe robbery at a cinema in Guildford. They asked the screw to wait outside.

'No, he stays. He's independent. If he goes, I go.' I looked at the screw and asked him to stay. 'OK, so what do you want from me?' I asked the two guys, showing no sign of concern.

'We are looking into a safe-breaking robbery at a cinema in Guildford and believe you may know something about it.'

'Don't think so, when was this?' I knew exactly what they were on about. That was the first of two jobs Bob and I did one Sunday evening.

'About a year ago. We have information that you were involved in this and we want to clear the books. We are not thinking of charging you, we just want it recorded as cleared.' – yeah, I bet.

'I don't think I can help you', I replied. 'Whatever it is has nothing to do with me.'

'We have a witness who identified you and another man.'

'I don't think so. You are on a fishing trip and wasting your time. I don't know what you are on about.'

'We can put you on an ID parade and sort this out.'

'You can do what you like. Will your budget go that far? I really can't help you, sorry an' all that, and if that's all you want, I'll leave you to it.'

I got up to leave and walked towards the door, when one of them said, 'There's a man doing three years for this crime and he has petitioned the Home Office, saying it was you and another person responsible.' This stopped me dead, as I had heard nothing of this. How could anyone point a finger at me when only Bob and I knew the score? I turned from the door and stared at him for a moment. 'You didn't tell me that', I said, feeling faintly annoyed, remember- ing how I had also done time for a crime I had not committed and how destructive it can be. 'Is your conscience bothering you?' Asked the smart one sarcastically, seeing my expression. Immediately my anger rose and I stepped towards the table.

'I don't have a f*****g conscience,' I said. 'I may steal a few quid occasionally, but I don't put innocent people in jail. I'll leave that to your f*****g mob, so don't lay your dirty deeds on me.' The nearest one rose sharply from his chair as if to attack me, and the screw moved forward to intervene.

'This is not a police station mate,' I said. 'Keep your hands in your pocket and go and f**k yourself.' I knew I could give them some verbal abuse without fear of reprisal, and my hatred of coppers had loosened my tongue. The screw took me back to my cell. I was feeling very p****d off with the encounter, which I will always remember.

I had been in Birmingham for six weeks when the sounds of discontent in the exercise yard started growing louder. I didn't need to be an agitator in any of this, as I knew I would be seen as one anyway – being a Londoner, in another city's prison, a long way from London, always had to be trouble. So, early one morning when the day shift came on, I was back on the 'ghost train' and taken to Winchester Prison in the south, much nearer to Brighton and Maria.

It was there, a few weeks later, that Maria brought Antony to see me, before leaving the following day for America. The Catholic priest arranged the visit in his office, and gave us a little time together to make each other promises which neither of us could keep – though I hoped, for me at least, it would not become a fantasy.

Shortly after they left for America, Bob left Lincoln through the recess gate, and I was shipped out of Winchester to Dartmoor to serve the rest of my time. (There were still only three prisons in the country for long term prisoners, though not for long, as the prisons were becoming a growth industry.)

Maria was not a letter writer – her written English wasn't easy for her, and after a few short weeks in New Jersey where her parents lived, her letters were drying up and becoming less personal and I was caught with that sinking feeling – it wasn't going to work. Maria was espoused to the American way of life, and her parents were much less committed to keeping any promises.

My mother had gone to Australia, so now my only links left in England were Maria's cousins in Brighton, who wanted to support me, but their links with America were strained. Day after day, for several weeks, I hoped for letters that were never written, and grew more isolated and depressed, hurting with frustration and growing anger with the system and with Maria for not caring for our relationship. My letters were growing angry and, therefore, self-destructive and would in themselves destroy. I had heard nothing from Maria in weeks and knew it was impossible to hold and safeguard our marriage without the commitment to it that was necessary. I knew that to survive, I needed to shut down and switch off completely, and hopefully pick up things when this was over. So I wrote to Maria and said this – she never replied.

Dartmoor had changed, the place was the same but the regime was more relaxed and easier to cope with. The 'silent' rule had gone and a few of the guards were more human, though overall, still Home Office thugs. Some still competed with each other for top score in the number of people they put in the punishment block, relishing the power the uniform gave them.

I was lucky, and given a decent job as assistant to a civilian heating engineer who maintained the boilers and archaic heating system. I would wander round the prison carrying his tools when the rest of the prison was locked-up. We became friends, and often he protected me from the abuse of the nasty ones. We shared some high moments, like flooding the hospital block when a pipe connection was leaking. He disliked most screws more than he disliked some cons. He was disapproved of by the uniformed staff because he wasn't one of them, and he wasn't intimidated by the heavy ones who, in fact, treated him with caution because he was a pal of the local magistrate who came to the prison often in an official capacity. His name was George, and I called him George. He helped me study, through correspondence, welding technology and electrical insulation and that would be useful in the future.

Most days, and especially Christmas times and birthdays, I would think of Maria and Antony and wonder – but they were out of reach.

Times change and governments change. A scheme was introduced for long term prisoners, called the 'hostel scheme'. In three selected prisons, accommodation was arranged so that each housed a dozen selected cons who were on the last six months of their sentence. These cons would be allowed out of the prison from seven in the morning each day until ten at night. They would be found employment outside of the prison and their wages would be handed in to the hostel warden in its sealed pay envelope. It was a nominal amount and would be deducted for rent and personal allowance, and the rest put by until discharge – why turn them loose with nothing if 50 per cent of them will be thieving the same day to survive? In principle, the scheme was a constructive idea, but in practice the rules that went with it were so draconian that 50 per cent of starters never finished and were returned to the prison. Well, it takes time for prison mentality to latch onto ideas that might have some merit.

One afternoon, once a month, there was an interview board for all the cons due for release in nine months' time – on average around twenty – and each month there were around six or eight vacancies coming up. I had eighteen months to serve when this scheme was introduced, and was still naive enough to believe that six months on the hostel was better than six months on the Moor.

But, as the months went by, cons were being returned to Dartmoor from the hostels for various slights or misdemeanours, and so some cons refused to participate. I was offered a place at Pentonville prison, in north London, nine months before release, and spent the next two months working around the prison with others waiting for transfer to hostels. There were about a dozen of us on this party, none of whom I had known before, though I had seen them on the various yards. Just as, a few weeks before, I had seen Tommy Macguire with his buddy, both doing fourteen years for a jewellery robbery. They were the Maida Vale pair I mentioned earlier, who did the robbery I had been lagged for. They were nicked right after a jewellery robbery, with over £100,000 worth of stuff – but the police said they only recovered £35,000.

On the working party, with others waiting for transfer to hostels, I met a guy named John Murphy, an Irishman in his early thirties who was also going to Pentonville and we became friends. I've no idea why he was serving a six year sentence. It didn't matter.

I remember my last day on the Moor, sitting on the side of the low iron bed a few inches from the cold concrete floor. In total, I'd spent eight years of my life there and that cannot simply be dismissed.

They were the prime years of my developing life, when the foundations for a good life should have been laid. Instead it had all gone crazy – or was it all crazy to start with? – and really was I alone to blame? Was it me, or was it the system, and was the system also its own victim? Did it all boil down to nothing in the overall pattern of things? Was mankind born just to reproduce mankind and pass on? I don't know. Mankind is human nature and human nature is the real problem, and it's amazing what mankind can inflict and what others endure.

The cell blocks were like tombs, full of the sounds of silence and so still, it wrapped itself around you. My whole body jerked with the piercing clang of a chamber pot lid crashing onto the concrete floor somewhere off in the far distance. Then the drumbeat of someone pissing in his pot, and an angry voice shouting in indignation, 'Honeymoon on Niagara Falls, you nasty bastard!' – and what could you do but grin? I looked at the bedroll I had made up in the corner, ready to go, and the lime-washed arched ceiling, dull with morning dampness. I felt a numbness more than excitement as I heard the heavy tread and the rattle of the screw's keys in the door.

Soon the day shift would take me down to the isolation block, to go through the slow, boring routine of discharge. Murphy and I were going to Pentonville together the following day; there were two vacancies in the hostel there which we would fill. Had there just been one of us going, we would have been taken to Yeovil Station, given a ticket and sent off, but two would have to have a screw as an escort; and it was almost always two – the escort had a free ride and a night out in London.

The escort was OK. We looked like three working class yobbos on a day out. He looked different out of uniform, and played a different role. He was polite and nervously reserved, and Murphy and I didn't say a lot as our third man was still from the 'sewers', and we weren't able to switch on with his listening ears.

The hostel was a Nissen hut inside the prison, between two wings (cell blocks). Twelve small rooms were separated by a central corridor, each with just enough room to take your clothes off and get into bed. At the end, a larger room for eating and a wash room.

All you needed, but rather tight. We got there about two in the afternoon, and were served a midday meal that was part of the main meal for the prison, cooked about five hours ago and kept warm on a hotplate. Then the hostel warden introduced himself, an old deputy chief officer who was clearly worn out by the whole scene. He gave us both a gate pass and a 10s advance, and said we could go out in the world till 10 p.m. but we must not drink.

Murphy had cousins and friends in Kilburn – as you know, the Irish have cousins and friends everywhere. We spent the evening there, looking in the pub for different relatives. I was never a serious drinker, was never really interested, while Murphy considered it the joy of all things, and there was a point when the odds were against Murphy making our curfew. He fell out of the taxi by the prison gates, then walked through them fresh as a daisy – unbelievable. We became good friends and often spent the weekends with his Irish pals. We always had to be in before ten, which wasn't easy as most Irishmen start the night at ten.

The next morning, we met the prison governor – it was sticky, 'ferret eyes' Bennett, once in the past the borstal governor. I looked for the smelly old red setter – long gone – and from Bennett came no recognition, just another brick in the wall.

I can't remember the old warden's name. He was like a timid mother hen, and a little fussy. He spoke to us as if we were wayward children. He sent Murphy and me off to the local labour exchange to find jobs; fifteen minutes' walk round the back streets, he said – an hour later we found the place.

I was given the address of a central heating firm in a place called 'Archway', about a mile from the prison. They had the maintenance contract for all of Charrington's pubs throughout London. I'd learnt enough from George to get by as a fitter, and was given a job to start next day on a tradesman's pay scale. I figured I was in with a chance. The job was light and straightforward. I was given a young assistant to help with anything heavy. We'd travel across London on the underground, or bus from place to place to clean a boiler. Publicans are not early risers, so we never started work before 10.30 a.m. Ben, my assistant, was always an hour late as he was having a heavy affair with a girl who was getting a bit too much for him.

Murphy wanted an office job, and wasn't having much luck, which didn't seem to bother him, though if he didn't get a job in a short time, he would be returned to the Moor.

By Friday I'd worked one full day and was given a day's pay, most of which I was allowed to keep for expenses in the week ahead. Saturday and Sunday were free days. Everyone cleaned the hostel for an hour on Saturday morning and after that they were allowed out for the rest of the day. On the Sunday I left the hostel to get a bus at the main road outside the prison that took me to Victoria Station and a train to Brighton, one hour away.

Maria's cousins, the Lenkiewiczs, still lived in Devonshire Place and I had arranged to see them that day. Victor and Helena were very friendly and good-natured people. They had two young boys, Richard and Andy, and they considered me now to be a member of the family. They had fairly close bonds with their American cousins and often sent me brief news of Antony. It was inevitable that the passage of time would have its effect on my life, but I needed to be both optimistic and realistic. It would be through them that I could re-establish a relationship with Maria, and I knew that Maria's parents weren't impressed with me. Nevertheless, they were caring for my child and I still harboured the hope that one day we would be able to rise from the ashes.

Victor and Helena gave me a very warm welcome, with open arms, and their warmth was genuine. Maria would have known I was to be at Helena's house that day and I thought there might have been a message, but there wasn't. We ate and chatted about this and that, and agreed to talk about serious things when the boys went out to play. Helena then got very embarrassed, and she told me that Maria had got married again. I knew at once that there would be no phoenix, and that the news would take time to absorb. We were all Catholics, and there hadn't been a divorce as far as I was aware, though I subsequently learned that Maria had gone to Alabama where they do 'Disneyland' divorces for a few dollars, which are then only valid in 'Disneyland'. Not that it really matters once the deed is done. I needed time to consider, and I was only halfway out of prison still. Some things are junctions in our lives, which stay with you.

I hadn't been expecting that kind of news and it set me back a bit. I knew Maria was desperate to be an American when we married, and she knew that I wasn't interested in America. In any case, I wouldn't be able to get a residence visa – up front that is, though there are always ways. To vast numbers of eastern Europeans, America was the land that dreams are made of and for a part of it, some people will sell their souls.

I was shocked and disappointed that no one had said a word, as if, I was not just a 'nobody' but didn't exist at all. Some things I could have understood, as I hadn't made life easy, and maybe I should have known better and not expected loyalty. Whatever, I tried to be a believer and there had been no room in my world for that. I needed time to sort out my own emotions. Maria had made an American marriage without an English divorce and I knew nothing about it. I was devastated. My vague hopes of a reunion were wiped out in a single stroke. But what of my son? I didn't send him to America to be raised by a substitute parent. I could understand Maria's desertion and could accept that, but not saying a word and not discussing Antony left me wounded.

8

Back at Pentonville, life continued. I would often go out after work with Murphy for a couple of hours, just to be out. He wasn't doing so good. He hadn't got a job, and wouldn't take a job he didn't want, and there was a suggestion he would be returned to Dartmoor unless he got something soon.

A couple of weeks passed and I had arranged to meet an old friend, Teddy Fleming, in a small club in Notting Hill. Teddy was due for release that Wednesday from the Moor and had said he would be in this club about eight and he gave me the address (in Westbourne Grove). I came out of Pentonville about seven and went to the bus stop outside. I had just missed one and had to wait for the next. The traffic was normal and I wasn't taking a lot of notice, then an old Ford saloon pulled into the kerb and the driver called my name. It was a guy called Johnny Hilton who, some months before, had occupied a cell on the landing above me and who I'd often passed time with on the yard. We were about the same age and he had a reputation of being a livewire, always full of energy. He introduced me to his companion, a young man in his early twenties called Philip Kelly. I explained what I was doing, and where I was going. Johnny knew Teddy Fleming, so he offered me a lift over.

The club was a small place over a couple of shops. Teddy was there drinking with the owner, and we all chattered away for an hour and I left about nine. These clubs are licensed for members only, and to be a member you put your name on their register. Using an alias was the common rule, and when the club was slack and wanted to look busy, the doorman would fill a few more names in.

It was now Friday 16 November. Murphy still hadn't got a job and it was becoming obvious that he would be shipped back to the Moor any time now, and rather than that happen he took off and at midnight he booked into the Regent Palace Hotel in central London for the weekend. On Saturday morning the hostel warden asked if anyone knew anything about Murphy and of course, no one did. Later that day, I bought a Christmas present for Antony and sent it off. Late in the afternoon I went to the cinema in Leicester Square and afterwards wandered around to look at the place where the Rainbow Club used to be, before returning to the hostel. The Regent Palace is just around the corner from the Rainbow Club.

Several years later I met up with Murphy, and he told me that he had seen me in Piccadilly that evening as he came out of the Regent Palace Hotel, 100 yards away. Later that night, he broke a window in the hotel and the management sent for the police. Two detectives interviewed him, and decided the breakage was an accident and that Murphy was drunk, and that was it. The following day Murphy picked up his seaman's papers from a friend who had been holding them, and a few days later joined a merchant ship and left the country. He didn't hear of the Co-op robbery, or of my arrest and trial, for several years, until he was finally arrested for leaving Pentonville Hostel and sent to Parkhurst.

But, on 17 November, that evening about 8.30 p.m., three masked men raided a Co-op milk depot and during the robbery, one of them shot and killed a Co-op worker. The three guys were Philip Kelly, Johnny Hilton and Bob Connelly. Kelly and Hilton were the two guys who I went to Teddy Fleming's 'coming home' evening with, and lots of faces were there, including Bob Connelly who I'd known for years. When I read the story of this Co-op robbery and shooting in the papers on the train to Brighton on the Sunday morning, I had no idea who was responsible and thought no more of it – but in no time, the police were rounding up the usual suspects.

Another ten days went by, and London disappeared in the worst fog for years. It was now 30 November and I had been at the hostel a month. I came out of the front gate as usual just after seven, to walk to the bus stop. There was the usual small crowd of people there, waiting for that day's discharges. I had walked about 30 yards, when two guys moved away from a car and stood in front of me. Both in their early forties, one in a light grey suit, the other in a brown one. 'Is your name Thatcher?' said the grey suit.

'That's right,' I replied. None of their names were known to me until much later, but it will be easier for me to explain these events to you by using their names now and explaining the rest later.

'We are police officers and we want a word with you,' said Detective Inspector Frank Williams, and his partner, Detective Sergeant Moore put his hand on my arm and wanted to hustle me into their car.

'Hold on a minute – not so fast.'

'We are taking you to the station for questioning,' replied Williams.

'You're not taking me anywhere until the prison is notified of what's going on,' I said. Another con had come out with me and he ran back to the prison gate while I stood there refusing to move. The driveway was actually on prison property and I wasn't going to disappear with these guys without someone knowing about it. I'm not sure if the prison would have had prior notice that I was going to be pulled; they are different empires, different interests – not always compatible.

When the con returned I got into the back of the police car between Williams and Moore, and a third guy got into the front with the driver. His name was Inspector Ian Forbes, and I vaguely recognised him as one of the coppers involved in charging me over the Maida Vale robbery. They were now a team from Scotland Yard's Flying Squad and they were bad news.

'What do you want with me?' I asked angrily. I was getting a little alarmed.

'You'll learn soon enough,' replied Williams.

'Where are you taking me?' I demanded.

'You'll see when we get there,' said Forbes, turning around to face me. 'You're in plenty of trouble.'

'With you f*****g lot anything's possible and you can go and f**k yourself. I'm having no dialogue with you a***holes without being legally represented.' And with that, had no further conversation. They drove me to a police station in the Tooting district.

We arrived there about nine, and I was taken to a detention room where Williams left us, while Sergeant Moore told me to empty my pockets, asking me to explain each item. I shook my head, all I had was a worksheet and a few coins. Williams returned with a Detective Inspector Charles Hewitt, who said to me, 'We have a chap here called Kelly, who's a friend of yours.' If he was expecting a comment from me, he didn't get one. 'We are holding him over that Co-op shooting,' said Hewitt, waiting for a reply. One thing I'd learnt over the years was never say to anything to these people on their own turf.

'Put him in the cells,' said Williams, 'and let's go to breakfast.'

No one came near me again till four in the afternoon, and I was getting very pissed off. At four the door opened and Williams came in. 'OK George,' he said, as friendly as a regular guy, 'you're cleared on this, and as soon as we can organise a car we'll take you back to Pentonville.'

'I can take myself back.'

'No, the boss wants us to take you, we won't be long.' He left, and the door was locked, and I was left for the next three hours to wonder. Then I was given back the few things taken from my pockets and lead to a car in the yard. An escort of three drove me back to the prison, where I was met at the gate by the hostel warden who wanted to know if I was upset – the prison had had the police bring me back to cover themselves in case I'd 'tripped over and broke my nose'.

Things were happening in the background which I knew nothing of until much later, but it will answer a lot of questions if I fill you in now. A few days before I was pulled in, the police had arrested Philip Kelly, as there was a connection with him to a car that was used in the raid. They held him for three days without sleep and he later told of having his head held in buckets of water when being questioned until he confessed and dictated a statement.

It was clear that the police were uncertain of the number of robbers involved, and Kelly told them four. There were three witnesses to this robbery; two saying they saw three robbers, and one saying he saw five – his name was Herbert James Cambridge. He wasn't a good witness, and neither the police nor prosecution took him seriously, though no one else could ignore him. He manned the gate lodge, a windowed hut at the entrance to the depot, which meant it would be extremely difficult to see into a passing car from a lighted hut. He said, in evidence, 'I saw three drivers as the car came in, then two more through the rear window as the car was going away and three and two makes five', though he only saw three at one time.

The shooting was a capital offence, and there were people opposed to capital punishment because mistakes had been made in the recent past. So the politicians had decided that the law on capital punishment would apply only to the person pulling the trigger, and that person must be clearly identified. Kelly was told he had to produce a trigger man or it would be down to him. Ideas were being put in his head and he was very scared. In his third confession, Kelly said he raided the Co-op depot with Hilton and Connelly. They jumped over the counter and he stood in the doorway with a gun, and a fourth man outside did the shooting. He didn't know the fella's name but he had met him in the Grove Club on the night Teddy Fleming was having a party.

The police then rounded up everyone who they thought had been to the Grove Club and produced mugshots for Kelly to identify the mystery fourth man – and that's how it happened to be me. They pulled me in and put my photo in front of him and he said 'not him', and that's how Williams cleared me.

The trigger man had to be identified, so Monteith (the guy in charge of this murder enquiry) and his 'mob' could have someone executed. Monteith wasn't doing too good as a detective, having lost his last murder trial. He was now trying to force Kelly to name a fourth man who could be the villain of the piece, and Kelly realised a fourth person would let himself, Hilton and Connelly off the hook on a capital charge. He was held in police custody for almost a week without charge, without a lawyer, and made five confessions naming different people.

Shortly after I was released, Kelly made another confession and identified a fella named Jimmy Gilbert as the trigger man. Kelly was then remanded in custody and given a court lawyer who told him not to make any further confessions. A week later, Superintendent Monteith discovered that Jimmy Gilbert had a perfect alibi.

The day following my release was Saturday, and by noon things were back to normal and I wandered around the West End and went to the cinema as usual. On Monday I was back at work, and life went on, until eleven days later, on 11 December. I walked out of the prison gates to go to work and Frank Williams and Detective Sergeant Moor arrested me.

Williams said to me, 'You're under arrest,' and they bundled me into their car and no one said another word. It was very weird, and quite confusing and all my instincts told me to remain mute. They were playing their games, ignoring me, and I wasn't going to ask questions. I was in the back seat again, between Frank Williams and his partner, Moore. They were still in the same suits, and in the front was Inspector Ian Forbes. It was just over an hour's ride before I was back in Tooting Police Station and not a word had been spoken after Williams had said, 'You're under arrest.'

I'm going to jump forward a bit, because it makes it easier for me to explain …

Some weeks later Frank Williams and Inspector Thompson gave evidence in court about this arrest, recalling an incriminating conversation taking place in the police car on the way to the station. Both were word perfect, written in their notebooks. Two other detectives gave evidence to support them, neither of whom I had ever seen before, and neither had ever travelled with me in any police car. In evidence they both said that they had copied the conversation into their notebooks from Inspector Thompson's notebook and their memories were identical to his. I don't know why Forbes and Moore dropped out and let the other two take their place, maybe they just didn't want to know.

Anyway, we got to Tooting and all four of them walked me to a cell and told me to strip naked, and then Williams said to Moore, Thompson and Forbes, 'Let's go to breakfast.' They locked the cell door on their way out and there was nothing I could do, except wait.

At 10.15 a.m. Williams returned with Thompson, followed by Superintendent Monteith and Inspector Hewitt. They looked at me for a moment and then Monteith said, 'Now you have been brought here, Thatcher, you are staying here'. I had no idea at that time the names of these guys, or who was who. They made no formal introductions.

Superintendent Monteith was a tall bony, quiet-spoken Scotsman in his sixties. Hewitt was about the same age and build as Williams, except he was more suave. About a year before this (which I learnt much later), there had been another killing during a robbery in Monteith's district and he had arrested a local guy named Sampson for it. At a subsequent trial at the Old Bailey, Sampson was acquitted. I don't know the details, but it would seem that this particular group of 'crime-busters' made their own decisions about who the bad guys were, and fabricated the evidence to support their theories. I told them in no uncertain terms that I would not cooperate with them without legal representation.

'We have information that you have been to the Grove Club in Westbourne Grove with the three men involved in the Co-op shooting and we believe you were involved too.'

'Then I wish to be legally represented.'

'Never mind about that,' said Monteith.

'I will answer no questions unless I am legally represented,' and with that I refused to speak, knowing full well I had no chance of getting a lawyer. After a few minutes Williams said, 'If he thinks we're kidding let's charge him.' The door was slammed belligerently as they left.

Ten minutes later they returned with the uniformed station inspector, a man in thick horn-rimmed glasses named Cuthbert. I don't know what the rules are now, but in 1962, the CID were not officially allowed to charge anyone. People were charged with offences by the uniformed station inspector. That was part of his domain and all documents relating to criminal charges were his responsibility.

'Thatcher, you are charged that on 17 November last, with others, you did murder Dennis Hurden by shooting, etc. Have you anything to say?' I shook my head. 'Then sign here.' He laid the document on the table for me to sign, which I did, and the time on that document said it was 10.30 a.m. – I had been in the station just over an hour. Charge sheets are serial numbered and cannot be duplicated. This particular charge sheet was the responsibility of Inspector Cuthbert Monteith and from the moment I was charged I would have no access to it.

As they left the cell, Hewitt tossed some papers on the small table and said, 'This will give him something to think about.' It was alleged to be a copy of the fourth confession made by Kelly, naming me as the fourth man. I didn't read it at that time, and didn't want to. There was a small window in the cell door and the face of an observer was watching me the whole time. I knew all I needed to know about confessions. They were evidence against whoever wrote them, no one else.

The 'mob' were desperate and I was in deep s**t, and I often wonder how they would have treated me had I not been a serving prisoner, still under the prison's jurisdiction.

About an hour later, two strange detectives came to the cell with a box of clothing for me to put on. It looked like it came from the sewer. It was old, stained and very smelly and much too small. I was then taken to a room where I was fingerprinted, then put in another cell. I saw no one then until about seven in the evening when six of them entered the cell: Monteith, Hewitt, Williams, Thompson and two others whose names I never discovered. They baited me and held me as one of them cut off a lump of my hair, threatening and foul-mouthing me the whole time. They grew increasingly angry as I refused to speak and after a while they left. All this was very frightening, and the only way I could deal with it was by keeping my mouth shut until I understood exactly what was going on. Needless to say, when the time came to question this event, it appeared never to have happened.

In court the next day, looking like the scarecrow from the *Wizard of Oz*, I complained and demanded my right to an lawyer, which the court appointed. I was remanded in custody to Brixton Prison where all those awaiting trial were held. Though it was not the norm, I was put into solitary confinement and was allowed no contact or communication with anyone. It was obviously in agreement with the governor and the police, and whatever the effect of it was, I couldn't learn anything and didn't really understand what it was all about, except that I was on a murder charge.

I needed to concentrate my mind. The people who made this charge against me had unlimited resources and I had nothing, except the knowledge that I wasn't involved.

The following weeks were difficult and, as the days went by, I began to feel positive that things would be sorted out at the pre-trial hearing set for the New Year. I had a lawyer named Michael Sherrard who would represent me.

I saw Kelly for the first time since the night at the Grove Club as I was led into the dock at the magistrates' court. He was already in the dock, handcuffed between two detectives. He looked at me with a pleading embarrassment and I could feel his shame. I knew then that he had been put on the spot and was jockeying for a safe position. He didn't want to die. He was only twenty-one.

As you can imagine, this period of my life had a profound effect on me. On top of learning that my marriage was over, I still wanted to get into a life more stable. Things were happening that even to my cynical nature, were unbelievable. They weren't make-believe, this was real, though I wished it wasn't. When I recall these events I still feel as if I've been hit in the head, and am full of sadness that torments me. A smouldering anger surrounds the very thought of these events and, if I tell it all to you, then maybe I'll be shot of it and maybe you can learn something from it.

This pre-hearing in a magistrates' court was the norm. The police would make out a case and the magistrate would commit it for trial – no case, no trial. The first two days were taken up with various witnesses giving evidence about what they said happened at the scene. The police case was that four armed men raided the cashier's office at the depot. Three masked men going into the office, one staying outside. The one outside shot and killed a Co-op worker. One witness identified Kelly as being in the doorway of the office but there was no other identification evidence. I matched no description from any of the witnesses. There was nothing from any of them to suggest I was a part of this business.

Then, on the third day the police gave their evidence, and I knew I was in lots of trouble.

First, Williams and Thompson gave evidence of my arrest and an incriminating car conversation which I couldn't believe. I sat in the dock tense with anger, and my lawyer, Michael Sherrard, clearly didn't know how to handle it. No one in those days ever called a policeman a liar, because no one wanted to believe it could be true. Superintendent Monteith and inspector Charles Hewitt then gave their evidence, and I was stunned beyond belief, learning for the first time that these two detectives were manufacturing evidence – I could not believe it, unbelievable.

'I told Thatcher he was going to be charged' said Monteith, 'and he said "I was there but I am saying nothing until I see a solicitor". This is the statement Thatcher made, which Inspector Hewitt wrote down'. Then Monteith handed the court an unsigned statement written by Hewitt – I could not believe it.

All statements of any nature written in police stations must be signed to be valid. The story that Monteith was giving the court never happened. This was more than the normal manufactured 'verbal' the police use – to someone of my background and character this was a personal insult. I was completely overwhelmed, trembling with disbelief, unable to speak and my escort sitting beside me in the dock put his hand on my shoulder, and later said to me, 'I thought for a minute you were going to jump out of the dock.'

My lawyer Michael Sherrard, was lost for words, clearly out of his depth. Later, in the cell below all I could do was rave at him for not seriously challenging the police. Eight of them giving evidence which was all b*****ks – some of them I had never seen before.

This is not fiction.

The mindset is that when the police accuse someone of a serious crime, they are guilty. But I had nothing to feel guilty about. I just wanted to get away from this place and these people. Sherrard had to go, and I would start again.

Connelly and Hilton were nicked, both charged and committed for trial at the Old Bailey along with me and Kelly, on 10 February 1963.

A few days later I was charged with capital murder and with a second charge of robbery.

No words can convey the way I felt, or the confusion spinning through my head. I was held in total confinement in Brixton Prison with no idea of what was going on. I tried desperately to concentrate my mind and be positive.

A week before the trial, I received a letter from a solicitor named Lissack saying that he had been appointed to represent me. He asked if I could leave instructions for him at the prison gate on Saturday evening as he wasn't able to get to see me. The trial was due Monday. I knew that anything I wrote to a solicitor and left at the prison gate would be passed to the police. I trusted no one, certainly not the prison people.

Monday 10 February 1963, 8 a.m.

I stood with my head against the cold bars of the cell window, anticipating the day with anxious thoughts. The snow outside in the walled prison yard was crusty moulds of pitted black marked by birds searching for food. Soon the day shift would return from breakfast and bring with them the escort to take me to the Old Bailey. I was isolated from the other prisoners and would not be allowed contact with anyone other than my escort, so I stood listening for their footsteps on the stone corridor. Knowing that I would accept, without comment, the filthy clothes the police had substituted for mine in order to create the image of a lowlife as I stood in the dock. From the prison cell, we would drive through the streets I had known in my teens, once as familiar to me as the bars on my cell window had now become.

We arrived at the Old Bailey in a black transit van which drove into the concealed courtyard in the rear. The two screws detailed for escorting me lead me, in handcuffs, through heavily barred gates, down a long corridor of cells to ascend the dusty iron stairway to the third floor, where I was locked in a narrow Victorian cell next to the screws' tea room. Scratched graffiti decorated the back of the door and angry slogans mixed with peeling paint marred the decaying brickwork. Twelve foot long, five foot wide. I counted the bricks to the ceiling, trying to ignore the stain-covered jersey irritating my skin. Nervous fluids flowing through me, while the seconds stretched into minutes with nothing appearing to be happening. Then, hearing the sound of keys in the lock I turned to see, framed in the opening doorway, the plumpish figure of a mackintoshed man standing rigid with hands in his pockets. The set expression on his thick-lipped face told me he had no intention of entering the cell. 'My name is Victor Lissack,' he announced somewhat abruptly, taking in my appearance with ill-masked disapproval. 'I am the solicitor appointed to represent you.'

'I received your letter a few days ago,' I replied uncomfortably, aware of his reserve. 'You collected the letter I left for you on Saturday?'

'Yes I did,' he said, 'but I was not allowed to see you because the prison was closed for the weekend. However, I was able to spend yesterday reading the deposition of evidence and your statement. I will prepare a brief for counsel later today. Your trial was listed to begin this morning but I have had insufficient time to find anyone to defend you. I have engaged a junior counsel to request a postponement.'

'Will you get that?' I asked, not wanting any further delay.

'I need a few days to arrange your defence.' he replied, 'and you will have to accept whatever QC I can get at short notice.'

'Ok'. I was trying to be objective and not doing too well.

'The barrister I would recommend is already committed to another case,' said Lissack, appearing more relaxed. 'However, I have had quite a lot of experience with murder cases and I will find someone to represent you. You are in fact the seventeenth person I have acted for on a murder charge. Three of those were capital, all of whom I have helped get reprieved'. He spoke with a sense of achievement, as if to assure me of his commitment. 'I have received no information from your last solicitor, so I don't know why he no longer represents you. The case against you, on the surface, isn't complicated. Either you have said the wrong thing when you were arrested or the police have decided you are guilty and want you put down.'

'Which of the two would you go for?' I asked, feeling stimulated by his directness.

'A lot of my work is presenting police cases at Bow Street,' he replied. My heart sank in a moment of alarm. The last thing I needed was a police solicitor. Whose Machiavellian idea was that? 'In my experience people either say far too much when they are arrested, or they say nothing at all. I don't like the police evidence against you; it is too short and too precise'.

'It's verbal.' I exclaimed with emotion. 'I had nothing to do with this murder and I have said nothing incriminating to the police. I'm not a f*****g idiot, for Christ sake.'

'The evidence will be challenged, Mr Thatcher,' he replied, 'and someone has slipped up here, as there aren't any cautions'. (When a suspect is questioned the Judges' Rules require the police to first administer a caution.)

'The Judges' Rules have no legal status,' I interrupted.

'They may be given some in a case of this seriousness.'

'I doubt it,' I said, trying to remain reasonable.

'We will be in court in a few minutes to ask for postponement, and I will see you afterwards.'

Five minutes later I stood in the dock of Number One court before Justice Roskill. I was separated from Connelly, Hilton and

Kelly by two screws. They each pleaded 'not guilty' to a charge of murder, and I pleaded 'not guilty' to a charge of capital murder. There was a second charge of robbery, but the court could only deal with the murder charge. The robbery charge would go on file.

A junior barrister rose in the well of the court and introduced himself as Michael Corkery, representing me on an application for a separate trial. Because the evidence against Connelly, Hilton and Kelly was not evidence against me, it was argued that I should not go before a jury. The application was refused, but Corkery was given a three day postponement as I did not have anyone representing me.

Thursday 14 February 1963, 9.45 a.m.

I was back in the cell below the court for about five minutes when the door opened and Corkery entered. He introduced himself, and told me that Christmas Humphreys QC would represent me, but that he was currently engaged on another case and would be free later today. Until then, he would act for me.

Most of the morning was taken up with witnesses to the crime scene. There were six witnesses to the robbery, and both Kelly and Connelly were identified as office raiders. All of the witnesses stated that there was no one of my description raiding the office. I am 6ft 4in and well-built.

The case was going down tremendously in the press. Every day it was on the front page, and the police were under real pressure to get results.

The prosecution's case was straightforward: four men raided the Co-op depot, three raiding the office, one remaining outside. While the raid was going on, the outside man shot and killed a Co-op worker. Kelly, Hilton and Connelly were the office raiders, and I was accused of being the outside man and playing no other part in the robbery. Under existing law, whoever shot the Co-op worker was guilty of capital murder and that person had to be positively identified to warrant the death penalty. The first witness for the prosecution was the old night watchman. From the transcript for the prosecution:

Q Are your names Herbert James Cambridge and are you the night watchman and do you have a little hut just inside the entrance to the depot?

A Yes Sir.

Q On the evening of 17 November, at about a quarter to nine, did a car drive in?

A Yes Sir.

Q A strange car?

A A strange car to me, Sir.

Q Did it turn left as it came in?

A It turned left as it came in.

Q Did you see anyone in it?

A I see three. Two and the driver and when the car got a little way out of my sight, I saw two more at the rear of the car, making five.

Q It was dark then, of course?

A Dark and drizzly, with rain.

Q Were there any lights on in the car?

A None at all, Sir.

Q Did anyone look at you from the car?

A At the back.

Q After it turned right at the corner, what did you see?

A I looked out of my sliding window. I could see the car come by and the rear of the car stopped right in my vision at the end of the path.

Q That is the path that leads …?

A That leads to the office.

Q Did you leave your hut to see what was going on?

A Yes Sir. I went around the road to catch the car coming out.

Q Did you get up to the corner of the roadway?

A I got to the corner all right, Sir.

Q When you got to the corner, did you see the car?

A Yes, Sir, I saw the car stationary.

Q Whereabouts was it, in relation to the door which leads into the cashier's office, where about was it?

A I would say it was about five yards that side of the door.

Q Did you see any person or persons?

A The only person I saw was the gentleman on the steps.

Q Tell us what happened. Did he appear to have anything in his hands?

A As I turned the corner, I heard two reports and as I turned, I saw Mr Hurden stagger.

Q You heard two bangs?

A Yes, Sir.

Q Were they one after the other quickly?

A Successive shots, Sir.

Q He did not fire at you, did he?

A Yes, Sir, there were two shots.

Q Just think. Do you mean there were four shots fired?

A I heard four, yes Sir.

Q Do you think you are right about that?

A I am certain of it, sir. I know what a rifle shot is. I have heard enough of it.

Q Then did you see any other men there?

A Two or three in the office through the window.

Christmas Humphreys entered the court after lunch to cross-examine the night watchman:

Q Describe where you saw this car come in.

A I was looking out of from my hut window; facing me, it came up the driveway.

Q And you had a look at it because it was a car you did not know.

A Every car, when it comes in here is owned by people, but has only one driver. This one had three.

Q Quite definitely three people side by side in the front?

A That is what made me suspicious in the first place.

Q Then would you describe this as a 'low down sports car'?

A A very low down sports car, yes.

Q A very low down sports car.

A Yes, that is what it seemed to me.

Q And there were five men in it?

A That is correct.

Q And you came round to where the car had stopped?

A Yes.

Q When you turned the corner and saw the car, was there anybody in it then?

A Only this chap on the steps.

Q All five people had got out of the car?

A Apart from the one who stood on the steps, that was the only person I saw outside the office.

Q And he had something in the crook of his arm?

A Well, it appeared to me like a sawn-off shotgun.

Q Just where was he standing?

A On top of the step by the office door.

Q Would you look, please, at photo exhibit seven. That is the back view of the car that came in.

A Yes. It don't look like the car I thought I saw.

Q That may be so, but it, in fact, is the car you saw.

In his original statement to the police, a few hours after the murder, Cambridge gave a description of the person he said he saw, as being 5ft 6in. To Christmas Humphreys he said, 'He was medium height, rather thin featured.' That is not a description of me, as I am 6ft 4in. Cambridge stood firmly by his evidence. There were five raiders but he only saw three at any one time. He was not a good witness.

Late in the afternoon, Justice Roskill adjourned for the day. I leaned over the top of the dock to introduce myself to Humphreys. 'I would like to speak to you,' I said hurriedly, knowing the escort would want to get me back to Brixton.

'Yes of course,' he replied amiably, 'I will send Mr Corkery down to see you in a minute'. One of the screws put his hand on my arm with a light insistence that we leave the dock and they returned me to the cell, and Corkery entered a few minutes later.

'Well, Mr Thatcher', he said, smiling at me as he entered, 'The crown's case of four men is looking a bit thin, it may well have been five'.

'It may have been three is more to the point.' I was disappointed that Humphreys seemed to think that he didn't need to talk to me. 'I don't understand why the old man wasn't asked if he could identify anyone in the dock, fitting his description.'

'That would be tempting providence' said Corkery.

'Oh come on, the old man should have been asked for his opinion'.

'That wasn't necessary, Mr Thatcher,' he said, looking astutely at me. 'When a person is charged with murder, people assume he is guilty. Mr Humphreys' strategy is to defend you against the indictment of capital murder. He doesn't have to prove your innocence. All he needs to establish is that there isn't enough evidence to prove your guilt.

'Sure, I wish he would talk to me about it,' I replied. The screws were waiting to take me back to Brixton. Corkery would see me again in the morning and I was left with the feeling that Humphreys wasn't interested in establishing my innocence. He was only interested in getting the capital charge sorted out. He probably thought I was guilty, anyway. I needed to be very careful of anything I said.

I was handcuffed and taken to the van in the court yard. The senior screw, a man in his early sixties, an old hand at the Bailey (the cells and dock were staffed by Brixton) began chatting about various counsel. Humphreys, he said, was a Buddhist and a senior prosecuting counsel at the Bailey, prosecuting many of the major murder trials of the fifties, including Ruth Ellis and Craig Bentley (and I was listening, not talking, as he turned to me, obviously attempting to fill me in). Bentley should not have been executed, he was only eighteen and didn't kill anyone. The screw was being informative, as if with a few casual words, he was telling me something, and in the process making me rather more depressed.

Humphreys was a household name, though beyond that I knew nothing of him, and would not get a clearer insight until I read his autobiography, *Both Sides of the Circle*:

> Most of my work was prosecuting because I preferred it. Witnesses called by the prosecution are generally telling the truth as best they may and the prisoner is generally guilty. Most defence briefs aim at cross-examining witnesses for the prosecution to persuade them to say the opposite of what they have just said and then call the defendant to tell a story palpably untrue and to persuade the jury, if possible, that at least the case for the prosecution is not proven. It is a job that must be done, for all are entitled to help

from trained lawyers to put forward their defence, but I preferred the dispassionate calm of prosecution as others revel in defence. I think that the average police officer is telling the truth. I refuse to believe that the planting of evidence or the physical bullying of defendants is more than a very rare occurrence.

Friday 15 February 1963

The same screw returned to take me back to the Bailey, thirty minutes before the case was due to resume. Corkery did not come to see me and I was sat waiting, caught with a sense of urgency to discuss the details of my defence that I had given to Lissack. I strived, with difficulty, to suppress a growing impatience. My innocence was being considered incidental, if considered at all. I was not going to get a real opportunity to communicate with counsel or anyone else.

After an hour I was taken into court and told to sit down, and the first witness of the day was called, the eighteen-year-old clerk, Clive Brooks, from the cashiers' office. A tall, slender, self-assured young man entered to take the stand. While the usher took him through the oath, my nerves seemed to settle. Somewhere in me lurks a natural optimism:

'Mr Brooks, at about 8.30 on the evening of 17 November, did you see someone come into the office?' asked Griffith Jones.

'Yes, Sir, Mr White, a roundsman, came in with his son,' Brooks answered. 'Then shortly afterwards, three masked men came in.'

'Just tell the court in your own words what happened.'

'Two of them carried revolvers and one had, what looked to me, like a sawn-off shotgun. One of them said, "This is a stick-up," and the two carrying revolvers jumped over the counter. One of these men told me to lie on the floor face-down, which I did. I stayed on the floor while the men ransacked the office and, after a while, they ran out through the counter door and I got up.'

'Did you hear any shots fired while all this was going on?' asked Griffith-Jones.

'No, Sir, I did not,' replied Brooks.

'Can you, do you think, identify any of the prisoners in the dock as the men you saw come into your office?' asked Griffith-Jones.

Brooks had already been asked this question at the magistrates' court, but neither Hilton nor Connelly had been there, so they were now asked to stand up.

'I think I recognise the man on the right,' said Brooks, pointing to Connelly. 'He was one of the two who jumped over the counter, but I cannot identify anyone else.' It was three months since this robbery occurred which, in the circumstances, makes identification of this kind rather suspect. The police had not held any identification parades because, I believe, the witnesses are thought to be more prone to be influenced by the sight of prisoners already in the dock:

'Can you give the court a description of the other man who jumped over the counter?' asked Griffith-Jones.

'He was stocky, I would say about 5ft 10in.'

'Can you tell us anything about the third man you saw?'

'The third man with the shotgun,' replied Brooks, 'didn't come over the counter. He was a tall person, about 5ft 11in, and when I lay on the floor I couldn't see him anymore.'

'Are you familiar with guns?'

'No, Sir.'

'Are you sure the third man was armed with a shot gun?'

'I thought it was a gun with a longish barrel. That was the impression I got, but I was occupied with the men who jumped over the counter,' Brooks answered.

'Were any of these three men as tall as you?' asked Griffith-Jones.

'No, none of them were as tall as me,' replied Brooks, who was 6ft 2in.

Well, at least, I thought, on Brooks' evidence, no one could seriously believe I was one of the three men who robbed the Co-op office, as I am taller than Brooks; and the night watchman's description of numbers and his description of the killer on the steps must, in reality, seriously dispel the prosecution's contention that I was that person.

Christmas Humphreys had no questions to ask of Brooks and so he left the witness box, to be followed by the senior clerk on duty that night, the twenty-six-year-old Alan Davis, who seemed ill at ease in the role of witness:

'You were working in the office with Mr Brooks when Mr White, a roundsman, came in?' asked Griffith-Jones.

'Yes. I saw the roundsman come into the office with his son.' Davis replied. 'I was facing the door when they came in and I then turned around with my back to the counter. Then I heard a noise and I looked towards the door again and three masked men came in. I only saw two of them.'

'How do you know there were three, then?' interrupted Griffith-Jones sharply.

'Everybody says there were three ...' replied Davis.

'We only want to know what you saw, not what you have heard from other people,' insisted Griffith-Jones. 'Just tell the court what you saw.'

'I saw two men,' said Davis. 'They were both masked with stockings and both had revolvers. One was about 5ft 10in, the other was thick-set. One of them told me to lie face-down on the floor under a table, which I did. I couldn't see anything after that, but I heard them opening drawers. I stayed under the table till I heard them leave. I did not hear any shots and I could not identify either of them.'

'Thank you, Mr Davis,' said Griffith-Jones, handing him over to defence counsel who wasted no time in cross-examination, and the next witness was called. 'Your name is Percival Henry White?'

'Yes, I am engaged as a roundsman by the Co-op Society,' he replied. White was a short person of 5ft 5in, in his early thirties, who appeared to me to be anxious to give a good impression:

'I gave a statement to the police on the night of the murder and I gave evidence at the magistrates' court. I've thought about this many times,' he told the court.

'And talked about it with your friends?'

'No, Sir, I never spoke about it to anyone. I have been more concerned about being a witness, keeping this thing to myself,' he replied [as if talking about his experience would have been breaking a confidence, which sounded very odd to me].

'Having parked your vehicle with your son, aged eleven,' said Griffith-Jones, 'you both went to the cashier's office and, while you were there paying in your money, did someone come in?'

'Yes, Sir, three armed men came in,' he replied. 'One of them said, "This is a stick-up" and the other two jumped over the counter. I was told by the man who said, "This is a stick-up" to crouch down underneath one of the pay cubicles with my son' [which apparently he did, holding his son in front of him]. 'The man who said, "This is a stick-up" was the prisoner, Kelly. He stayed by the door, holding a gun with a longish barrel, it was bigger than a '38.'

'You are quite positive that the person you saw standing at the door was the prisoner, Kelly?' asked Griffith-Jones.

'Yes, Sir,' replied White.

'Can you tell us anything about the other two who jumped over the counter?'

'One of them, Sir, was about 5ft 5in, my stamp,' White answered. 'The other was about 5ft 9in. I was frightened.' [Connelly is 5ft 8in, Hilton 5ft 10in, Kelly 5ft 11in.]

'Did you see anyone other than the three men in the office?'

'No, sir,' replied White.

The court adjourned for lunch, and I was led below to find Victor Lissack waiting for me. He had lost his earlier reluctance to enter the cell and was less formal. He held a large, blue-covered barrister's notebook out towards me. 'Mr Humphreys would like you to set out your answers to the police evidence in this book, Mr Thatcher,' he said with a faint trace of embarrassment. 'You will see that Mr Humphreys has set out each phrase individually on the left hand pages. He wants you to add your comment opposite on the right hand page.'

'You're joking!' I replied in amazement. 'What's up with the account I've given you?' I opened the book. Humphreys had set out Inspector Frank Williams' evidence in widely spaced phrases on the left hand page.

'I imagine,' said Victor Lissack, 'that Mr Humphreys wants to deal with the evidence as concisely as he can, and this is his way of doing it.'

'Why doesn't he come down here and discuss it with me?' I asked. 'If we don't communicate on a personal level, we won't communicate very well at all.'

'I can do no more than pass your comments on,' he replied, not comfortable in the role of middle-man in this way. 'I'll collect the book from you in about forty-five minutes.' He left me. I leaned against the wall for what seemed a long time before writing anything in Humphrey's book.

The court was in session again and, very shortly, the frail figure of another little old man in his mid-sixties entered the witness box. 'Let him have a chair,' said Justice Roskill, turning politely to the witness and inviting him to sit down:

'Your name is Mr Rogers?' asked the Prosecutor Griffith-Jones. 'You are retired and had been to the fish and chip shop on the night of 17 November? And you were on your way home, passing the Co-op depot?'

'Yes. I was walking down the road at the side of the depot towards the footbridge that crosses the railway lines. I was about 30ft away from the side of the depot when I heard two bangs and someone holler twice at about five-second intervals. I walked to the foot bridge and was crossing over. I was on the top of the steps to go down the other side, when I heard a car coming towards the foot bridge from the direction of the depot where I had just come. It was travelling at considerable speed. It pulled up sharply at the bridge. I was on the opposite side, going down the steps. I saw two men get out of the car. I didn't see the other one. They came up the steps to walk across the bridge. They were walking much faster than I could. I had got to the path on my side and was 20ft along the path when the first man passed me. He was about 20ft in front of me when the other two passed me. When I got to the end of the path, the first man, the tallest of the three, had got to another car parked at the side of the road. He pressed the starter and the engine stalled. The other two men came along and got in the car. The engine started and the car drove off towards Streatham.

Only three men walked past me to the car. One ahead of the other two, who were more or less together. I took the number of the car.'

Rogers had seen the raiders' car race up to the footbridge as he was crossing, saw three men pass him over the bridge and drive away in another car – three men only.

What was to follow would now be a very serious conflict of personal interests, all in an atmosphere of growing tension, where public image would override justice. I looked around the courtroom at the benches reserved for lawyers, and noticed that they were becoming very crowded. Then, the low-pitched murmur of conversation that spread around the courtroom between the testimonies of witnesses hushed as the slim, grey-suited figure of Inspector Frank Williams entered the box:

'You are with the Flying Squad at Scotland Yard?' said Griffith-Jones, invoking what awe he could muster from a fascinated audience. 'At a quarter to eight on the morning of 30 November last, you arrested the defendant, Thatcher, in Caledonian Road?'

'Yes, Sir,' replied Williams, opening his notebook. 'I said to Thatcher, "We are police officers. We are making enquiries respecting the murder of Dennis Hurden in Mitcham on 17 November, 1962, and in connection with these enquiries, I propose to take you to Tooting Police Station, where you will be questioned respecting this matter." Thatcher said, "You are talking about the Co-op shooting. I've never been to Mitcham in my life." He was taken to Tooting Police Station.'

All b*****ks – when the police arrest a suspect they tell them nothing, in the hope that the suspect will start asking questions that can lead to a dialogue.

Williams, in the course of time, would arrest Ronnie Biggs and also give evidence at his trial:

I said to Biggs, 'We are police officers. We are making enquiries respecting a robbery at Aylesbury.' Biggs replied, 'You are talking about the train robbery. I've never been to Aylesbury in my life.'

Williams would be suspended three times for corruption and finally resign at the age of fifty-two, during the corruption purge at the Yard.

I sat looking at him across the courtroom with little bubbles of anger bursting inside me. In any other circumstances I would have treated his deception with contempt. But here, it was not just me he was deceiving. The faces of the jury were absorbing his words and my thoughts switched to the morning he was talking about, in the detention room at Tooting Police Station, with Sergeant Steve Moore and Inspector Ian Forbes, when my reaction to their dialogue had reached a point of stalemate and I thought, for a second, that they were going to resort to violence. 'We have no need of that,' Williams had said. 'We have other ways of doing things.'

'Is there any objection to his using his notebook?' asked Justice Roskill.

'Yes, my Lord,' replied Christmas Humphreys, to my surprise. Obviously he was not going to object to Williams' evidence over lack of conformity to the Judges' Rules that Lissack had referred to, which added another dimension to my sense of insecurity. An appeal against conviction can only be based on questions of law raised during a trial, and Christmas Humphreys was not attempting to build up such a stock. I wondered why, as Williams continued giving his evidence:

I said to Thatcher, 'A man named Philip Kelly is in custody and he will be charged with being concerned in this affair. From what he said and other information in our possession, we believe you were also concerned.' He replied, 'I don't know anyone named Kelly and I've never heard of him.' Inspector Hewitt said, 'That does not seem to be true. We also believe you know an associate of Kelly named John Hilton, alias John Gary Hilton, and another, known as "Scotch Bob". What do you say about that?' Thatcher said, 'I've no idea what you are talking about. I do not know any of the persons you have mentioned.' I said to him, 'The murder took place on the evening of Saturday 17 November 1962. Will you please explain what you were doing on that date?' Thatcher paused for some time and then said, 'Yes, I remember clearly now. I was in a cinema quite near Kingsway. I stayed there most of the evening until late. You can check because the show was *Mutiny on the Bounty*.' I said, 'Why are you so sure that you saw this film on that particular night? Have you kept half your ticket?' He replied, 'No, I threw it away, but I am sure about the date because on the following morning I read about the murder in the *News of the World*.' Inspector Hewitt said, 'What did you do after leaving the cinema?' He said, 'I don't think I did anything. I just went home early.'

More b★★★★★ks:

> Later that day, I saw Thatcher with Inspector Hewitt and Inspector Hewitt said to him, 'Your story about being in the cinema on the evening of 17 November is not true. Are you talking about the Royalty Cinema?' He said, 'Yes, that's right.' Inspector Hewitt said, 'Then you must be wrong because the film entitled *Mutiny on the Bounty* did not commence until 19 November.' He replied, 'You're a liar'. Later that day Thatcher was told by me that he would be released pending further enquiries.

Pending further enquiries! In these circumstances, the prison authorities would have held me in custody pending the outcome. As far as the bit about calling Hewitt a liar – that was nothing more than the wishful thinking which even the prosecution seemed unprepared to pick up. On the face of it, it would allow them to introduce my history. For, when you call someone a liar, you are challenging their good character and they, in turn, can question yours:

> 'Mr Williams,' said Christmas Humphreys, on his feet to cross-examine, 'take your mind back to 1 December, the day after Thatcher's release. Did you go with Chief Inspector Monahan to Brixton Prison to see the prisoner, Kelly? And did you show him a photograph of a man called Gilbert and did he identify that photograph as that of the fourth man involved in this murder?'
>
> 'Yes,' replied Williams.

COURT OF CRIMINAL APPEAL

FATHER KEOGH'S EVIDENCE

REGINA v. THATCHER
REGINA v. CONNELLY
REGINA v. HILTON

Before MR. JUSTICE ASHWORTH, MR. JUSTICE WINN and MR. JUSTICE THOMPSON

The COURT began the hearing of these appeals by George Frederick Thatcher against his conviction of capital murder and of Charles Connelly, of Walworth Road, Walworth, and John Garry Hilton, of Priory Road, Hornsey, against their convictions, at the Central Criminal Court before Mr. Justice Roskill on March 12, 1963, of the murder of Dennis Thomas George Hurdon on November 17, 1962, at the Royal Arsenal Co-operative Society depot in Mitcham.

Mr. Christmas Humphreys, Q.C., and Mr. Michael Corkery appeared for Thatcher; Mr. Lewis Hawser, Q.C., and Mr. Felix Waley for Connelly; Mr. Charles Lawson, Q.C., and Mr. R. J. Lowry for Hilton; Mr. J. M. G. Griffith-Jones and Mr. S. A. Morton for the Crown.

STATEMENTS AND LETTERS

MR. HUMPHREYS said that three days after the trial began prosecuting counsel broke to the defence the news that Kelly, while on trial for murder, had spoken to two men in prison and written three letters. Kelly's letters said in terms that it was he who had shot Hurden.

Copies of the letters were prepared and legal argument began on how they could be used in the trial. The Judge refused application for the letters to be put to the officer in charge of the case, Superintendent Monteith, for the two prisoners to whom Kelly had spoken to be called as witnesses as being of vital importance, or to put the letters before the jury himself.

Kelly did not give evidence at the trial. Statements he had made to the police at an earlier stage were not evidence against Thatcher. Once what counsel submitted was inadmissible evidence against Thatcher was removed, and, considering Kelly's confession, there was insufficient evidence that Thatcher was the man who fired the shot.

It was impossible that Thatcher would be given justice in a trial of all four men together.

Two witnesses who had seen Hurden shot by a man on the steps of the depot office while the robbery was going on inside, had given a description of the killer incompatible with it being Thatcher.

A statement by Kelly had first brought the three other men to the attention of the police. Parts of the statement and of what Kelly said to the police were inadmissible, but had been repeated so often in the trial that the jury could not keep them out of their minds.

The weight of the appeal was rather to say that it was unsafe to convict Thatcher of capital murder than that it was injustice to find him Guilty of ordinary murder.

MR. JUSTICE WINN said he could not follow how the discrepancies in Kelly's statement lent force to the submission that there should have been a separate trial for Thatcher.

NEVER BECAME EVIDENCE

Counsel replied that for 19 days Kelly's irresponsible writings and words had been rammed into the jury's minds. They must have had the general impression that Thatcher was the man who shot, yet, in the end, Kelly did not give evidence and what he said never became evidence against Thatcher. The moment it became clear he was not giving evidence, injustice began to be done, and in the end injustice was done.

Counsel said that he recognized that in any sensational murder many people came forward with false confessions. This case was different. Kelly was already working to be tried for murder when he wrote the three letters, and they could not be waved aside as having been written either for the press or under fear of "frighteners", because there was no evidence of that.

The evidence of the two Brixton prisoners was tainted by the fact that they were criminals, but there was no evidence that either of them knew the other accused before. They did not receive one penny from the letters and they had no reason to lie. Their attitude was, "we could not care less about this man".

If Kelly, having "grassed", was in fear of what was going to happen to him in the long years ahead of him in prison, there were various things he could do. It did not follow that one of them was likely to be to plead Guilty of capital murder. The much more human reason for Kelly's action was that he was a man with a secret. There came a time when no man could hold a secret like that to himself any longer. He was going to blab it out somewhere to get it off his chest.

The letters were eventually admitted at the trial and counsel read them to the Court of Criminal Appeal. They contained the sentences: "If the police catch the other two, I will top." "I have led the police to believe Thatcher done the killing. It wasn't true." "I pulled the trigger." "If they top Thatcher it will save my neck." "If Thatcher gets done, I will come the truth at the trial."

Counsel added: "He did, at the Old Bailey, say, 'I killed Hurden'. That was the only thing he did say, except to plead Not Guilty."

Counsel submitted that Kelly would not have given fellow prisoners statements—for the benefit of the press—which would be damning evidence against him at his trial. Arrangements had already been made for Mrs. Kelly to receive £1,000 from the press for a story.

Before the Court rose for the midday adjournment counsel applied to call as a witness a Roman Catholic priest to give evidence of what Kelly had told him in prison on a date before writing the letters. Counsel—This was not under confession, because he would not be allowed to reveal that, but in the course of general conversation with a man he was trying to help.

The priest's statement had been brought to the attention of the defence by crown counsel last week. Kelly had agreed in writing to the evidence being given.

MR. GRIFFITH-JONES opposed the application.

MR. JUSTICE ASHWORTH said the Court would give its decision after the adjournment.

After the adjournment MR. JUSTICE ASHWORTH said that the Court gave leave for the fresh evidence to be called.

KELLY'S PERMISSION

FATHER JOHN KEOGH, Roman Catholic Chaplain at Brixton prison since September, 1961, said he wished to make it clear that he had never heard Kelly's sacramental confession. He had Kelly's written permission to give evidence and had also taken the advice of his superior.

FATHER KEOGH said he met Kelly in his cell in Brixton at the end of January. "He posed a problem to me. He said: 'I am worried about this Mitcham job because I shot the bloke, not Thatcher'. He sought my advice and I told him that I would have to think over what his obligations were."

Counsel—What was his demeanour, attitude or state of mind?

FATHER KEOGH—I heard the word "frightened" used today. I could honestly say he was not frightened of other prisoners. I would say he was anxious more than frightened as to what his own obligations were. He told me that he was not frightened of other prisoners; he did not care about them. Kelly had told him that when he was picked up by the police he "sold them a line" and played the innocent, and they had believed him up to the hilt.

Counsel—What do you understand was the line he sold them ?—He misled the police into believing that he was a small-time man who was terrified and thought it better to tell them all about it. He said in reality he was not frightened. He told the police that Thatcher had done the shooting. He misled them as regards that.

What advice did you give him ?—I told him first of all that since he had misled the police about Thatcher, that in the event of Thatcher being condemned to death he, Kelly, should confess. I told him that in view of the fact that Thatcher had not yet been found Guilty he could delay his confession until such time as he saw what would happen to Thatcher. I decided that

if he confessed at that stage he was leaving himself no chance of escaping the death penalty. I felt he was entitled to that. I told him he should, even at the expense of his own life, come forward and confess if Thatcher was to be hanged.

Some days later, said the witness, he told Kelly not to repeat any false allegations against Thatcher.

After MR. GRIFFITH-JONES had said he did not wish to question Father Keogh, MR. JUSTICE ASHWORTH asked if he could see Kelly's written permission.

FATHER KEOGH took an envelope from his pocket and a sheet of paper was handed to the Judge.

MR. JUSTICE ASHWORTH asked whether the witness should fear from Kelly's remarks that he had been threatened.

FATHER KEOGH—It is common knowledge that if a man has been involved in implicating his companions in a crime it is to be expected that there would be repercussions.

MR. JUSTICE ASHWORTH —So if there were not threats by word of mouth he would know the danger and be conscious of it at the time ?—Yes.

MR. HUMPHREYS said that a witness had described the killer as 5ft. 9in. or shorter. This fitted Kelly's description, but Thatcher was 6ft. 3in. tall.

With all the conviction he could muster counsel said that he submitted that there was no sufficient evidence on which any jury, rightly directed, could have found Thatcher Guilty of capital murder. Kelly had sought the advice of his spiritual adviser, who said that if Thatcher was found Guilty of a murder which he committed he must speak.

The hearing was adjourned.

Solicitors.—Mr. Victor J. Lissack; Messrs. T. W. James & Wheater; Director of Public Prosecutions.

The Times' article detailing the evidence given by a Father Keogh during George Thatcher's appeal.

George Frederick Thatcher has been awarded an Arts Council grant of £50 for his first play, *The Hundred Watt Bulb,* but what he is likely to receive for it is a spell in the punishment block at Albany Prison, Isle of Wight. Thatcher is serving a life sentence (commuted after several weeks in the condemned cell) for the murder of a milkman during an armed robbery at the Co-op Depot, Mitcham, in 1962.

His play was sent out of the prison without permission to David Halliwell (writer of *Little Malcolm and his Struggle against the Eunuchs*) who is directing it for Quipu productions at the Little Theatre Club for the next fortnight.

Halliwell visited Thatcher in prison after seeing an advert in the *New Statesman* ("Lifer needs help"). "I was very impressed by him. It is certainly difficult to believe the man I met could be capable of a crime of this type. He is cool, collected and very intelligent." Thatcher has always protested his innocence of the murder, and Halliwell encouraged him to write the play as a way of attracting attention to his case.

The Arts Council did not know who Thatcher was when they approved the grant for the Quipu production, including the playwright's £50—" but we do not know that we would have acted any differently". Thatcher has already said that he wants his money split among the actors.

The Home Office say it has not yet been decided what punishment is appropriate. Halliwell says: "Thatcher will be quite prepared for it. He has only been free, on parole, for six weeks in the past 15 years. His view is that they can't do anything more to him and he must try anything he can to establish his innocence."

Shaikh Sulman bin Daij al-Khalifah, the Bahraini ambassador, set off a string of firsts when he presented his credentials to the Queen yesterday. He was the first Bahraini envoy to go to the palace (and it was also the first time the new marshal of the diplomatic corps, Major-General Fitzalan-Howard, was there in his present capacity). When the Queen goes on her Far Eastern tour on Tuesday she will be the first reigning British monarch to visit Bahrain, itself the first of the small Gulf states to declare its independence and become a member of the United Nations last year.

Booker again

More changes are on the way for Britain's biggest literary award, the £5,000 Booker fiction prize. After missing a year in 1970, and altering the award last year so as to coincide with the winning novel's publication, the Publishers Association are now in the throes of giving up much of the administration to the National Book League.

It seems an appropriate change. Martyn Goff, the NBL's effervescent director is already on the Booker committee (it was he who directed the controversial Bedford Square Book Bang last year), and the League and the Booker Prize coincide in their aims—to promote the sale of books. All the same I can't help feeling that it is time the prize settled down. Four years should be long enough to solve teething troubles.

Incidentally I hear that another big book prize is on the way—from a major paper manufacturing complex which is working out details of a Booker-like operation.

Wilson sells

Harold Wilson's political memoirs seem to be doing considerably better in their (abbreviated) German version than so far in the original English.

The opposition leader was in Bonn yesterday for the launching of *Die Staatsmaschine* (as *The Labour Government, 1964-1970 : a Personal Record* has been retitled). After the excision of sections on purely domestic issues, the text is about one-third shorter.

It became known yesterday that 5,000 of the first print order of

An article detailing the Arts Council grant awarded to George Thatcher for his first play, *The Hundred Watt Bulb.*

HMP Isle of Wight, viewed from Noke Common, Newport, where George would spend most of his life sentence.

George with his older brother, Bill, and mother, Liliian, in 1931.

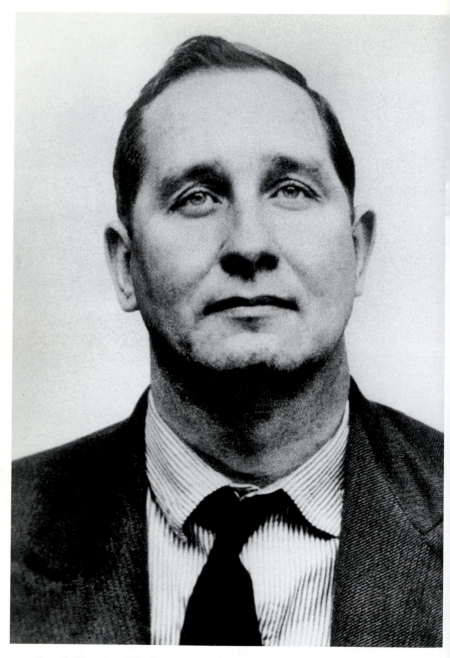

Ronnie Biggs, one of the Great Train Robbers, following his arrest in 1963. He and George became friends during their time in prison. (Mary Evans Picture Library)

George in 1972.

George and Val on their
wedding day in 1980.

George on holiday in
Australia in 1983.

George and son Antoine sharing a joke at the local in 1985.

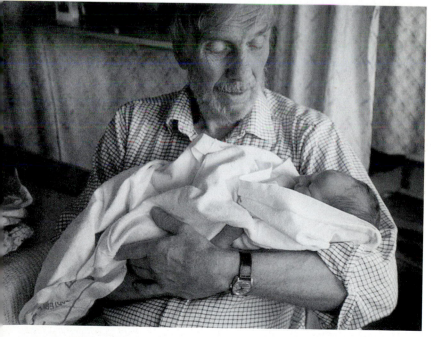

George with baby grandson Jack in 1993.

George in 1996.

George with Val and Floss
the dog in 2010.

'Williams, you have been looking at your notebook. When did you make your note relating to the alleged conversation with Thatcher?'

'My first notes were made in an office upstairs in Tooting Police Station about an hour and a quarter after I arrested Thatcher.'

'Who was with you when you arrested him?'

'Inspector Forbes and Sergeant Steve Moore, who is attached to me,' replied Williams.

'You saw Thatcher, you say, at about 9.30 with Inspector Hewitt and put questions to him. Who made the running?'

'I did. I put all the questions to him,' replied Williams.

'Some questions about a cinema and his whereabouts? I suggest to you that that conversation about a cinema took place at 7.30 that evening, just before his release.'

'No, Sir, that conversation took place in the morning.'

'I suggest the conversation went more like this: Mr Hewitt saying to him, "You have come through this very well. For the record, can you remember what you were doing that day?" Something like that. You had a bit of a conversation about a film he had seen on 24 November and he was released at about 8.00 p.m.'

'No, Sir, that conversation took place in the morning.'

'You made your notes about it in conjunction with Inspector Hewitt and everything he has in his notebook is verbatim with what is in your notebook?'

'His memory is the same as mine,' replied Williams.

'M'Lord,' said Christmas Humphreys, 'if I am not completely conversant with my instruction, I apologise, but I think I have challenged what I wish to challenge, although I may not have put it to the officer all that which my client may say.'

'That's odd', I thought. Williams is saying nothing about arresting me with Moore on the second occasion on 11 December. I had written it down in Christmas Humphreys' notebook and he was not taking it up. I sat puzzling over this as Williams left the stand, to walk past the front of the jury box to the row of empty adjacent benches reserved for police witnesses. These benches faced the judges' rostrum and were in very close proximity to the jury box, allowing any whispered comments the police witnesses might make to be audible to the jury. I watched Williams take a seat in the front row. He carefully avoided looking towards the dock, and the prosecution called the next witness, Inspector Ian Forbes, who had not been listed. He was being introduced to the court now to rebut a comment made about him by the lawyer defending Hilton. Although Forbes was saying nothing about me, his appearance gave Christmas Humphreys a chance to ask him:

'Were you with Inspector Williams, the last witness, on 30 November when Thatcher was taken to the police station?'

'Yes, Sir,' replied Forbes. 'There was one other with us, Sergeant Moore.'

'My client has some difficulty remembering the identity of all these officers,' said Christmas Humphreys to Justice Roskill, [which was a fair comment, as only Monteith had introduced himself, so I was only able to identify them now when they appeared in court and gave their names. My first encounter with Forbes, however, had been ten years earlier, when he was a sergeant in the Flying Squad and I had been beaten up in Paddington Green Police Station for 'resisting arrest'].

'You travelled in the police car with Thatcher on 30 November?' asked Christmas Humphreys.

'Yes, Sir,' he replied.

'I only want to ask you, on instruction, whether you at some time said he was being put on an identification parade,' said Christmas Humphreys.

'No, Sir, I had no idea what was going to happen after we took him to the police station.'

Forbes' Scottish accent came clearly over the courtroom. He had shaved for the occasion, and looked at ease in the box. I could see, nevertheless, that he didn't want to be involved in this case and I fancied Williams' aide felt the same way:

'You never mentioned an identity parade to him?'

'No, Sir,' replied Forbes.

'Do you agree that he wanted a solicitor present for any interview?' asked Christmas Humphreys.

'He may have,' said Forbes, 'though he said nothing about it in my presence.'

'Not in your presence?'

'No, Sir.'

'Thank you, Mr Forbes,' said Christmas Humphreys. 'I have no further questions.'

Forbes left the stand to sit beside Williams and the next police witness appeared:

'You are Detective Sergeant Harry Louch?' asked Griffith-Jones, identifying this person to the court. 'You were with Detective Inspector Thompson when Thatcher was arrested and taken to Tooting Police Station on 11 December …'

Hold on a minute! I don't know this man. He had nothing to do with my arrest on 11 December and he didn't travel with me. I was arrested by Williams and his aide, Sergeant Moore:

'Would you tell the court what conversation took place in the police car?' asked Griffith-Jones.

'Yes, Sir,' replied Louch, opening his notebook and reading from it, 'Inspector Thompson said to Thatcher, "We are police officers. When you were last detained, you denied all knowledge of the men Kelly, Hilton and Scotch Bob. Evidence now shows you know these men very well. You are being taken to Tooting Police Station in connection with the Mitcham murder in which these men are concerned." Thatcher replied, "Don't be so foolish. Nobody can be identified." This conversation took place in the police car.'

Nonsense. I felt myself trembling. There had been no conversation, and this man was not travelling with me and never travelled with me, ever. But, that aside, Inspector Thompson had not been in my presence in Tooting Police Station while I was there on 30 November either, so he had no personal knowledge of anything pertaining to me, which meant that this fabricated verbal was inadmissible hearsay:

> 'On the way to Tooting Police Station in the police car,' continued Louch, 'Thatcher said, "I thought it was too easy last time when they let me go. I have been worried since. You must have been stringing me along." Then later, in the police car, he said, "What do the others say about it?" Sergeant Stagg said to him, "Philip Kelly, who you may know as Galvin, says you were with him and did the actual shooting." Thatcher replied, "He would never say that. He would put himself in the middle as well. How do you know all this?" Inspector Thompson said, "Kelly has made a statement in writing." Thatcher said, "Well, I want to see it." Inspector Thompson said, "You will be able to do so when you get to Tooting Police Station."'

That really was mind-bending. I had read the deposition enough times to be blue in the face. Louch, according to the record, had never been in Kelly's presence, so he had no personal knowledge of anything to do with Kelly. On their own showing, they were producing hearsays (what someone else had told them). I looked at the long, crowded rows of barristers, many of whom were observers, and I began to imagine amongst them a sense of unease.

> 'Sergeant Louch,' said Christmas Humphreys on his feet to cross-examine, 'how many of you were present in this police car?'
> 'Mr Thompson, Sergeant Stagg, myself, DC Smith and a driver, Sir, five in all,' he replied.

This was crazy. It was Frank Williams and his aide, Sergeant Moore, who had arrested me and taken me to Tooting on both 30 November and 11 December.

> 'I do not dispute what you say as to his being taken to the police station. Well now, in the car, you say he was talking?' said Humphreys. 'When did you make your notes?'

'When we got back to the station. He was placed in a detention room. I was called into the Inspector's office and he said, "These are the rough notes I have made. Do you agree?" I said "Yes" and I copied them into my notebook, Sir.'

'You just made a copy. He writes down what he thinks has been said and you make a copy of it?' said Humphreys. 'At no time did you have the opportunity of an individual recollection?'

'Of course, yes, my recollection was the same as his,' replied Louch.

'By every word? By every word?' asked Humphreys.

'Yes, Sir.'

'Nothing to be added?'

'Nothing that I could remember, Sir.'

'Nothing to be varied?'

'No, Sir.'

'Nothing to be taken away?'

'No, Sir.'

'Because I suggest to you, he never opened his mouth in the car.'

'That is not so, Sir.'

'Was he handcuffed?'

'Yes, Sir.'

'So four of you have got him in a car with handcuffs and you say he is obligingly talking as you went along. Was any caution given to him?'

'No, Sir.'

The court adjourned for the weekend, and I quickly leaned over the dock to hand a note to Mr Humphreys, hoping he would come down and see me, but Michael Corkery came instead. 'Well you haven't had a bad day,' said Corkery entering the cell, smiling, 'and Mr Humphreys will try to see you on Monday morning.'

'Mr Lissack said something to me yesterday about Judges' Rules,' I greeted him, with barely controlled exasperation. The earlier calm I had felt at the beginning of the day was now replaced with frayed nerves and confusion. 'Why aren't you making a show of challenging the admissibility of this police garbage, for Christ's sake?'

'Mr Humphreys felt that an objection, quoting Judges' Rules would be overruled. He doesn't want Justice Roskill getting into the habit of overruling objections,' said Corkery, ruffled by my agitation. 'He is, however, going to object to Monteith's evidence.'

Oh, yes, I got the impression that Humphreys didn't like challenging the police or reading my instructions, a nagging voice inside of me protested. I was beginning to feel like I needed to be careful of what I said to Corkery. And Justice Roskill would have a copy of my form in front of him to balance against the interest of Monteith. I might just as well bang my head against the wall.

I was taken back to Brixton for the weekend, drained of emotional energy and with faint hope of a recharge. The optimism that normally lurks in me was all mashed up at the edges. I spent the weekend contemplating the burden of having a defence counsel who was at heart a prosecutor, who believed that police officers never manufacture evidence, and whose ambition it was to be a judge.

Monday, February 18 1963

The trial was due to continue at 10.30 a.m. Just before 10 a.m., the prison van drew up into the enclosed courtyard at the rear, stopping a moment for the gates to be locked behind us. Over at one side, in one of the three reserved bays, was parked a sleek, expensive sports car. 'That belongs to your counsel,' said the screw beside me, following my vision.

'Does it?' I replied in mild surprise. 'That's not the type of car I would imagine Christmas Humphreys to own.'

'No not him,' said the screw, 'the younger one.' – Which immediately struck me as odd.

'How is he allowed to park there?' I asked in curiosity.

'He's a Treasury counsel. He works at the Bailey.'

'You're joking!' I said in surprise.

'Not at all. He's with the establishment and one of their prosecuting counsels.'

As we walked to the cells, I felt depressed by this information. All prosecuting counsel at the Bailey are employed by the Treasury. If Corkery was a Treasury counsel and Griffith-Jones the senior

Treasury counsel, was Griffith-Jones Corkery's boss? What were their interests and loyalties?

Nothing had happened by 10.30 a.m. I had waited and waited, anxiety turning to impatience. The sound of other prisoners being taken to their courtrooms had ceased. I banged on the cell door to draw the guard's attention, incurring an angry retort in the process. 'You aren't wanted in court this morning,' he shouted through the closed door. 'Someone will be down to see you in a little while. If you bang the door again we'll come in there and shut you up.'

'You can go and f**k yourself,' I replied under my breath, relieved to know what was going on, and thinking I was actually going to get some dialogue with Humphreys. For half an hour, I sat chewing over things I wanted to say, desperately trying to be calm enough to be coherent. The door opened, and two screws escorted me down the long corridor to a small waiting room in an alcove at the end, where Humphreys and Corkery, in wigs and gowns, were waiting with Lissack in his raglan mac.

'Well, Mr Thatcher,' beamed Humphreys as I entered, 'a most remarkable event has occurred. The prosecution have obtained three letters written by Kelly to one of his friends. These letters came into the hands of the prison authorities on Saturday, who handed them over to the police …'

'Has this got anything to do with me?' I asked.

'They completely exonerate you,' replied Humphreys, smiling. 'We were given photocopies when we arrived here this morning. I want you to see them.' Corkery held a slim volume of papers towards me, which I started immediately to read. 'They are, as you can see, rather lengthy and I must apologise for the haste of this meeting. The court has been adjourned for a conference with the Lord Chief Justice due to begin in a few minutes, which I have to attend.' I was trying to read the difficult scrawl and listen to Humphreys at the same time, my head in a muddle. 'You will see these letters contain a great deal of descriptive detail,' Humphreys chuckled with amusement, 'and some rather scurrilous comment.'

I was too bewildered to read thoroughly and skipped over the first page of a long account of an interview with the police, giving a different story from what they had given at the magistrate's court:

They leaned on me and put words in my mouth ... I'll tell you
the full score. I killed Dennis Hurden and I know f**k all about
Thatcher till the Old Bill stuck him up. He wasn't on the job with
me. I didn't even know his name. The Old Bill just wanted to fit
him up. That's how he came into the picture ...

Humphreys was in a hurry to leave for the conference, so our meeting ended before I had finished reading. The situation was absolutely
unreal. 'I do not know what is going to happen, Mr Thatcher,' said
Humphreys, retrieving the photocopies from me. 'I will, of course,
see that you are kept informed.' He walked out of the room leaving
me with Corkery and Lissack.

'These letters should put the cat among the pigeons,' said Corkery,
with a trace of a grin. 'What do you make of them?'

'I need a little time to take it all in,' I answered, through the
muddle of my confused thoughts. Corkery's casual remark was
almost disarming and might well have been, had I not known he
was working for the establishment.

'Do you think this crime was executed in the way the prosecution have it?' he asked.

'I don't know,' I replied. 'They haven't got it right with me, and they
haven't got it right according to those letters, or according to the Co-op
witnesses. I just don't know, and armed robberies are not my thing.'

'But you were convicted of armed robbery the last time you were
on trial at the Bailey?' said Corkery, in a matter-of-fact way and
I knew that he had read my history, according to the police files.

'That's right. And that conviction was obtained by police deception.' I held my breath for a moment to suppress an angry outburst.
He was referring to the Maida Vale robbery in 1952 that I had had
nothing to do with. 'There's no court record of that trial, Mr Corkery,'
I said, when the amount of anger in me passed, 'that disappeared
when too many questions were being asked about its miscarriage
of justice. The only armed robbery I've been involved in was in '48,
when I was convicted of robbing the Ranee of Sarawak, who, incidentally, told the court, "The robbers were perfect gentlemen."' The
memory of such an odd description of robbers still sounded amus-

ing. 'The point is, don't get the wrong impression of me from police files. I'm not a cowboy.'

'The police seem to think you are.'

'Sure,' I sighed, 'but they aren't always blessed with an abundance of good judgement. And they don't pull the wool over your eyes, Mr Corkery, they just manipulate you. You were a soldier. This Co-op raid wasn't a military operation, you know. I'm not impressed with the story that a guard was left outside. If there was anyone outside, which, on the face of it, there wasn't, he would be a driver and wouldn't get out of the car.'

'Then you think Kelly would have been the trigger man?' asked Corkery, 'and he wanted to throw the blame on the driver?' That reminded me of what Monteith had said to me in the police cell the night after I was charged – 'If you were just a driver on this job, now is the time to say so, because it will be too late in a couple of weeks' time.'

'No, that's not what I'm saying, because I don't know,' I replied in all honesty, 'there's so much wheeling and dealing going on. This statement of Kelly's for instance. It was made in Tooting Police Station three days after he was arrested. To my mind that implies extortion. I know Monteith and Hewitt have written a confession for me which is all b*****ks, so did they do the same with Kelly? They are desperate for a capital conviction on this case, because they threw out their last murder trial at Tooting. And to get a conviction on this one, they have to have a situation at the robbery where the killer can be identifiably isolated from the group, so they can say, "It was him". And they really don't give a sh*t who "him" is.'

'Do you really think they wrote Kelly's statement?' Corkery asked.

'I don't know,' I replied. 'They wrote mine, so they may have written his. We know Hewitt altered Kelly's statement two weeks after it was originally written.' I shrugged. 'Your guess is as good as mine.'

'The alterations and additions were dictated by Kelly,' said Corkery.

'Sure they were. Hewitt has said so.' I shrugged again. 'But if there wasn't a driver or anyone outside, it would be difficult to find a candidate from the office. Someone outside would make it easier, and so far you've had Jimmy Gilbert. Then me. Now Kelly has said *he* shot this man, Hurden, and he's named another man in his letters as one of the robbers.'

There were sounds coming from the corridor outside, of courts adjourning for lunch. The screws wanted me back in the cells, so the interview ended.

At 1.45 p.m., Lissack returned. The screws outside let him in. 'There is a parcel of clothing for you with the chief officer. He is going to give it to you in a minute,' said Lissack, pushing the door shut. 'The court is going to resume at 2 p.m.'

'What happened this morning?' I asked, anxious to know.

'All I can tell you is what I have been told by Mr Humphreys,' said Lissack. 'It would appear that the prosecution want to amend the indictment against Kelly to one of capital murder, introduce the letters as evidence and proceed with the case,' his tone expressing disapproval, 'but they are not able to do that or change horses in mid-stream. They either quash the indictment against you, by offering no further evidence and having you formally acquitted, then amend the indictment against Kelly and begin again, or they proceed without the letters, not allowing them to be introduced during the case for the prosecution.'

'Is that what they are going to do?' I asked.

'Yes,' replied Lissack, nodding his head. 'If the defence want these letters introduced, we must first prove their authenticity.'

'Is there any question of that?'

'Absolutely none. However, the prosecution have recognised the danger of having the police exposed to questioning of the letter's contents, so the court is unlikely to allow them in while the police are on the stand.'

'Is Humphreys opposing that?' I asked, thinking to myself, if that is what the prosecution want, then it has to be opposed. Lissack shrugged, indicating his uncertainty.

'I think,' he said, hesitating a moment, 'the prosecution want you to introduce those letters in your defence, so they can accuse you of having your "friends" make Kelly write them.'

'You can't be serious!' I exclaimed, 'who the hell are my "friends"? That's absolutely absurd.'

The screw was at the door with a parcel of clothes. Lissack looked at his watch and turned to leave, when suddenly I was overtaken by an awesome premonition that I was going to be convicted and everything around me was crazy.

The courtroom appeared to buzz with curiosity as Justice Roskill addressed the jury. 'I am sorry,' he said, 'you have had what may have seemed to you to be a wasted morning. I will only say that there were good reasons which made it desirable that we should not continue, but we will now go on from where we left off on Friday.'

'You are Detective Constable Ronald Smith,' said Griffith-Jones to the man in the witness box. 'On 11 November last, with Inspector Thompson and two other officers, you escorted Thatcher to Tooting Police Station … '

I leaned forward to look carefully at the calm demeanour of this person. Then I scribbled a note to pass down to Humphreys. I had never seen Smith before, and in the whole of his life, he had never escorted me anywhere. Humphreys glanced at the piece of paper and then up at me with the placid expression of someone in meditation, just informed of something quite unacceptable. I thought, he must think I'm a screwball.

Smith's evidence was identical to that given by Detective Sergeant Louch on Friday afternoon. Adding the strength of numbers to the lie, I thought, as Smith finished with me and then gave an account of Hilton's arrest which I had to listen to while I waited for Humphreys to cross-examine him.

'Thank you, Mr Smith,' said Griffith Jones and Christmas Humphreys rose to his feet:

'Where did you get the material for your evidence?' he asked Smith with a quiet air of seriousness.

'From Inspector Thompson's notebook, Sir. I copied down exactly what was in his book.'

'Have you done that before?' asked Christmas Humphreys.

'Yes, Sir,' replied Smith, 'I've done it before.'

'I suggest to you that Thatcher never opened his mouth on that journey,' said Christmas Humphreys, agitating me by not challenging his presence in the car.

'He did, Sir,' replied Smith.

'What you have in your notebook, then, is a faithful copy of your superior officer's notes?'

'Yes, Sir.'

'Have you ever, on any occasion, differed by one word from what your superior had written down?' asked Humphreys. 'Any time in your life as a police officer?'

'I can't say as I have, Sir, no,' replied Smith.

Smith's account of Hilton's arrest, at a flat in Earls Court, had been embroidered with verbal, and Hilton's counsel, Mr Lawson QC, wanted to question it when Humphreys sat down:

'Officer', said Lawson, 'do I understand that in the case of Hilton and the notes you have been referring to, the same principle holds good as held good in the case of Thatcher? That is to say that you had no independent recollection yourself, but had copied down somebody else's notes?'

'No, it didn't happen on that occasion, Sir,' replied Smith. 'After we arrived back at Tooting Police Station, I went to Detective Inspector Thompson's office with Detective Sergeant Cherry and Detective Inspector Thompson wrote his notes. Whilst he was writing them, he said, "to the best of my recollection so-and-so happened," and I agreed with that, and then, "so-and-so happened," and I agreed with that. That's how the notes were made.'

'So, if we look at your notebook,' said Lawson, 'you have down in exactly the same words everything that Inspector Thompson has down in his notebook?'

'To the best of my recollection, yes, Sir,' said Smith.

'Without variation of a comma?' asked Lawson.

'I don't know,' replied Smith.

'Without the variation of a single word?' asked Lawson.

'I don't know, Sir,' replied Smith, getting cocky. 'I wouldn't know.'

When Hilton had been taken from the flat to Tooting Police Station, three detectives stayed behind and with them, three newspaper reporters. Several hours passed, then a cab had arrived with Connelly. The cab driver was called as a witness:

'Your name is James William Smith?' said prosecuting counsel to the cab driver. 'At about 11.30 p.m. on 8 January, you picked up a fare near the Elephant and Castle. He was carrying a bundle of bedding and he asked you to take him to a house near Earls Court?'

'Yes, Sir,' replied the cab driver. 'When we got there, he asked would I give him a hand in with the bundle by opening the door for him. He gave me two keys and said one of them fitted the door in the basement, but he wasn't sure which one. I went to the basement door, but I could not open it. Then a young lady opened the door from the inside and we went in. The fare said he thought the room door he wanted was the second on the right.'

'And then what happened?' asked prosecuting Counsel.

'I went to put the key in the door and a gentleman behind us appeared. He called to somebody inside the room to open the door and we were told to go inside.'

'Go on, please?'

'The gentleman said he was a police officer and he asked me for some sort of identification. I didn't know what it was all about and I gave him the information he wanted.'

'Were there others in the room?'

'Yes. Three or four,' answered the cab driver. 'I was told that I could not leave, so I sat down. They searched the fare and took his belongings off him.'

'Can you recognise your fare in the courtroom?'

'Yes,' replied the driver, pointing to Connelly.

'When were you allowed to leave?' asked prosecuting Counsel. 'Was it before or after your fare?'

Connelly seemed to know his way around, but this bunch of 'honest' coppers could not be inhibited by an impartial cab driver.

The hearing for the day almost over, my head was full of question marks. I felt an overwhelming desire to get away from all this, to rolling hills and clean open space, to the fox in the meadow at the side of the moors, more natural than the circus surrounding me. 'Come on,' said the screw, touching my arm, 'let's go.' I followed him down the stairs of the dock, through the iron gates in the corridor below, along the passage to the cells, where Lissack was waiting, greeting me with a measure of courtesy I had not experienced in months. 'You feeling all right?' he asked when the cell door was pushed closed behind us. I nodded, bringing myself back to reality. 'I would like a few minutes with you to get your thoughts on these letters we were given this morning.'

'Well,' I replied, faltering, 'I never really had a chance to take them in, but I think they ought to be given to the jury like the rest of Kelly's statements, because at least you could be sure he had actually written them.'

'Mr Humphreys is going to try and get them introduced when he gets an opportunity tomorrow,' said Lissack.

'It would have been a good idea to have had some proper dialogue on my defence,' I replied. 'As it is, I can't help feeling you're all playing games around me.'

'I'm not, Mr Thatcher,' Lissack answered, with undertones of embarrassment. 'I am a solicitor. I cannot tell counsel how to conduct a case. That would be seen as an impertinence.'

'Sure,' I sighed, sensing the limitations of his role in the jealously guarded territories of the legal profession. 'But I do believe I ought to be better informed and given more chance to express an opinion.'

'Yes, I agree,' said Lissack, pondering a moment before tapping on the door to draw the guard's attention. 'I'll try and see you in the morning.' The screw's key crashed in the heavy lock, making us both flinch with its unexpected violence. 'You ready, Sir?' he announced, nodding to Lissack. He had left the key in the lock and was holding the end of the long key chain in his hand. He moved smartly to one side to allow Lissack to pass, then pulled the chain to close the door.

'Can I get to the toilet?' I asked hurriedly.

'I don't know, mate. I only lock the doors,' he replied, banging it shut.

Tuesday 11 February 1963, 10.30 a.m.

The trial continued with evidence of Connelly's arrest.

'Members of the jury,' said Justice Roskill, 'I must remind you again that the evidence you hear against each defendant in this case you must separate in your minds from that for the other defendants.'

The first witness of the day was Detective Sergeant Donald Fulford:

'I was returning to the premises in Earls Court and saw the taxicab outside. Connelly got out with a bundle of bedding and spoke to the taxi driver. They both went down into the basement and I followed them. The taxi driver put the key in the door of the room where Hilton had been arrested and I called out to Detective Constable Hall, who was inside the room, to open the door. I told Connelly and the taxi driver to go inside. Connelly said, "What's going on?" and I said, "I'm a police officer. What is your name?" and he said, "Connelly". I said, "My gov'nor wants a word with you." I searched him and took possession of the items on him. There were three officers and three pressmen in the room. I told Connelly and the taxi driver to sit down. Then I went to phone Inspector Thompson and returned to the room ten minutes later, and Connelly said, "I want you all to know I don't know what this is all about. I have made no statement if they try and verbal me". When Mr Thompson arrived, the taxi driver and pressmen were told to leave and …'

'My Lord', said Lewis Hawser [Connelly's defence counsel], rising to his feet, 'I have an objection to anything further …'

The jury left the courtroom, and Hawser continued:

'My Lord, might I ask the witness one or two questions before making my submission?'

'Of course, you can,' answered Justice Roskill.

'Mr Fulford,' asked Hawser, 'according to your notice of evidence, you are going to say that when Inspector Thompson arrived, he said to Connelly, "Are you Charles Connelly?" and the reply was, "Yes". Then Inspector Thompson said, "We are police officers. I have reason to believe that you were concerned in the Mitcham murder." Was Connelly cautioned at any time?'

'No, Sir,' replied Fulford.

'Connelly was under arrest?'

'Yes, Sir.'

'My Lord,' said Hawser, 'I put my submission on two grounds: rule two and three, together with rule six of Judges' Rules – "A person in custody should not be questioned without the usual caution being first administered."'

After an hour of legal argument, Justice Roskill overruled the objection and the prosecution continued with DS Fulford's account of what happened:

'Inspector Thompson said, "I have reason to believe that you were concerned in the Mitcham murder." Connelly said, "How did you find us? Who blew the gaff? Johnny must have done it." Mr Thompson said, "I am taking you to Tooting Police Station in connection with the Mitcham murder." I then left the room.'

'Mr Fulford,' asked Hawser, in cross examination, 'can I just ask you a little bit more about the statement made by Connelly. There were three police officers, three pressmen and the taxi driver in the room and after a while Connelly stands up?'

'Stands up?' asked Fulford, 'What for?'

'To make a statement.'

'No, sir, he was sitting down when he did that. He said, "I want you all to know I don't know what this is all about. I have made no statement if they try and verbal me." He said that in general to everyone in the room.'

'He wanted the pressmen and the cabman to witness the fact that he was not going to make a statement at all?'

'That's right, Sir,' answered Fulford.

'You said Inspector Thompson arrived, he told Connelly he believed he was concerned in the Mitcham murder, he ordered the pressmen and taxi driver out and Connelly immediately made a very damaging statement, amounting to an admission?'

'Yes, Sir,' replied Fulford.

Fulford left the witness box to take his place among the growing number of detectives on the benches by the jury and the next witness appeared, Detective Constable David Hall:

'You were one of the officers in the room when Connelly was arrested and the sequence of events you have recorded in your notebook are identical to those of the last witness?'

'Yes,' replied Hall.

'That Connelly made a statement in front of a cab driver and three pressmen to the effect that he was frightened the police would try and put one over on him and he wanted them to know he was not going to make any statement to the police, but, immediately they left the room, entirely of his own free will, in front of four police officers, he incriminates himself by saying, "Who blew the gaff? Johnny must have done it."'

'Yes, Sir.'

'Very convenient, don't you think?' asked Hawser.

'Yes, Sir,' replied Hall.

'Very obliging.'

'Yes, Sir.'

'And your recollection of words and events is identical to the other police officers'?'

'Yes, sir,' answered Hall, without faltering, and I wondered if they were all members of the actors' union.

Later in the morning, the lean grey figure of Superintendent Monteith left the table beneath the dock to take the oath in the witness box. His evidence was detailed, beginning with his investigation of the murder, then various interviews with Kelly, before coming to me:

'We come, then, to 11 December 1962,' said Griffith-Jones, referring to the brief in front of him, 'the second occasion that Thatcher was brought to the police station.'

Monteith was saying nothing about the first occasion on 30 November when he refused to allow me a solicitor and that I was naked, or that he interviewed me on 30 November:

'You saw Thatcher with Inspector Charles Hewitt at about 10.15 a.m.?'

'That's correct.'

They had come into the detention room with Inspector Frank Williams and Inspector Kenneth Thompson, but they, Williams and Thompson, were not now in the story Monteith was giving:

> 'What did you say to Thatcher?'
> 'I said,' replied Monteith, reading from his notebook, '"We have information that you have been associating with three men, named Galven, Martin and Connelly at the Grove Club, Westbourne Grove. Galven's real name is Kelly, Martin's real name is Hilton, and you have been using the name of Kitchen." He replied, "Yes, I have been there but not during the past week." He admitted using the name of Kitchen.'

None of that dialogue in that form had occurred, no names of anyone had been mentioned:

> '… and I said to him', Monteith continued, 'It is alleged you were concerned in this robbery at the Co-op in Mitcham.'

Yes, Monteith did say that to me and I told him I would answer no questions unless I was legally represented. I refused from that point to acknowledge or reply to their banter and Williams interceded, 'If he thinks we're kidding, let's charge him.' They then left the room. They returned ten minutes later. It was the responsibility of the station inspector to charge people. He read the charge to me and asked me if I understood. I nodded in reply and he asked me to sign the charge sheet to acknowledge that I understood, which I did. The time on the charge sheet was 10.30 a.m. I had been in the station for just over an hour. Hewitt threw a document onto the table. I had no idea what it was, and he said, 'This will give you something to think about,' and they left:

> '… I said to him,' Monteith continued in the witness box, '"as a matter of fact, Kelly says you did the shooting. Here is a copy of the statement made by Kelly. You had better read it." I cautioned him and left him with the statement. At about 11.45 a.m.

I received a message that Thatcher wanted to see me and, with Inspector Hewitt, I went to the detention room …'

'My Lord,' said Humphreys, getting to his feet, 'I object to the rest of this officer's evidence.'

The jury left the courtroom and Humphreys asked Monteith a few questions on which to base his objection:

'I understand, Mr Monteith, that the statement given to Thatcher, exhibit 73, contained alterations and additions from the original statement and they were unsigned.

'You hoped, of course,' asked Humphreys, 'that Thatcher, on seeing that statement, would make some observations about it?'

'I cautioned him and left him with it.'

'You hoped,' asked Humphreys, 'Did you hear my question? That he would make some observations about it?'

'My mind was completely neutral,' replied Monteith.

'Was it?' asked Humphreys. 'A statement which attacks Thatcher, and you are saying your mind was completely neutral as to whether he had something to say in reply?'

'Yes. It was only fair that he should see in writing what somebody else had said about him,' said Monteith.

'I must challenge your statement that you cautioned him and put an alternative story to you. I will not trouble you with the earlier part of the conversation about the club, that is not relevant, but you said something to the effect: "It is alleged that you were concerned in the robbery in the Co-op in Mitcham," and I am putting to you Thatcher's reply, "I will answer no questions until I am legally represented, which is my right!" Did he say words to that effect?' .

'No, Sir.'

'Do you agree that, if at any time he refused to speak until he had a solicitor present that was his right? asked Humphreys.

'I do not agree,' replied Monteith.

'You do not agree?' asked Humphreys again.

'No,' answered Monteith.

'That a man brought in for questioning on a murder charge is not entitled to have a solicitor?' asked Humphreys.

'I never said that he was not entitled to have a solicitor. He did not ask for one at that time,' replied Monteith.

'I suggest to you that he asked for a solicitor. Then one of your officers present said, "If he thinks we're kidding, let's charge him."'

'That is entirely untrue,' replied Monteith.

'And that he was charged, naked under a blanket, at 10.30 a.m.'

'He was charged at five past twelve in the afternoon,' replied Monteith.

'The station officer who did the charging read the charge and Thatcher was asked to sign it? asked Humphreys.

'Thatcher was not asked to sign the charge,' replied Monteith.

Not asked to sign the charge sheet? I frowned in puzzlement, thinking Monteith is preparing the ground in case he's asked to produce it:

'Would he be given a document? asked Humphreys.

'After he had been charged, he in fact was given a document setting out the offence with which he was charged,' said Monteith.

'Would you look at exhibit 75,' said Humphreys. 'That is the document, is it?'

'That is the document which was handed to him after he was charged,' answered Monteith.

'Which contains the printed caution,' said Humphreys. 'Was he then left with a copy of Kelly's statement and the words of Inspector Hewitt, "Here, this will give you something to think about"?'

'I gave him Kelly's statement,' replied Monteith, 'and I said to him, "Here is a copy of a statement made by Kelly. You had better read it." And I cautioned him.'

'Then you left him with it,' said Humphreys, 'and you say you go back to see him an hour later, with Inspector Hewett who takes with him some statement forms. You believe that Thatcher wanted to see you. You went back expecting to hear his comments on that statement?'

'I did feel in my mind there was a possibility,' answered Monteith.

'In these circumstances,' said Humphreys, 'would it not have been right for you most carefully to have cautioned him?'

'I had already cautioned him,' replied Monteith.

'Do you wish to call any evidence on this from the defendant?' Justice Roskill asked Humphreys.

'No, My Lord,' said Humphreys. 'In my submission, I do not consider it necessary. I would argue this – even on the assumption that the officer is correct, his evidence is inadmissible. Rule 8 of the Judges' Rules. Your Lordship will find it on page 465 of the '35 edition of Archbold's Criminal Pleadings, part of paragraph 118: "When two or more persons are charged with an offence and statements are taken separately, the police should not read those to the other persons, but each of such persons should be given by the police a copy of such statements and nothing should be said or done by the police to invite a reply. If the person charged desires to make a statement in reply, the usual caution should be administered."'

I listened with a weird sense of fascination to the legal arguments that followed, over something that had not happened, and over words that were never spoken. And in his conclusion, Justice Roskill ruled:

'I am quite satisfied that there has not been any breach of Rule 8, but in case it should be said later that I am wrong, I ought to deal with this. The prosecution has invited me to take the view that, even if there had been a breach of Rule 8, it was not a serious breach in the sense it in no way lead Thatcher to make a statement which was not completely voluntary. Therefore, on that basis, I should think it right in the interests of justice in this case to admit the Superintendent's evidence.'

I couldn't believe this!

Humphreys rose from his seat with a ruffled air of dissent and requested time in the jury's absence, to discuss the introduction of the three Kelly letters:

'My Lord,' said Kelly's counsel, jumping to his feet, 'my client wrote certain letters while in custody. I understand Mr Humphreys would like to put them before the jury in cross-examination, if

> Superintendent Monteith and the prosecution have indicated they
> think it necessary to use part of these letters in their cross-examina-
> tion of the prisoners, though they oppose the introduction of them
> at this stage. I do not wish to use them in any way.'

Still in a daze from Justice Roskill's amazing comment of 'voluntary
statement', I listened in snatches to the developing argument on the
floor of the courtroom. My mind unable to concentrate on that, as
it wrestled with a nagging demand for insight into the funny business of the charge sheet. It pounded away at my thoughts; I knew
I had been charged at 10.30 a.m., the time was typed on the sheet
and I had signed it. That document must exist somewhere, because
police forces zealously keep documents, and its existence exposes
the fraud of Monteith's evidence.

'Tomorrow,' I heard Justice Roskill say, 'if you come here armed
with authorities, I will be glad to listen to arguments on the issue of
these letters …'

The proceedings were ending and a moment later I was taken
down to the cells, where shortly Lissack came to see me. 'Looks like
I have to accept the inevitable,' I said, voicing my disappointment at
yet again not having Humphreys to speak with.

'There isn't anything further I can do about that,' replied Lissack,
sounding both peeved and embarrassed. 'I shall see Mr Humphreys
in the morning and convey to him anything you want to say.'

'Not quite the same thing, is it?' I sighed. We had been over
this so many times it was now ridiculous. 'What is he thinking of
doing about Monteith and the charge sheet?' I asked, the question
still tormenting me. Monteith could have fabricated a confession
for 10.30 a.m. just as easily as 11.45 a.m., so why complicate the
issue by changing times? Unless he had to say I was charged in the
afternoon, to justify keeping me out of the court that day, in police
custody till the following morning. 'Are the prosecution producing
a charge sheet?' I asked, anxious to get an opinion.

'I don't know,' said Lissack, pondering a moment. 'It won't be
good for you if they do.'

'Oh, yes, it will,' I replied, instinctively knowing the prosecution
would produce the charge sheet if it supported Monteith's and

Hewitt's evidence. But they were not producing it, because Monteith was lying and they knew it.

'You can't be sure of that,' said Lissack, with less conviction than his response implied.

'The changes are,' I said, speaking thoughts aloud, 'the station Inspector who charged me, and we know who he is, because his name is on the piece of paper he gave me when he charged me …'

'Is the time on that?' said Lissack.

'No. It's just a piece of paper with the details of the charge on it', I replied. 'The time is on the charge sheet itself and the chances are that a uniformed Inspector won't mess about now with a document that bears his signature, and I think we should call him as a witness.'

'We can't do that,' said Lissack. 'You won't get a police officer in the witness box to contradict another police officer. You must be realistic.'

'Then what about the occurrence book,' I replied, 'which the desk sergeant fills in? He will have recorded the time and charge in that. So ask for that to be produced.'

'The police will sit up all night if they have to and write a new book,' said Lissack, shaking his head at my suggestion. 'You are being naive.'

'Am I?' I sighed, with a mixture of impatience and doubt. 'They are official documents and I think we should ask for them to be produced.'

'I will speak to Mr Humphreys in the morning,' said Lissack. 'And I'll get back to you.'

Back in Brixton Prison for the night, I lay awake trying to see the wood through the trees. Why had Monteith altered the time they charged me? Clearly they had made up their minds that my association with Kelly and Hilton at the Grove Club put me in the frame. There wasn't any evidence, so they would write a few confessions. Hewitt wrote the statements. Williams and Moore brought me to the station, then went to breakfast, and Williams and Monteith arranged for Cuthbert to charge me at 10.30 a.m. But they didn't allow any time for confessions, and confessions or admissions had to come before any charges, so they changed the times?

The police took a cardboard box of my stuff (letters, receipts etc.), from my room at the hostel to Monteith's office. The box was returned

to me during the committal at the magistrates' court when Sherrard
was representing me, and he searched through it and removed a hand-
written note from a Chief Superintendent Dick Lewis to Monteith.
Dick Lewis was Monteith's boss. The note said: 'Make sure you get
a statement.' Sherrard showed it to me for comment, then gave it to
Monteith. I can only surmise the note came from Monteith's desk
into my box. But after Hewitt's statement, I made the connection
– Dick Lewis was behind Monteith, and Monteith would not have
manufactured evidence without the back-up of his boss.

12 February 1963

Shortly after being back in the cell at the Bailey, the door opened
and Corkery came in. I was wondering what the day would bring.

'Good morning, Mr Thatcher,' he greeted me. 'Mr Lissack said
you were concerned about the original charge sheet. Well, Mr
Humphreys thinks it should remain in dispute, along with the rest
of the police evidence. After all, there isn't any evidence apart from
what the police have to say to warrant a connection in his opinion.'

'Where I come from, Mr Corkery,' I said, 'it's against my religion
to have any form of dialogue with the police and certainly nothing
incriminating. There are eight coppers giving evidence against me,
all saying I was making admissions. Eight of them, one of me. Give
me a break. The police have decided I'm the villain of the piece and
have manufactured their evidence to prove it. I wish I had the ability
to defend myself.'

'You *must* be represented.'

'Then represent me, Mr Corkery.'

The courtroom, as I entered the dock, seemed more crowded
with lawyers than spectators. The long rows of benches were full of
people in gowns who had come to listen to the arguments. It looked
odd in contrast to the empty jury box:

'I have taken the opportunity,' said Justice Roskill, reopening the
discussion on the Kelly letters with a statement of his position, 'of
reading what authorities I can find. So far as it is a matter for my

direction, I am not prepared to allow these letters to be used or referred to in cross-examination before they are properly proved. If you want to prove a document,' he addressed his remarks to the defence counsel, 'in a civil or criminal case, what you have to do is call somebody who is familiar with the handwriting and can identify the handwriting.' He turned to the prosecution. 'Is that not so, Mr Griffith-Jones?'

'That is so,' Griffith-Jones replied.

'I am asking your Lordship's ruling,' said Humphreys, 'on my right to do that through a police officer who knows Kelly's writing.'

'If the answer you get is "Yes"', said Justice Roskill 'it does establish that they are in Kelly's writing. If the answer is "No", it does not. That is so, is it not, Mr Griffith-Jones?'

'That is so', he replied.

'But the mere fact,' said Justice Roskill, 'a witness says "Yes", does not make them evidence at that stage. If you wish to argue the contrary, My Humphreys, I will listen.'

'I shall wish to argue to the contrary,' said Hawser for Connelly.

'So shall I,' said Lawson for Hilton.

'I have not said these documents,' said Justice Roskill, 'are irrelevant. What I have said is that they must first be properly proved …'

'You've got no chance of proving them through Monteith or any of his subordinates', I was thinking as the argument developed and I watched the clock on the panel above the clerk's head slowly tick the morning away till Lewis Hawser vigorously picked up the argument for Connelly and Humphreys sat back to let him get on with it:

'In my submission,' Hawser continued after long reference to legal reports, 'Once the handwriting has been proved, then there being documents emanating from one of the accused and relevant documents in this case, the jury is entitled to see them and we are entitled to put them forward. It is part of the general case put forward here that Kelly made certain oral and written statements. The position now is that Kelly has made certain further written statements and in my submission, providing we establish they are in his handwriting, then we are entitled to cross-examine upon them and put them in front of the jury.'

'When the documents are proved,' replied Griffith-Jones, 'I can make no possible objection to the contents going before the jury. But it would be wholly wrong to allow these letters to be used in cross-examination of a police officer before they are properly proved.'

'In the circumstances of this case,' submitted Lawson, after further heated discussion, 'it is for your Lordship, for the court, to enquire into circumstances in which these letters came into existence. A great deal of cross-examination of police officers in relation to them is required. The case the police present is on the basis: "This is what Kelly has said to us, and all the accused have told us Kelly is right". Therefore, I invite your Lordship to say that it is for the court in these circumstances to put them forward.'

'I don't propose to take that course,' said Justice Roskill with an avalanche of words that only a lawyer could interpret. They made little or no sense to me by this time. 'I do not think it right for a trial judge to exercise the discretion which he undoubtedly possesses to adduce evidence which has the effect, or may be through by observers to have the effect of tipping the scales one way rather than the other. The scales must be kept evenly balanced. I will allow Mr Humphreys to ask Superintendent Monteith if he can express an opinion about the handwriting of these letters, but beyond that they must not be referred to or read obliquely, directly or otherwise. I am not prepared to allow police officers to be cross-examined upon them until they have been properly proved and I am sure you appreciate what I mean by the word 'obliquely'. Now let us have the jury back.'

A few minutes later, the jury were in the seats and Monteith had returned to the witness box:

'Let me briefly summarise,' said Griffith-Jones, 'to bring the jury back into the picture. We had reached 11 December. At 10.15 a.m., Mr Monteith, you saw Thatcher and told him it was alleged he had been concerned in the robbery at the Co-op depot and that Kelly had said he, Thatcher, had done the shooting. You gave

Thatcher a copy of Kelly's statement. You cautioned him and left him with it. At 11.45 a.m. you received a message that Thatcher wanted to see you. When you got into the detention room, what happened?

'When I got there, he said to me, "I've read the statement a dozen times. The chap that wrote it must be screwy. You know I was in on the job. If he says I did the shooting, I am going to say it was him." I then said, "You are going to be charged with being concerned in the murder of a man named Hurden at the Co-op in Mitcham on 17 November, 1962," I cautioned him and he said, "I was there, but I'm saying nothing until I see a solicitor."'

Shockwaves of angry disbelief had swept over me when I had heard that garbage for the first time at the magistrates' court, but now I felt a strangely numbing sense of embarrassment, as I relived the reality of sitting naked in the detention room. It *was* 11.45 a.m., just as Monteith had said it was. I had been charged then for over an hour, and a piece of paper with the details of the charged typed on, that the station inspector had given me was on the table, with the document Hewitt had tossed there. I did not know the document was a photocopy of Kelly's statement till I finally read it, and then Hewitt and Monteith re-entered the room. 'How do you feel now?' Hewitt had asked. I did not answer. Instead, I picked up the station inspector's piece of paper and held it up to Monteith's face, pointing out to him the printed words of the caution that were on it. 'I want to contact a solicitor,' I had said with all the force I could muster.

'What do you think I am – a c★★t?' he had replied in anger and left the room. Now that was a million miles away from the 'confession' Monteith had just presented to the court:

'Did you make a note of that?' asked Griffith-Jones.

'Inspector Hewitt wrote it down on a statement form,' replied Monteith. [Exhibit 73A.] 'Inspector Hewitt was in the detention room with me.'

Little did I know that one day Monteith would come to terms with his life and commit suicide by blowing his brains out. If this was not all going down in the courtroom transcript, I would not believe any of it. I shook my head vigorously for a few brief moments to clear it and breathed deeply while I listened:

> 'We come to 8 January,' Griffith-Jones was saying, 'Hilton was brought to the police station and you saw him …'
>
> 'I saw Hilton with Chief Inspector Monahan at 9.30 p.m. in the detention room. I said to him, "We are police officers. You have been using the name of Martin and in November last you visited the Grove Club at Westbourne Grove." He replied, "Yes, I have been using the name of Martin". I said, "it is alleged you were concerned in the robbery at the Co-op depot" and I cautioned him …'

'My Lord,' interrupted Lawson, Hilton's lawyer. 'I object to the rest of this …', and the jury were again sent out. Then, after a short cross-examination of what Monteith was going to say in evidence, Hilton was called to the witness box to recall his own story:

> 'Superintendent Monteith and Chief Inspector Monahan came into the room. Superintendent Monteith said to me, "My name is Monteith. This is my colleague Chief Inspector Monahan." They sat down at the table where I was sitting and at that time another man came into the room and introduced himself to me as Chief Superintendent Lewis and he said to me, "I've come in here in an unofficial capacity to see you. I want to help you, even though you may not think so." I had never seen him before. He said, "You know that this is a murder and I want you to put in writing the part you played in this robbery. You must think of yourself and not of other people and if you do this, you will help yourself and the police at the same time." He said, "If you confess to your part in this robbery, there is a possibility that you could get charged with only robbery and not murder. You must think of the possibility of Connelly and Thatcher turning against you when they take the witness box, and now I shall leave you alone with my colleagues and I shan't see you or speak to you again and I shall deny ever doing so."'
>
> 'At any time was any caution offered to you?' asked Lawson.

'No,' replied Hilton.

'Mr Monteith,' said Lawson 'says he said to you, "We are police officers. You have been brought here because it is alleged you were concerned in the Co-op robbery."'

'He never said that to me,' answered Hilton. 'He handed me a copy of a statement and said, "If you read this you will see that Kelly has put you away." I made no reply and he said, "I'm going to leave you for a while to read this and then come and see you again."'

'That is all I want to ask at this stage,' said Lawson, and Hilton returned to the dock for Lawson to present an argument that the remainder of Monteith's evidence was inadmissible, which quickly invoked Justice Roskill's ruling.

'Suffice it to say,' he said, 'having seen both the prisoner, Hilton, in the witness box and Superintendent Monteith in the witness box, I have no hesitation whatever in accepting what the Inspector said. I therefore overrule Mr Lawson's submission on the footing the Superintendent's evidence is correct.'

The jury returned and Monteith continued, and the thought occurred to me that Justice Roskill would save the country a fortune by instructing the jury to convict everyone and send them on their ways.

'What did you say after cautioning Hilton?' asked Griffith-Jones, of Monteith who was now confident after Justice Roskill's statement.

'I said to him, "Philip Kelly and a man named Thatcher have already been charged with being concerned in this matter. Kelly has told us you, Connelly and he, held up the cashier's office with guns and Thatcher, who was outside the office, was the one who did the shooting." Hilton replied, "Kelly is right. I was on the job with him and the others. I would rather top myself than shop them." I gave him a copy of the statement and said, "This is a copy of a statement made by Kelly. I will see you presently after you have had time to read it." I saw him half an hour later, again with Chief Inspector Monahan, and Hilton said, "I have read Kelly's statement. I agree with every word he says, but I am not going to grass like Kelly." I told him he was going to be charged. I cautioned him and he replied, "I have been expecting that, but I will deny that I have said anything to you."'

'Early the following morning,' asked Griffith-Jones, 'at about 11.45 a.m., Connelly was brought to Tooting Police Station and you saw him with Detective Inspector Thompson?'

'Yes,' replied Monteith, 'I told him who I was and I said to him, "I understand you are known as 'Scotch Bob'?" and he replied, "Some people call me that." I said to him, "You are going to be charged with being concerned with others in the murder of a man named Hurden". I cautioned him and said, "Here is a copy of a statement made by Kelly". He said, "I know about Kelly's statement. I do not disagree with him. He is dead right, but I will not put anything in writing."'

'Thank you, Mr Monteith,' said Griffith-Jones, handing Monteith over to the defence for cross-examination and the court adjourned for lunch.

A few minutes later, Corkery visited me in the cells, 'Mr Humphreys received a letter this morning from Mr Jimmy Gilbert. Mr Gilbert said he was interviewed by the police and they accused him of being one of the Co-op raiders. They told him Kelly had accused him of doing the shooting and they were going to charge him, till they discovered he was in custody at the time of the crime. Mr Gilbert said he is available to give evidence on your behalf if you wish to call him. However, Mr Humphreys would prefer you not to call any witnesses in your defence. He believes you do not have a case to answer on the charge of capital murder and he will submit a plea of "no case to answer" when the prosecution have finished presenting their case. This will probably fail, but if you call no witnesses, Mr Humphreys will get the final speech at the end of the trial and, in the circumstances, he would like to be in that position.'

'I'll need to think about that,' I replied. 'Mr Humphreys has kept his distance from me, so I can only assume he has some idea of what he's doing.'

'He is keeping your background away from the jury, Mr Thatcher,' said Corkery, 'which rather inhibits examination of police witnesses.

Though he does not believe it necessary to prove the police have got carried away because there isn't really a case against you on this indictment.'

'I hope the jury see it that way,' I replied doubtfully.

'The jury do not have the last word,' said Corkery.

'Don't they? So, what are you going to do about the charge sheet?'

'Quite frankly,' said Corkery, 'Mr Humphreys is frightened of asking for that document to be produced, because it could be very dangerous for you, if you force the issue. We feel it will be better to leave the time in dispute between you and the police.'

'The prosecution won't leave it there if they could produce a charge sheet without my signature; it's as simple as that. And there's no point,' I said, turning to the subject uppermost in my mind, 'in asking Monteith to identify Kelly's handwriting. You won't get anywhere with that till we get Kelly in the witness box.'

'I understand Kelly is not going into the witness box.'

'You're joking!' I replied.

'His counsel will have advised Kelly not to give evidence,' said Corkery. 'And the police won't want him examined.'

'Hold on a minute,' I said, my thoughts jumping with suspicion. 'Is that some sort of deal? Is that why he hasn't been charged with capital murder – pay-off for not giving evidence?'

It must have been the police's idea to hold me in confinement, so I could have no communication with anyone or learn what was going on. I could not at that stage understand why Monteith and Hewitt were changing the time they say I was charged. My signature was on the charge sheet. The prosecution must have known that. I felt that I had become a pawn, trapped in a spider's web. 'Why do you think the police picked on you, Mr Thatcher?' asked Corkery.

'Association. They need a body, and with my form, I make a good candidate,' I said, aware that Corkery's main interest was with the people he worked for. 'When the police decide to frame someone, Mr Corkery – and it's not uncommon – they get support all through the system, and with capital murder, it's premeditated and this is not the first time I've been fitted up.'

Kelly's letters were never produced, none of his alleged statements were signed and the charge sheet never appeared.

I met Christmas Humphreys with Corkery and Lissack in a room beneath the court and explained to them that the time on the charge sheet that was read to me, and which I signed to acknowledge that I understood, was 10.30 a.m. – and that should prove conclusively that Monteith and Hewitt's account of events was a fantasy. The charge sheet of 11 December was held by the station inspector, not Monteith. Monteith would not have access to it because it was in a different department from his. Christmas Humphreys was cautious. I could see he was hesitant, and clearly reluctant to pursue the issue; he much preferred to leave it in conflict, while I was a bit nervous about the wrong document appearing, so the ball was in his court. Could a charge sheet appear with Monteith's time on it, I kept asking myself. Then why hadn't it been produced?

Charge sheets are individually serial-numbered, like cheque books, and to produce it in evidence could only be done by the station inspector who recorded the charge. And would he allow himself to be compromised in public? It was a document that couldn't be duplicated. The prosecution should have produced it the moment it came into conflict and, because they didn't produce it, I wondered why. And Justice Roskill, the trial judge, should also have had it produced. But everyone suddenly became frightened of this document and this was serious stuff; my life was on the line here and the reputation of the police was in the melting pot.

The only real evidence against me was what Monteith and his 'mob' had to say of events in the police station. I insisted that Lissack should obtain a copy of this charge sheet and he later told me he had seen it and it was timed 10.30 a.m., but that he was unable to get a copy. Then it disappeared, and no one has ever seen it since. Lissack was ambitious, and subsequently became the first solicitor to become a trial judge.

This sequence of events took place in the early sixties, and it doesn't have the same frightening effect on me that it did at the time. Nevertheless, turning over the embers depresses me and in the ashes there remains a glowing anger. The whole thing was such a rip-off. I was really on my own, and I couldn't trust anyone. I was surrounded by hostility and false images. It was plainly obvious to everyone that the police had decided I was part of this crime – or maybe they didn't really give a s★★t, as long as they had an acceptable candidate. I was still serving a sentence for a Co-op robbery, so *modus operandi*, and this bunch of 'crime-busters' were, in effect, challenging the establishment and the judiciary to support them. With my form, whose side do you take?

I can see it clearer now in retrospect, though obviously only my little piece of the saga – and I can take you through my eyes, the bits I could see. There was a great deal going on behind the scenes that I knew nothing about and I can take you through the trial, one day at a time, most of which I recorded years ago, when everything was fresh. The trial lasted a month and the judge, Justice Roskill, was so clearly in favour of the police evidence, in tone of voice and facial expression, that only the deaf and blind couldn't see his prejudice and influence on the jury. Fortunately for me, the court was always packed with observers, because the trial had become front page and there were images at stake. I had to be convicted, otherwise the credibility of the police would crumble and heads would roll, and the spin-offs would rock the establishment, because the strong arm of the law must not do s★★t like this, and Chief Superintendent Dick Lewis, Monteith's boss, must not be part of, or endorse, such a swindle! All parts of the same whole, and their type of corruption we can all do without.

The jury found me guilty of being the fourth man, outside – the trigger man – and Justice Roskill gave me a b★★★★★king and sentenced me to death.

Kelly, Hilton and Connelly were all convicted of being in the office, and guilty of non-capital murder. As I was being taken from the dock, Kelly said to Justice Roskill that *he* shot Dennis Hurden, the Co-op worker, and Roskill sentenced him to life imprisonment. I haven't seen Kelly since. He was sent to prison in the north and released several years later. After that, I don't know.

Hilton and Connelly were also given life. All three had been convicted of being in the office, with me convicted of being outside doing the shooting. That's what the prosecution wanted, and that's what they got. But, beneath it all, I hadn't really been convinced it would happen.

This was really heavy duty, so don't ask me how I felt. Some feelings are too controlled by instincts to make a lot of sense. Justice Roskill wanted a conviction in support of his team, but the day wasn't passing unnoticed and many a harsh word would become hot air.

9

With an escort of three prison officers, I was taken to Wandsworth Prison in south London, where I was led from the gate entrance of the prison to an outside staircase attached to one of the prison wings. This leads straight into the passageway between the gallows and the holding cell. The holding cell was through a large door on the right – wide enough for three to pass through if the condemned man needed physical assistance to 'nowhere'.

The average time anyone spends in this cell is seven weeks to the day of their execution, so you see, anyone being put down will have to sit and wait about seven weeks, by which time their head will be so f****d up by the torture of the coming event that they will need assistance. Premeditation is the name of the game and most of the assistance would come in liquid form in the food the prisoner ate.

The holding cell was crowded with people in uniform: the governor, the chief officer, the priest, the doctor and his assistant, and two of the really heavy Home Office thugs from the punishment block below this landing. The cell was actually two ordinary cells knocked into one, and the other two screws in the cell were to stay with me after the welcoming committee had watched me undress and the doctor had checked my bum for alien objects. The governor asked me who I was, and did I understand what I was there for, and would I like a sleeping draught – no, this wasn't the time to be blocked out completely, I was blank enough. So they left me with my two minders.

The idea was to hold me in this extended cell for whatever time was necessary to complete the procedure of clearing away the legal paperwork. There would be an appeal, but not before I had signed the application form, and I needed space. My mind had misted over. I was numb – in total isolation, even though, as things were at this moment, I would never again be alone. Ever since the sentencing, two guards were with me, every minute, day and night, always within reach, safe-guarding me from harm! An iron bed against one wall, a table and three chairs, an alcove for a toilet. The bare necessities, where one minute will be a day and every day would be forever.

The two screws who spent the first night with me had volunteered to fill in for the regular watch who were on their way from other prisons. It was policy not to have any of the regular local staff of the prison on death-watch, but to have volunteers from other places. There would be four – two on, two off – for twenty-four hours in twelve hour shifts. The first two came the following afternoon, and spent most of the night discussing the overtime they hoped to make.

On the first night I couldn't sleep, and sat at the table with the volunteers, playing cards. I needed a bit of company and these two were making an effort to be impartial. During the night, they told me a few bits and pieces about what was and what wasn't allowed – no newspapers, no radio, no contact with the outside world. Visits were thirty minutes, once a day, and close relatives only. I knew Helena from Brighton would want to see me, but there was no way I would subject her to the distress of that, so visits were out. And they told me I was entitled to a pint of beer a day, which rather surprised me. Who do I see about that? The prison doctor who visited me twice a day, along with the governor and a handful of others. I wasn't a drinker, as I don't particularly like the taste of beer, but I would ask for it and, after that, the chief hospital officer would bring me a bottle of beer which he opened in front of me and poured into a mug. On the first couple of occasions I swigged a mouthful and threw the rest down the toilet. I didn't really want it, but I was determined to have it, and after a few days I'd share it between the two screws rather than dump it. I felt no animosity toward them, or any desire to abuse them.

Much later I discovered, through the con who cleaned the hospital surgery, that the beer was doped and I would wake up in the night to find my two minders asleep at the table. They knew no more about it than me.

Once a day, when the rest of the prison was locked up for the midday meal, I was taken out for a short exercise, walking up and down between my minders, one on the left in front and one on the right, behind. We would sometimes trip over each other when we turned round, and I would only stay out long enough for the cell to be searched and cleaned and, on going back into the cell, I was forced to strip and discard my prison clothing for a fresh set. The prison shirt was so heavily starched that it felt like untanned leather – not the way they normally come from the prison laundry – and, knowing the paranoia of Wandsworth, I knew all the clothing coming into the condemned cell would be organised by a screw, not a con, so what was the stiff shirt implying? Another screw with a problem? As it was, I couldn't blow my nose or do a crap without a guard standing over me.

I knew from experience that I had ten days to lodge an appeal, and I knew an appeal would be automatic. A few days later I got a letter from Lissack, the solicitor, asking me to sign appeal forms, for an appeal already scheduled for a hearing in a couple of weeks.

I would wake about 6 a.m. after a restless night, my mind a blank but unable to shut down. The two night shift would be dozing at the table at the foot of the bed and I'd lay, engulfed in the silence, wondering, deceiving myself. This isn't real, they can't possibly go through with this. At the thought of it I'd switch off immediately.

The sudden piercing call of a blackbird outside the cell window cut into the silence like a sword, its unexpected sharpness startling the world into a new life, another day, and each day hence I would lay in the silence, waiting for its morning call and the sounds of the prison – heavy keys in solid locks, the tramp of boots on slate and the side door in the alcove opening. Odd screws would pop in for a short chat with my minders – an excuse to look at me – and I would lay in bed, pretending not to notice.

'I've popped in to welcome you to Wandsworth and see everything's OK,' said the landing screw, looking at me. 'You don't want to let this con lay in bed all day – make him get up with the rest of the nick,' giving me something to get p****d off about and focus on.

Breakfast – porridge and a slice of bread.

The doctor and his assistants at 9.15 a.m. 'Are you all right? Is there anything you need?' I would shake my head and they would leave. Then the governor and the chief at 10 a.m. 'Are you all right? Is there anything you need?' At 10.30 a.m. the priest would enter and say 'Good morning. Can we have a chat?'

'Sure,' I said as the two screws moved away from the table and we sat down.

'Is there any family or friends I can contact for you?' he asked me in that slightly pious way that some priests adopt when talking to the 'lowlife' of unknown temperament.

'No.'

'Your family in Brighton?'

'No.'

'You sure?'

'Yes – I want them left out of this,' I said, aware of his concentrated stare as he tried to weigh me up. 'What I need is an ally with an open mind.'

'I can't give you any guarantees. But I can help you spiritually.'

'Help me see the wood through the trees – my spirit is not in danger.' His name was Brian, and he would call every day and spend an hour or more. He talked like a con – 'f★★★★g' every few words and telling me it was a word that didn't mean anything. He used it – I didn't. Was he talking to me in this way as a route to my confidence? An attempt to be understanding, or actually a good guy trying to help me through?

We talked a lot in the three weeks leading up to the appeal. He told me personal stuff he'd gone through and love affairs. Probably lots of things he wouldn't have told me if he hadn't thought I was about to die. I knew more about his life behind the façade than he knew of me. I would only talk in detail about the manufacturing of evidence and the complacency with which it was accepted. We talked for hours about corruption – they surfaced and submerged – that was all I wanted to talk about. He listened as I unloaded some of my disbeliefs, leaving nothing to believe in. I knew he was part of the system, even though he would insist he was trying not to be. He would write reports and pass opinions and would be involved. No one is ever neutral. 'Can I come again?' he asked as he was leaving.

'Of course, whenever.' He was, I guess, in his early forties, pleasant looking and in good shape, easily likeable and recently appointed, the first ever full-time Catholic priest in the prison service and, with a little devotion, would one day have his own empire within the system. I hadn't spoken to anyone in several months and needed the contact.

'You are different from the image I have of you from the papers.'

'Yeah – I bet.'

Apparently, all the national dailies had made this trial a front-page event and, after the conviction, they had a field day in their competitive world of fiction writers. 'It doesn't matter what anyone says about me, Father, unless you believe it.'

For several days I had lain awake, listening to the morning sounds, waiting to hear the alcove door opening and the outside landing screw come in to speak to my minders and pass a few snide remarks about me. I let it go a few times, hoping this one would lose interest. He was obviously a uniformed 'macho' of no substance and I was beginning to resent his intrusion. He was out of bounds and I knew I could abuse him without any kickbacks. I lay in bed, pretending to doze, waiting, knowing this one would come and I would pounce like a creature of prey. 'You get up in the mornings,' he snarled at me. I jumped up in the bed and screamed at him like a lunatic, and he was gone. So predictable – if it wasn't so serious, it would have been funny. My minders said nothing, but they would have to write it up in the occurrence book when they changed shifts and, later in the day, Brian told me that screw would not be bothering me again, and I asked if that was part of the drill, to try me out!

'Your counsel want to come and see you,' said the governor on his morning visit.

'OK. When?'

'On Friday at one o'clock. Your appeal is on Monday.'

'OK.' I had signed the appeal forms and sent them back to Lissack. That was it. I had heard nothing further, though I knew things would be happening. I had twice been doing time in Wandsworth when executions took place, so I knew how things were done. Lissack and Corkery were led into the cell through the alcove door and we stood leaning against the wall. 'We have an affidavit from Kelly, saying you were not involved in this.' Corkery was searching me for a response.

'What does that mean?' I asked.

'We can put this forward in your appeal.'

'Hold on a minute. What has Kelly got to do with me?' We stood looking at each other for several seconds. 'Was anything Kelly was supposed to have said in evidence in any way against me?'

'Kelly didn't give evidence.'

'So nothing he is supposed to have said is in any way evidence against me, but it's been put before the jury. That's a rip-off. The issue here is whether or not I made admission to something. That has nothing to do with me and I don't care what you think, I expect you to defend me.'

'That is where we are …' I cut him off, wanting to unload some of the tensions festering inside of me.

'Why do I feel your interest lay elsewhere, and you and Humphreys are coasting?'

'Mr Humphreys …' said Corkery.

'Hold on …' I said, desperate to unload. 'The police have put me here, and you are sitting on the fence.' Corkery was sharp, articulate and ambitious. He contained his indifference with ease and I could feel his reluctance to get involved. 'Why do you think the police selected you, Mr Thatcher?' he again asked me.

'They need success. They are under pressure, and that's coming from the top.' I looked at him with searching eyes. 'They haven't got it right and they don't give a s★★t. They have vested interests.'

'With your form, it's very dangerous to attack the police.'

'You're telling me?' The threat of execution concentrated the mind, and the deeper I searched mine for ways out of this, the less I felt the threat. It wasn't going to happen. The trial had been a failure in many ways for the law-and-order 'mob'. The police challenge to the judiciary to support their way of doing things was too blatant. It had created a problem in the high ground of those in charge, left questions as to who was in charge.

I never saw or spoke with Corkery again.

The weekend was before me, and it was just a block of meaningless time. I wanted it to end and to get back into the arena. I wanted to be invisible, out of the spotlight and left alone, as nothing seemed to be real.

At 9 a.m. Monday morning, I was handcuffed in the back of a transit van on my way to the appeal court with three screws. Two of them my minders from the cell.

Appeals are the reverse of trials, and normally their function is to decide whether or not the law has been observed and they are dealt with in a few minutes. In trials, the prosecution states the case for the crown and the accused opposes it. In appeals, the accused argues the law and the prosecution defends it, and the case stands or falls on the judgement of whoever is interpreting the issues. In the law there are always opinions for and opinions against, so judges can go either way – after all, it's their field of play.

From the cells below the appeal court I was led down a corridor to a door that opened directly into the defendants' dock, and I was surprised to discover that this dock was on the same level as the judges' rostrum and was actually attached to it at right angles, so the defendant and the judges looked down together into the well of the court, where the lawyers and observers were. I was seated no more than 3ft away from Justice Winn, one of the appeal judges. I could turn my head and speak to him.

The appeal developed into a complete review of the trial and lasted for five days, with witnesses being called who hadn't been available at the trial. Halfway through the morning on the Friday, the prosecution finished arguing for the verdicts to be upheld. Christmas Humphreys rose to his feet to argue some more, but the senior judge, Justice Ashworth, held up his hand and told him to wait a moment while he conferred with Thompson and Winn – the other two judges. They moved together to whisper, just 3ft from me and I could hear every word they said to each other.

'We must grant this appeal,' whispered Justice Ashworth.

'Yes,' whispered Justice Winn.

'But we must consider public opinion,' whispered Justice Thompson, an arm's length away.

I can see it all and hear their words as clearly today as then, and I knew immediately that the threat of death was gone. My head was all over the place, and all the hidden tensions that I'd somehow managed to conceal were now released, leaving me in a total state of confusion. What now? Was I meant to hear that? Were they looking for a compromise, a face-saving exercise, and what worth did any of them consider me in all this?

I was public enemy number one at that time. The hype the press had given me after the conviction left nothing to the imagination. Even Antony got his photo on the front pages of the nation's press, with stories of my intention to bring him back to England and a lot of other garbage, most of which I knew nothing of for several months, because I was allowed no access to radio or press. And by the time I was, it was history. Although most of it was hurtful stuff, it really meant very little to me. I was up against the world, as we all are at different levels, and the only people on my side were the friends who knew me.

There never was any evidence to involve me in this murder, and this panel of judges knew more about the evidence than I ever will. Did they mean me to hear what had been whispered, about public opinion?

Ashworth looked at Humphreys who was still on his feet:

'Before you say anything, Mr Humphreys, we are going to grant this appeal in part,' he said.

'There is the question of separate trials, milord,' said Humphreys. 'I would like to speak with my client.'

'Would you like us to adjourn?' asked Ashworth.

'No need for that, milord, I can talk with him here,' Humphreys replied, coming over to me to stand beneath the dock and I leaned forward to look down at him.

'Should I argue for a separate trial?' he asked me.

I had only spoken to Christmas Humphreys once, for about fifteen minutes, halfway through the trial itself when I insisted on talking to him about the non-production of the charge sheet and the difference in the times the police were using in evidence. I wasn't interested in another trial. I'd had more than enough of this one and I was under no illusions. The dealer would stack the deck if there was another trial. I felt that Christmas Humphreys had been very subtle in his cross examinations – too subtle in fact – and I could feel he was uncomfortable challenging the words of high-ranking police officers. Eight had given verbal evidence, all vaguely incriminating, several I neither recognised nor recalled. They were back-up for Monteith.

Years later in his autobiography, *The First Circle*, Humphreys made it clear that he believes police officers are all integrity.

He was opposed to capital punishment – and in all the murder trials he recalls, he doesn't mention me. I was alert enough to understand he was defending me on the capital charge, and beyond that he wasn't interested. He had, however, saved me from the vultures and, in the game played in that arena, he had won the day, I had to go to the wall to protect the police image.

I looked down at him, searching his face, trying to communicate with my eyes, and I shook my head. We both understood, though our reasons were different. He nodded and returned to his pew and said, 'I have nothing further today, Milord,' and sat down.

'Very well,' said Ashworth. 'We will give our ruling in a little while. The court is adjourned.'

I was taken back to the cells. 'I will leave the door open,' said my escort, leaving me alone for the first time. He was an old hand and had done time on the Moor. We knew each other by sight. He was wise to the ways of the world and spent his life doing time with prisoners. 'There you are', he said, handing me a cup of tea. 'I bet a week's wages you would win your appeal.' I looked at him with gratitude.

I sat waiting in the cells below the appeal court. The door was opened wide and two screws were now waiting with me. I didn't speculate on what might happen next. I sat with my eyes closed as if in a trance, deep in a sense of relief. My head was in a hollow place. I needed space and I knew there would be another day. I had to get out of the limelight, so emotions could settle and opinions be more realistic.

About three in the afternoon everyone was back in court and Justice Ashworth began reading their judgement. 'We are granting this appeal against capital murder,' he said, 'and quashing the conviction against Connelly.' And in so doing, he wiped out the death penalty, quashing the jury's verdict, acknowledging the fact there was insufficient evidence to support the prosecution theory of four robbers, with me, the killer.

'However,' continued Ashworth, 'as the defendant Thatcher had admitted to the police that he was there, we are substituting the verdict to one of non-capital murder, and sentencing him to life imprisonment.' That was a major cop-out. Substituting a jury's verdict.

I had been convicted of being the fourth outside man who the crown accused of being the killer. Now, to acquit me of capital murder meant I wasn't the fourth man, and that should have left me with no part to play in the crime. However, by acquitting Connelly, it could now be suggested I was one of the office robbers, even though the prosecution insisted that I wasn't. So the whole venture was now speculation. That made no sense.

I stood up in the dock, not wanting to hear any more. I just wanted to get out of there. Ashworth stopped reading and instructed the screw in charge of the dock to take me away, so he could continue. They were altering the verbal, supporting the police, and any further protestations from me would be useless. I didn't hear the rest of what Ashworth was saying after I was taken from the dock, and at that moment in time, I didn't really care, as I was the ball in the field of play and I had no options.

Monteith and his buddy, Hewitt, were the two 'I was there' inventors, and I often wonder how they lived with that. Monteith retired after the case, and Hewitt and most of the others took early retirement when under investigation for corruption a few years later.

'Would you like a cup of tea?' the senior screw asked me again, as I was led into the open cell below.

'Oh yeah,' I replied.

'Sugar?'

'One please.' I sat down on the cell bench seat.

'I bet a week's wages you would win your appeal,' he said as he handed me a cup of tea. 'Keep your nose clean and you will be out in eight or ten years.'

Eight or ten years punched me in the head. I was overwhelmed with relief at having my life back, but I wanted desperately to be alone. To have space to myself, to gather my thoughts to look into the future. I wanted a life away from all this deceit and double standards. 'The solicitor wants to see you,' said the screw, leading me into the corridor. 'How do you feel now?' asked Lissack, looking pleased with himself. I nodded in response, not wanting to talk. 'Connelly has been released on a nominal bail, as the prosecution want to put him on trial for the robbery indictment.'

'Can they do that?' I asked.

'We will have to wait and see,' he replied, 'and I've seen the charge sheet. It says you were interviewed at 10.30 a.m. and charged at 12.05, and it wasn't signed.'

'Then what you've seen is not the charge sheet because I signed the charge sheet.'

'Can I do anything for you, Mr Thatcher?'

'Yes, you can give me the transcript of the trial.'

'Yes, of course.' He looked ill at ease. 'Hilton has lost his appeal. Now there are just the three of you convicted.'

'What do you think, Mr Lissack?'

★   ★   ★

A month later, Connelly was put on trial at the Old Bailey. The judge refused to try him, as the evidence for the robbery was the same as for the murder, and a second trial using all the same evidence would be double jeopardy. The prosecution got a further delay while they found a judge willing to try the second indictment. They argued that once a person had been charged with an offence, they had the absolute right to a verdict and the crown should have the same right.

Connelly was tried and given ten years. His conviction compounded the fact there was no part in the crime for me, so I applied for a verdict on the second indictment of robbery and was refused. Time had passed and emotions were more stable.

Sitting silently in the cell, waiting for the transport to freight me back to Wandsworth, I wasn't really functioning. I could look into the recent past, but see nothing of the future. Things would happen around me, most of which I would know nothing.

Kelly would be released after ten years and I would hear nothing of him, and it would be a year before I met up again with Hilton. He told me then that he, Kelly and Connelly robbed the Co-op, and there never was a fourth man. That man was invented to take the blame for the killing.

Hilton would be released after twelve years, get involved in another robbery and get a further fourteen years in prison. He was then convicted of another murder and will now never get out.

A statement by the 'Met' commissioner in the *Daily Telegraph* a few months later, saying 'We will convict the criminals by hook or by crook,' said it all. What happened to me was not a one-off, and I met many prisoners in different prisons who the police had framed and who were actually innocent. The police decided who they wanted to hold responsible for various crimes. They made up evidence in support, and in the following year, 457 Scotland Yard Detectives were either tried for corruption or took early retirement.

My mother used to say, 'There is nothing wrong with the world, it's the people in it.

Years later in Parkhurst Prison, I met a guy named Sanders doing fourteen years for a series of bank robberies which he knew nothing about. The man from the Yard investigating had said that Sanders made oral admissions to him and so Sanders was convicted. Some time later, a member of the bank-robbing team was arrested by this detective. I can't remember the copper's name, but he had a reputation of being a real nasty b*****d. The guy he arrested was named Bertie Smalls and they did a deal. Smalls would be the first 'supergrass' and would plead guilty to the series of bank robberies, giving evidence against the team. In exchange, Smalls would not be sent to prison. Smalls told the coppers that Sanders had nothing to do with any of the bank raids. To add credit to Smalls' evidence, Sanders had to be freed. He was put on appeal, said he was drunk when arrested and could not remember making a verbal confession, but could remember saying that he didn't – his conviction was squashed.

Oral confessions were common practice in criminal investigations. It wasn't just me being ripped off. It was the whole system. In the years that followed, many innocent people would go down:

There was the 'Birmingham Six'. Two of them I met in Gartree Prison, a father and son. The IRA planted a bomb in a pub in Birmingham, killing several people. Twenty-four hours later, six Irish men travelling home to Belfast on a ferry after a reunion party were arrested. They were beaten, abused, verballed and convicted, and given life sentences. It was several years before the court recognised their innocence and released them. None of the police involved were called to account, and none of those responsible for the bombing ever identified. When innocent people are framed, the guilty get away.

The 'Maguire Eight'. A family associated with the 'Six' were arrested for aiding them. They were abused, verballed and convicted, and they spent many years in prison before their conviction was quashed. Totally innocent people.

The 'Guildford Four'. Another IRA bombing and four innocent people convicted, one of them a seventeen-year-old English girl. They were held in prison for several years before their innocence was established.

George Davis. Given twelve years for a robbery he didn't commit. His supporters dug up the cricket pitch the night before the test match at Headingley to bring attention to his injustice.

John Murphy from Luton, and others whose names I can no longer recall …

I was put away on police evidence for the Maida Vale robbery, which I didn't do, and some other guy did three years for a safe that I robbed. The quality of the judiciary and the law enforcement 'mob' is not perfect and there are too many who believe that near enough is good enough.

Down the line, somewhere in the future, I would find a voice …

10

Two of the screws who had been minding me for the past few weeks in the death cell, were sitting silently in the back of the transit van as we headed back to Wandsworth following the outcome of the appeal. They had made no comment about events, and would sign off when we got back to the prison and return to the jails they had come from, losing several weeks of overtime, as they were now redundant. For a moment I recalled their conversation on the first day they arrived, as they sat at the bare table and I lay resting on the bed. They were calculating their overtime. We hadn't developed a relationship during the many hours shared, as we lived in different worlds and their way of life was alien to me.

When we arrived at Wandsworth, we drove to the reception block. I went through the normal reception procedure and was located in the hospital wing for observation. The only difference between the hospital cells and regular cells was that the door had a hatch which opened on the outside and, shortly after being locked up there, the hatch opened and the con working as the hospital orderly appeared. He was curious and wanted to talk. He told me about the business with the sedatives in the beer.

The following day I was relocated into the mainstream, and set to work doing two hours in the mornings and two in the afternoons, stitching mailbags – eight stitches to the inch – for the government Post Office, and paid one penny a bag. It was soul destroying until you become immune. If the weather was right, you got thirty minutes, twice a day, shuffling round the exercise yard. No prospects, just survival, and no one with ears to complain to.

There always seemed to be known faces on the familiar exercise yard in Wandsworth – someone to talk to of events in the outside world. You would sometimes hear the other side of stories that made the headlines; the vices and various habits of the rich and famous; or the high-flying politicians caught with their pants down. You'd find out what books to read, and who was who.

The days were short and the nights were long. Long lonely hours thinking of what might have been – the family and life lost – and trying to let the wounds heal.

Reading was a very large part of life then, in those early days of the sixties, and the library trolley was wheeled round the landing once a week. You were given three books to see you through, and they were often very boring stuff with pages missing, but for a nominal fee – a small amount of tobacco, maybe– the con on the trolley would sort you out something he thought you would like, and you would slip him a list of categories or titles or articles to look for. Same as in the real world, you got what you paid for. Tobacco was the currency, and if you sewed enough mail bags, you could get ½oz of 'shag' a week to smoke and spread around and, because I'd made a bit of a reputation as a working villain (whether true or false), I got small favours from other cons and never any aggravation.

Nevertheless, I felt very subdued and my pride was shattered, and I wanted it recognised and re-established, and I had nothing going for me except the knowledge that I wasn't going to let the predators wipe me out.

After a few months at Wandsworth I was transferred to Parkhurst Prison on the Isle of Wight. The prison there was originally built two centuries earlier, to house prisoners who were being transported to Australia. I didn't get to Parkhurst early enough …

Australia is an island in the Pacific Ocean about the size of America and was acquired by a sea captain named Cook a couple of hundred years ago to become part of the British Empire, just as, a few years earlier, America was taken over by the adventurers – 'The Empire Builders' who put down any of the locals who showed objection.

Parkhurst held about 600 prisoners and, for the past few years, had been used to house prisoners serving 'preventive detention'. Preventive detention (PD) was part of the Criminal Justice Bill introduced in 1948, and the idea was, if a person was sent from a magistrates' court to a higher court for the third time, he was automatically sentenced to prison for a period of seven or fourteen years, with one sixth off for behaving according to the rules. So, shoplifting a tin of beans could result in fourteen years imprisonment if it was your third offence.

A lot of PDs were homeless derelicts who couldn't cope with a regular life, and many were content with the three regular meals they got in prison. Some were on their second trips – deliberately committing an offence to get back in. They weren't really equipped for a regular life but made good currency for the over-ambitious in the business of crime and punishment. With the preventive detention section of the criminal law came more liberal rules and attitudes towards the way PDs would be treated, which resulted in a much better atmosphere and level of tolerance within Parkhurst. Anyway, you don't need me to analyse the standards of a system that was a worm-ball of contradictions.

The PD section of the 1948 Criminal Justice Bill was eventually abolished in 1962, and PDs were being released earlier than originally intended. Parkhurst was changing into a prison for guys with long sentences, and I arrived there in the afternoon on the day John Kennedy was assassinated.

As I hadn't actually been released from the sentence I was serving when I was given the life sentence, it meant that the time I had been inside counted towards visitation rights. In those days, Dartmoor and Parkhurst weren't easily accessible to prisoners' families, because of the prisons' locations. So, after a period of four years, a prisoner had the right to be transferred for one month to a local prison for family visits.

During the years I had been inside, Maria's relatives, who lived in Brighton, had kept in regular contact with me – they were Polish Catholic and didn't approve of Maria's attitude towards our marriage. We had become good friends and they wanted to keep a family link with me. The nearest local prison to them was Lewes – just a few miles away. Those were the days when very few people had cars and everything depended on public transport so, after a year in Parkhurst, I was on the move to Lewes for visits. Lewes prison was where I had done time as a young prisoner, but it had since changed over to a short-term locals' prison.

To get there from Parkhurst took anything up to two weeks in transit. Once a week the prison bus came to Parkhurst from Wandsworth with a bunch of new cons, and it took away anyone heading in the other direction. It then returned to Wandsworth, where you had to wait for the prison bus to go to Lewes to pick cons and bring them back to the London prisons, for whatever reasons – court appearances, medical reasons etc. Normally this procedure of getting from one prison to another took about seven days.

When I arrived in Wandsworth I was put into a cell in B wing to wait for the Lewes bus the following week. Next morning I was let out for thirty minutes' exercise with the rest of the block, and I met up again with Ronnie Biggs, who had recently been given thirty years for his part in what was then known as the 'Great Train Robbery', the 'crime of the century'!

Ronnie was in his mid-thirties – the same age as me – but I was a couple of inches taller. We had both lived in south London as teenagers. He was a regular guy – inoffensive and good natured – and, in the world of crime, known as game and reliable. He was married and lived with his wife Charlotte, a very typical south London girl, in one of the outer suburbs on the way to Brighton. He worked and earned a living as a carpenter, and only occasionally got involved in the other things. We had done time together in Lewes prison as young prisoners and we hadn't met in years. He had been serving a three year sentence as a young prisoner back then, for burglary which he had committed with my brother, Bill.

Bill had climbed through the window above 'Del Montiers' delicatessen in the Lambeth Walk one night, and stole a foot square biscuit tin full of money while the family who ran the place were playing cards in the next room. Del Montiers made great ice cream and I don't think the biscuit tin was meant for the tax man. Their place was opposite Jane's Café where we played dice on the pavement outside. Bill told me that when he was nicked for his stunt, he had rows of silver coins lined up on his cooker at home.

Ron and I walked the yard in Wandsworth twice a day for half an hour during the week that I waited to go to Lewes, and we discussed the qualities of life and the comfort of various establishments – who was who, and what was what, and what we could expect for the foreseeable future. Ron, like me, was still dazed by the burden of empty years of uncivilised treatment and confinement. His crime never warranted thirty years, and that kind of sentence had never been handed out before. It had been a bold and daring venture.

It caught the imagination of the media and the excitement of many, and the wrath of the establishment.

It was a very one-off crime, and involved about a dozen guys. I can't remember now who started the ball rolling — a Scottish guy who worked for the Post Office in Glasgow — and the actual robbery was organised by a guy named Bruce. Every week a heap of used currency that was being replaced with new currency was put into mail sacks and transported from Glasgow to London on the overnight mail train. Two guys dressed as linesmen signalled the train to stop near Aylesbury, a few miles north of London. They took over the engine and forced the driver to move the train down the track to where Ronnie and the rest of the robbers were waiting. They then unloaded twenty-odd, very heavy, mailbags full of money, and disappeared into the night. There were several hundred people on the train, all unaware of what was going on. The amount of money stolen was astronomical, creating all kinds of envy, jealousy and greed from hangers-on and the 'mob' in Scotland Yard's Flying Squad. A very small amount of this money was ever recovered, and a large chunk of it went to Scotland Yard for favours they reneged on. But that was their nature, and the way things were. No one gets away with a crime of that nature, there are too many people involved, across the field, too many tongues to wag, too much pressure for culprits, and opportunities all round. The spin-offs got exploited.

Ron and I talked a lot about our experiences and the current trend on the crime scene, and it wasn't a good picture. We were both at that age of our lives where the loss of the next twenty years was frightening, and then what? Free at the age of fifty-odd, in a totally changed world, with nothing but what you stood up in. A complete stranger in a strange land and fit only to be an object of curiosity; and almost certainly an unable-to-cope derelict. We talked of leaving the premises, and what the chances were, and where to start and where to go, and where to find the help that would be needed and how it would have to be forever. We fantasised in a make-believe serious way, but I knew that I couldn't face the prospect of failure and I wanted a complete sense of freedom without constantly looking over my shoulder. For me, there were too many negatives on the outside, no money, and with no money you go nowhere, you don't even eat. I didn't have the capacity to be a fugitive with the certain knowledge that I would be gunned down by the 'heavy mob' – and some a★★★hole would be a hero. I needed more space to consider what I could do with my life to bring some lasting quality into it, as I had nothing going for me.

'I'll see yer when I get back from Lewes, if you're still here,' I said to Ron, as we left the yard for the bang-up. Tomorrow I was heading to the coast.

Lewes was more lax than I was used to, and I was the only lifer they had there, so it was easy-going. Helena, Maria's cousin, visited me twice a week and brought me up to date. She had a soft spot for me and considered me a part of the family. She never had any news from America, which made her sad.

Three times, Bob came to see me in Lewes. He was out and about and as reckless as ever. He had been in a serious road accident a few months after he escaped from Lincoln. Three passengers were killed and he finished up with a permanent, partially stiff leg – and six months extra time. Under the visiting rules, only family and long-standing friends were allowed to visit. I sent all my visiting passes to Helena's family and Bob became a member. He was driving a very expensive white Elite sports car, parked outside the front gate on false plates. His attitude was 'If you look right, you are right.' He understood I didn't want to be a fugitive.

Back in Wandsworth, en route for Parkhurst, I spent a few more days on the yard with Ron. He told me he had a bundle of money stuck away, his share of the train robbery; and there were people around interested in having some of it, and that money in itself makes most things possible. There were also guys around ready to give a helping hand just to be associated with the 'big time'. Ron had made up his mind that he had to leave. There was nothing else for him, and nothing he could do on his own. It had to come from outside.

The train robbery had taken place near Aylesbury, and Ron had been arrested by a certain Detective Inspector Frank Williams, who said in evidence that when he told Ron he was being arrested for the train robbery, Ron is alleged to have said, 'I've never been to Aylesbury in my life'. The crime I had been framed for took place in Mitcham, and when Williams gave evidence of my arrest he said that I had said, 'I've never been to Mitcham in my life'. Standard dialogue with a name change? They didn't need to be original.

Frank Williams, at that time, was a pal of a guy named Freddie Foreman who ran a pub in south London, and Foreman was an associate of Alfie Gerrard who was part of the 'Richardson' and Kray twins' scene. Williams had his feet in both camps. Williams got promoted after the train trial, to Superintendent, but the Yard was getting so many complaints about his wheeling and dealing that they put him in charge of the 'Rubber Heel Mob'. That's the nickname for the internal investigation team at Scotland Yard who investigated complaints of corruption within.

I had a friend in the nick who was a celebrity burglar. He had a reputation for his courtesy towards his victims. He would always catch them in bed in the middle of the night, and would talk to them rather than scare them. He would give the ladies a kiss as he left with their jewellery. He made it easy for the cops to catch him, as they did one day with £80,000 worth of gems he had just stolen. But only twenty of them were officially recovered and he was given eight years, and was really p****d off. So he made an official complaint to Scotland Yard that his arresting officers had nicked most of the jewellery. The Yard sent Frank Williams along to the prison to investigate the complaint. Williams' reputation had preceded him, and this guy wouldn't speak to him when he realised who Williams was, and was so p****d off that he wrote to the commissioner, saying he didn't want a crooked copper investigating crooked coppers and could he send along a straight policeman to interview him. I helped write the letter, and we never got a reply. Then, a couple of years later this con committed suicide. I can't remember his name now.

Gerrard and Foreman were heavies at that time and got rid of Frank Mitchell for the Krays, and then Ginger Marks another time. Gerrard was taking care of a large sum of money from the train robbery, and was helping to organise the lifting of Ron from Wandsworth. We never discussed the details of this. I wasn't part of it. I was only passing through, so we spoke in general terms, and I didn't need to know as there was nothing I could do to help. Had I been with Ron in Wandsworth for any length of time, things may have been different, who knows?

When I entered the world of confinement I was not a good reader, and all I can ever remember reading was *Tarzan of the Apes* by Edgar Rice Burroughs, when I crossed the Atlantic to Baltimore on a slow old coal-burning cargo boat – that's about it. But in jail you read, and often remember. We were talking one day about an article I'd read in *Life* magazine a few years earlier in Dartmoor – some time in the mid-fifties. It was about a banker somewhere in a mid-western state of America, names and fine details I can't remember, just the interesting bits. He bought a holiday apartment in Rio de Janeiro and took his pregnant wife there for a holiday, where she had their child. He left her there, and returned to the bank and ripped off several million dollars, returning with it to Rio where, for all I know, he lived happily ever after because he could not be extradited. I think it's something to do with the first amendment in the Brazilian Constitution, to do with the parents of children born in Brazil.

Many years ago, the French had a penal colony in South America where they sent their convicts. The place was known as 'Devil's Island'. Although Devil's Island is only a small island off the coast and only ever had a couple of prisoners on it, as most of the prisoners lived in compounds on the mainland. The whole place was called Devil's Island. Read *Papillon* if you can find it, and want to know more. When the convicts had done their time, they were exiled for that long again before being allowed back into France. Most of French Guyana was jungle, so those who were exiled and those who escaped had to scratch a living and integrate with the jungle tribes. Many of them prospected and discovered diamonds, and drifted to Brazil with their wealth, where they started families, often with native Indian girls, and helped establish Rio de Janeiro. Many of those gleaming white high-rise hotels that decorate the shoreline on that long sweep of Copacabana's sandy beach were funded by escaped convicts who had prospected the jungles, and their influence set the constitution so that escaped prisoners could not be extradited if they had a family in Brazil. They built the sky-line on the waterfront that rose on the shimmering horizon as the sun came up, and once a sixteen-year-old galley boy had watched it rise in wonder.

Could I not turn back the clock?

Betty Webster, my first proper girlfriend, used to tell me I was a dreamer.

I told Ron about the new maximum security unit that was being built in the compound where the punishment unit at Parkhurst was. It would house a dozen high-profile prisoners, and was especially designed for the train robbers – years of total isolation, where the opportunity of escape would be non-existent – and it would be ready in another six months.

I arrived back in Parkhurst still feeling subdued, knowing something had to fill in the gaps, knowing that a long period of empty space was ahead of me – long, lonely, empty times with nothing at the end of it that I could see. I would fight the justice system and all their hypocrisies, and the whole system itself if I could. And I would, in my own way, not be wiped out. I would tell everyone I could that I had been framed by a bunch of crooked coppers. Most would not believe me and not want to believe me, but I'd keep telling them, and a lot of them would learn that things are not always what you think they are. This was a period of our time when careers were being built and it was fashionable to frame all the usual suspects, and it was happening in a big way. I met many of them over the years and could tell you lots of stories.

A couple of weeks back in Parkhurst and I was given a plum job. Fortunately the governor was a liberal person, and seemed to give the best jobs in the place to guys serving the longest sentences and I was the first lifer there. He was a suavish character with a reputation amongst his staff for being more interested in propping up the bar at the Royal Yacht Club a couple of miles away, than finding fault with those in his care. It is traditional for the governor of Parkhurst Prison to be an honorary member of the club, going back to the beginning when Parkhurst was a transit centre for cons being shipped to Australia. Alistair, the current governor, felt he was in the right place at the bar of the Royal Yacht Club.

Anyway, he gave me a job as a waiter in the dining room of the prison's staff canteen. This was a separate building within the prison walls where breakfast dinner and tea was available to screws, administration and civil workers. The canteen was officially run by an auxiliary screw (that's a civilian worker with a uniform and keys, but not really a proper screw) and four cons, a chef, an assistant and two waiters, and the canteen was open 6.30 a.m.–6.00 p.m. seven days a week, and the place was never locked.

Actually, the canteen was run by the 'Chief', a south London crook who was a really nice guy, called 'Paddy Onions'. He said who he wanted working with him, the place ran smoothly and always broke even, and the food was good. The screw did the paperwork and everything was sweet. Paddy Onions was a friend of a friend and that's how I got the job when a vacancy came.

We ate well, and everyone treated us decently. When the screws came into the canteen they took their hats off and behaved like normal people, and, after a while, everyone got used to my being there. The screws would forget that I wasn't one of them as they talked shop over their meals, and I got to know where each one was coming from; and I made the most of it, staying in the job for five years – only locked up 9 p.m.–6.30 a.m., and I could wander round some parts of the prison on my own and was even allowed to keep tropical fish in the dining room. I worked hard and served my own interests.

I got into painting pictures, and made a couple of good friends. I had fresh, clean clothes from the laundry every day and, once a week, sent a parcel of pilfered goodies back with the dirty linen. Paddy Onions was, in every way, a good guy to me. I don't know what he was doing time for, he didn't say – I didn't ask, and I didn't really care. It was something to do with cars and finance companies. In the years after the war, finance companies were so eager to finance car sales that they were ripe to be ripped off. Second-hand cars were sold on bomb sites by the wide boys, then the sale was upgraded and financed by half a dozen different companies.

Paddy was a great cook, maybe not so good with books, but really good with food. He was popular with the screws and would give them free meals in return for small favours. One of his ambitions was to go to Las Vegas with a pocket full of money, and stay there until he had nothing left except his fare home. I don't know if he ever made it. I heard that, some years later, he answered a knock on his front door and someone shot him. I don't know why. Life was changing in the outside world; thieves were becoming gangsters and shooting each other, and others were disappearing leaving nothing behind except gossip and rumours.

In the years I worked as a waiter, many things began to happen – setting the trend for the future, as prisons began to become a growth industry. More and more prisons were needed, and little people started to build new empires.

Paddy was unlocked at 6.00 a.m. and taken over to the canteen to light the stoves and put the kettle on, and us three followed at 6.30 a.m. We all worked through till 6 in the evening, when we were taken back to the cell block for a couple of hours' chat or TV with the other cons. Life was not a hardship, and could have been a lot worse.

Then, one afternoon the news came on the radio that Ronnie Biggs had escaped from Wandsworth, from the yard in B wing, during the afternoon's exercise period. A ladder had come over the wall, and the screws on point-duty were blocked from interfering while Ron left the premises. We found out later that he'd gone on from Australia to Rio de Janeiro. I had been working in the staff canteen for four years when Ronnie Biggs was located in Rio, and the screws in the canteen were wetting their pants with excitement. They had this 'Nobody gets away from us' attitude and, talking about it in the canteen with the fat, overweight thug who ran the punishment block, I said, 'You won't get him back, bet you a bar of chocolate.' I'm still waiting.

'Biggsie's' departure from Wandsworth upset a few people, and new electronic prisons were being constructed to hold such prisoners ½ mile from Parkhurst. The 'train robbers' unit in the Parkhurst compound would give them no contact with anyone outside of the unit and the conditions were very claustrophobic. It was rumoured that they kept one cell empty for Biggsie. The politicians got so paranoid about losing prisoners like him that a whole new department was set up to deal with the security grading of prisoners, and the security grading of prisons themselves.

Four grades of prison and prisoners – A to D – 'A' being maximum security, 'D' minimum, with a couple of grades in between which were a bit of each. Category A prisons held all four grades of prisoner, though the lower grades would eventually be moved on to lower grade places. In the first grading of prisoners I was graded B.

On Sunday afternoons, on a separate compound from the cell blocks, the prison football team played in the local amateur football league. All the matches were played at home, and the visiting team used the staff canteen as their changing room.

One day, the governor got a letter from a south London amateur club, asking if they could come and play the prison team. They came and they lost, and the following day all future matches were cancelled because it seemed that most of the London team were ex-cons! One of them was Frankie Fraser, who was recognised by the chief officer as they were leaving. The team entered the prison with their hold-alls which they left in the canteen while the match was played, and I emptied the bags for 'presents' before serving the visitors tea. The cook's name was Tommy Lockram, a south Londoner doing five years for something to do with laundering money from the train robbery. He had been extradited from Australia at the same time that Ronnie Biggs left Australia for Rio.

Then, there was the morning we were told that the train robbers' unit was ready, and there would be an extra dozen for lunch. The Flying Squad from Scotland Yard, escorting the escort of prison officers, bringing the train robbers to the new unit – a totally over-the-top exercise. These guys were thieves not anarchists. But, as a Commander Dick Lewis of Scotland Yard had been put in charge of prison security, you can understand him giving an easy job to a few of his pals at the Yard, and the hype was good for the image. Dick Lewis was Monteith's boss when I first had the pleasure of meeting Monteith's style of coppering. I always knew Monteith would not have pulled the stroke on me without a nod of approval from his boss, just the same as the mafia, I have no love for Lewis.

Anyway, there we were, a dozen gangsters for lunch at two in the afternoon, when the main diners had finished and gone – what should I do? We had a crisis meeting in the kitchen with the chief officer, because none of us wanted to serve this meal and, after many voiced opinions, it was decided that they would have egg and chips. No choice, no dialogue, and one waiter – we tossed, and I lost. It was either serve them or get fired, a choice I never want again. I really had to switch off for that one and pretend this wasn't happening.

As the days went by, I was feeling less outraged by the deeds of Monteith and Hewitt. They had stolen my life and I was bitter and twisted by it, but one day it might catch up with them – who knows.

Then, one day, it came over the radio that Ronnie Biggs had been arrested in Rio by Superintendent Slipper of the Yard, commonly known in the underworld as 'Slippery'. The following day, it appeared that Slippery hadn't notified the Brazilian authorities of his intention to take Ron back to England, which they considered rather arrogant so they threw Slippery out of the country and Ron was given the right to remain in Rio since his Brazilian girlfriend was pregnant. Ron had been skint when he got to Brazil, and was making a living as a carpenter.

Often in the early days, when I had a pocketful of money, I'd waste it going to very expensive night clubs and West End shows, or to see Ella or Nat King Cole or Sammy Davis Jr. It's so easy to get caught up in different habits and lifestyles when you have no desire to be anything other than short-sighted and crazy. Well, apart from getting caught when I should have seen it coming, I have few regrets. Of course, I missed the young and growing-up years of my son, the family unit, the shared responsibility of loving a child, and showing him the way, having him grow up with the knowledge that both his parents loved him and the brothers or sisters he may have had. I had no idea where Antony lived until he was about six years old. Helena couldn't tell me, and I was very cut off from the outside world which I knew that, one day, I would have to re-enter. I needed new friends, apart from Helena and her family. I knew no one who wasn't crooked – but maybe there aren't many people who aren't in some way crooked, who knows?

The PDs were finished. I remember a white-haired old boy of seventy one of the last PDs to leave Parkhurst. Discharges were released at seven in the mornings, and would pass the staff canteen on their way to the front gate, and we always watched them go and wished them luck. This old guy was in tears. The place had become his home and he had nowhere to go. As the last of the PDs left, and the place filled up with regular long-termers, things began to change and become more rigid.

11

I had a long-standing friend, named Billy Gosling, who was about to finish his sentence, and I needed people on the outside to take an interest in my conviction. I had rocked the boat with some members of the establishment by continuing to send protests, shouting corruption. They were the only avenues available, although I knew it was a waste of time, because any complaint about police corruption was sent, for comment, to the very coppers who were being complained about – a joke. Everything was censored and recorded in your record – and the official line followed – so that, after a few years, my record was 2ft high.

I breathed fire and had six heads, but the stubbornness in me refused to switch off, even though I was constantly being told to duck my head so that I'd be released sooner – whatever *that* meant. The hopes and expectations I'd had when I'd been released from Dartmoor were shattered beyond recovery. I went through all that, and in many ways I was walking around in circles, looking into empty spaces. I was too insulted to let it ride. My world was closing in, and my credibility needed re-establishing. Though I don't quite know what that means.

The rules still only allowed correspondence with family or old, established relationships, and then only on a very limited level – one letter a fortnight. Though this was changing to one extra letter a week, paid for from your prison earnings, about six shliings a week. My mother, brother, Bill, and Helena would write to me a couple of times a year, but that wasn't enough. Beyond the walls was becoming another planet. I tried using other cons' canteen letters for a while, but that was very slow and complicated.

When Bill Gosling got out, he put an ad in *The New Statesman* – my name and prison number, seeking friends and correspondents. We chose *The New Statesman* because it was left-wing politically, and was a weekly read for 'liberal-thinking' people. I didn't want to become a side-show for weirdos. Bill would collect any response from a box number and vet it, then interview anyone he thought was genuine, and then they would write to me as a long-lost friend, to get around the rules.

Soon I had new friends punting for me in ways that I was unable to. One, a lovely lady named Molly (not the same Molly as 'hot pants' Molly!). Her husband had died a few years earlier. She had the franchise for Kodak film in the UK, and ran a business in west London. She became very friendly with Bill, who went to work for her until she retired and moved to Florida, which is where I last heard from her. I didn't have enough letters to write often. Anyway, she got me a lawyer named Bernie, a young, ambitious guy with a Beatles haircut, who became very successful and sadly died young. We were good friends, and the prison authorities were unable to restrict or interfere with correspondence between us. Of course, they censored it all – though legally, they had no right. I wrote a synopsis of my arrest and trial for him, and Molly had it printed and bound and sent to every politician in the country, and anyone else that might be interested, including authors and actors, as well as the chief of police.

A playwright named David Halliwell, who's still around and who we hear from occasionally, encouraged me to write plays which he produced and directed in various theatres. In times to come, David would contact an American friend who was doing a study for his masters' degree on the behaviour of 'men in groups' at Rutgers University in Edison, New Jersey. His thesis was published – I have a copy somewhere. Anyway, through him, I got hold of Maria's address, also in Edison, and, after several months of persistence I was allowed to send my son a weekly postcard, which didn't count against the weekly letter allowance I was then entitled to. I sent those cards for several years, until I found out he wasn't getting them.

Anyway, a new maximum security prison next to Parkhurst was being constructed, called Albany. Its main purpose was to house Category A prisoners, and things were slowly changing as I swapped jobs from waiter to tutor's assistant. Working for the tutor organiser was different again, I was back in the mainstream of the prison, in as much as I became part of the regular routine, except when the cell doors were open. I could walk around the place on my own and the screws would open gates for me into the various sections of the prison and let me wander, because the tutor was my boss and I was his 'errand boy'.

His name was Brian, pushing forty, a tubbyish and medium-sized Scotsman, same age as me. He and his wife had been primary school teachers before he took on the tutor's job. He was actually employed by the Local Education Authority, and the prison department had an arrangement with them. Brian knew nothing of prisons, or the mystique of prison culture. He was apprehensive in those early days about his relationships with both cons and screws, and he needed an assistant. So, when he was having a meal one day in the canteen he asked me if I was interested. I had been eating well for the past five years in conditions that were brilliant compared with what was on offer in the wings. Nevertheless, I was running dry and finding it more difficult to pander to screws who were another breed of 'lager louts'.

I was beginning to enjoy painting and taking it seriously. I knew I would never be brilliant, but it was absorbing, demanding, creative and very challenging, especially as I was partially colour blind and had difficulty with the subtler tones. I needed more time to concentrate and be alone, and working for the tutor would give me free time without pressure as well as unlimited access to art materials. All materials of every nature supplied to government institutions, from toilet paper to battle ships, came through the Ministry of Supply who, every year, would send a catalogue to the tutor's office with order forms. These catalogues contained the full range of art materials of the very finest quality, and just about everything else. One of my jobs would be the annual ordering of educational material, and these orders were never questioned, just supplied.

Brian was the official head of the Educational Department and, at that time, the *only* member. He was a civilian who was looked upon as an outsider, and not seen as a member of the 'brotherhood', some of whom were being resistant. However, being a department head, he was included in the prison's administrative system, which meant that the day started for him at the governor's office with all the other chief's. Here, the official mail was discussed and any other business of importance. Brian would come straight from there to his office and we would have coffee and discuss events; and I would tell him which screws to look out for.

Classes were in the evenings, 6 p.m.–8 p.m., and six cons were needed to make a class, which would take place anywhere there was a space. Any subject, six cons = a class.

Brian employed his wife to teach the handicapped, and to get daytime classes going, and in a little while they had enough classes to employ a civilian assistant and take on a second office, and the last I heard he was doing good and had his own empire. I discovered he was a member of the 'Orange Order', one of the political groups at loggerheads in Northern Ireland.

I started a film club that would show current films every weekend. Each member paid a fee from their prison earnings to cover the running cost, although it was often in debt. On the back of this, an educational film club was suggested, something that was free and entertaining as well as educational. There was no budget for this, so Brian let me do it, and I spent months writing to embassies, institutions, major industries, and anyone else who might have a film library that they could make available free on request. A class of ninety, on a Monday evening in the chapel, watched all kinds of stuff, from motor racing and football matches to holidaying in Georgia and open mining in the outback, deep sea fishing and all sorts. It ran for almost a year – until one day, a packet of films arrived from ICI, showing the method of manufacture and all you need to know about explosives …

As I explained to the management – we were only on their mailing list, *they* sent it!

Any letters I wrote were signed by Brian and sealed, then I would take them to the censor's office for the outgoing mail. I abused this system a few times and felt disloyal to Brian, but his back was covered and the risk was mine. We organised a Christmas parcel for every single parent and family on social on the Isle of Wight, and soft toys for the children's home.

Nevertheless, the atmosphere was cooling in the wings, as more cons were arriving with longer sentences and harbouring deeper feelings of resentment.

1971 – eight years later

The four wings of the prison were linked together by two corridors, and one of the cells had been converted into a medical room for drug issue. Every morning when the cell doors were opened, a line of cons would form to collect their drug of the day, mainly Librium in the mornings, and Librium and Mogadon in the afternoon. Sedatives were so easily available that a huge percentage of the prison was under the influence most of the time, we called it the 'liquid cosh line'. It was a standard joke that the thousand gallon oil storage tank at the side of the exercise yard should be filled with Librium and everyone issued with a pint mug.

The guy who was acquitted after Monteith's previous murder trial was now doing a long sentence in Parkhurst for an unrelated crime. His name was Sampson, and he dropped dead one day on the exercise yard as a result of too much Librium over a long period. Prescription drugs were freely available and used as a form of control.

Dick Lewis had been promoted to commander, and I firmly believe he was the force behind Monteith's corruption. Anyway, Lewis had been given the job of security grading all prisoners in the UK, and was visiting Parkhurst when I was delivering class material around the nick. I ran into him and the deputy governor at one of the gates into one of the wings, and he said 'hello' and wanted to talk to me. I blanked him out and walked away, embarrassing him. A week later I was upgraded to Category A, lost my job and had to be escorted everywhere by the screws. I was put on a yard party with a bunch of other cons, walking around the prison, tidying up, and thinking that, even in the nick, I couldn't avoid the crooked arm of the law.

Then Bob Dylan came to the island (Isle of Wight) as the main attraction in a music festival, and at night there were strange lights in the sky and faint music in the air. I had the flu at the time, like nothing you can imagine, and suffered three days of hallucinating nightmares you wouldn't believe.

There was a riot in the association rooms. Frankie Fraser had got himself a sentence after the football nonsense (see Chapter 9) and was now in Parkhurst. Whatever, his presence in Parkhurst was bound to have its effect, as the atmosphere was getting tense with rumours of cons being beaten in the punishment cells and screws foul-mouthing just about everyone.

There were only two screws in attendance in the association area, where there were a couple of TVs, a snooker table and a small kitchen for making tea, if you had any. This area was only used for a couple of hours twice a week, from 6–8 p.m. in the evenings. Apparently, Frank Fraser had a disagreement with one of the screws and wouldn't back off, so the other screw rang the emergency button. Being 7.30 in the evening, the prison was on short shift, and the alarm bell was connected to the screws' drinking club where a bunch of them had already had a few. Five minutes later they were in the association area with riot shields, breaking heads and seriously out of control. When it was over, a lot of cons needed stitching up and a few screws had time off to justify the damage. Nine cons, beside Fraser, were hospitalised and then charged with assault – though none of *them* were carrying riot sticks. Fraser was hospitalised for two months. The prison was shut down for two weeks for damage control and for the 'ghosting' of Category A prisoners to the new maximum security prisons that were coming on stream in various parts of the country.

Two days after the disturbance I was put into solitary confinement in the punishment section for foul-mouthing a screw. I wasn't over the flu or thinking straight. When you understand that a prison officer needed no qualifications, just the ability to obey orders and follow the leader, you understand that you can't always get it right. I didn't have any qualifications either, just the aftermath of flu.

I stayed in solitary for three months and didn't see another con or speak to anyone else until one Saturday morning. The door opened at 6 a.m. and four screws told me they were transferring me. Later that day I was back in Wandsworth, and located in the punishment unit. I would be in solitary confinement until they were instructed to move me somewhere else, and when I saw and asked the governor why, he said, 'For your own protection.' The disturbance at Parkhurst had been given the hype of a mega-riot, and any con coming from there on a Saturday transfer was obviously a villain needing attention.

I used to smoke nicotine in those days, about half an ounce of Holborn a week. It was all I could afford, and the rules were, you got canteen once a week. I was in Wandsworth for two weeks before I was given a canteen order. I was getting the wrong attention, so I gave up smoking and they could stick it up their a★★e.

After another four months I was ghosted to Albany, back on the Isle of Wight, which was now ready for Category A prisoners. I was the first, and went straight into the segregation unit for the night. About ten in the morning I was led into the governor's office with my two-screw escort at my side. The governor was behind his desk and the chief officer next to him. A brief introduction, and the chief officer was someone I'd known as a screw years earlier on the Moor. He passed a remark about my conviction, which upset me, and I told him very angrily in the only words I could find after seven months of silence, that he should keep his mouth shut about things he knew nothing of and that my internment was a fraud.

That wasn't a waste of time.

I spent the next three months in isolation, with no explanation, but I knew that every month a visiting magistrate came to the prison and that he would have to sign the order that kept me in isolation every month. Sooner or later, one would check me out. At midmorning on the second day in Albany I heard a key in the lock and the door opened. There stood a young Irish Catholic priest, too run down to be anything else, asking to come in. He wasn't part of the system, and saw me as just another person. It was November, and he started to drop in on me for a chat almost every day, never talking religion or anything pious. He came from a poor Irish background, took life as it came, and was happy with what he did. A couple of days before Christmas he asked me if he could have Christmas dinner with me in my cell, he would arrange an extra ration from the kitchen.

Then it was February and the door opened and there stood a magistrate, asking me if I was all right.

'No, I'm not.' His expression was serious. 'What am I doing here? Why am I segregated? What is the reason?'

'Yes, I'll look into it,' he said, and closed the door. Later that day I was relocated to A wing, the first of five containment blocks that made up the bulk of the prison. Everything was new and electronically controlled. The five cell blocks stood in line, four storeys high, connected by a long corridor with five steel gates opening into each wing. On the other side of the corridor was a series of glass-walled rooms, used as workshops and classrooms, and at the end of the corridor was a large gymnasium with a stage.

One of the workshops was used for sorting and recording the old service records of individual servicemen going way back beyond the last century. Very boring, though sometimes very interesting. These records were sent in boxes from one of the government archives, and contained all sorts of paperwork going back to the beginning. I never worked there but I knew someone who did. Occasionally amongst these papers were postage stamps donkeys' years old, often very valuable – and constantly disappearing and changing hands for peanuts.

The blocks were designed to contain prisoners in small groups. Twenty-four to a landing and eight to a spur, with gates and bars everywhere. Each block held ninety men, and already there were guys there I knew – several Category A men and Fred, a locksmith from the days in Dartmoor. Each spur could be sealed off with a gate that was normally left folded back against the wall. The lock on this gate was the same as all the others, one key opened the lock and overrode the electronic locking system. I walked into Fred's cell one day and he had the gate lock on his table.

Behind the cell blocks was a very large two storey factory that manufactured timber furniture for eight hours a day, and I was given a job in quality control under one of the civilian instructors. I worked there for almost three years, until one day, I'd had enough.

Life plodded on, and I met a young American guy who was in the same eight-cell unit as me. His name was Bill. He was twenty-two, and his dad was a colonel in the American air force and all his life Bill had lived on air force bases all over the world. He was currently a dedicated freewheeling hippie doing six years for a kilo of cannabis resin. Way over the top. It had been his misfortune to have been busted, in a friend's flat, by a Detective Inspector Kellard, the head of Scotland Yard's Drug Squad at the time. There were only three people in the Drug Squad then, Kellard and two assistants. Kellard was as crooked as a $3 bill and eventually got the push.

I can't remember whether that was for nicking dope and passing it on, or capturing a suspect with the same lump. He presented Bill to the world as a high-flying-around-the-world dope dealer, and the papers loved it – so Bill got six years.

Bill was young and in a strange environment. He'd heard horror stories of young guys locked away with sexually frustrated men. He'd never been in prison before, and was very curious. He was given a job in the same group as me so we got to know each other and became friends. He was no big time wheeler-dealer, just an easy going hippie and, after a while, he had me smoking the weed with him and two other 'tokers' before lock-up each night.

The only previous experience I had had with dope was back in 1947 when I joined an old, coal-burning tramp ship in Cardiff, South Wales. Most of the crew were coloured, from Tiger Bay – a notorious area in Cardiff. I became friendly with a light-skinned South African a couple of years older and we went out the night before we sailed to see some of his friends in their local pub. They were smoking what they called 'bush' – and we call 'grass'. I smoked it, and preferred nicotine. Now, thirty years later, I got into resin, which was probably the best thing I could do in the circumstances. It stimulated other senses and blocked out a lot of the s**t.

There was a central stairwell on the landings, caged in with gates, and around this there was space to walk, with windows where the landing screws would sit sometimes. Someone thought it would be a good idea to have a flower box, where Bill planted some seeds for a lark. He pulled them out when they were a few inches high before the joke went wrong, luckily nobody knew what a cannabis plant looked like – just another weed!

I was heavily into doing mosaic pictures at the time, using egg-shells, and I did one for Bill, 20 x 30 on a board nicked from the factory. Under the picture was a hollow compartment the size of an exercise book. I was productive, and allowed to hand out pictures to my visitors, several at a time. I had a good stock of paints and brushes, from the tutor's office, which followed me around.

David Halliwell came to see me one day. Molly had left for Florida and nothing was happening outside over my conviction so David suggested I try writing a play to attract attention, and, after a lot of head scratching, I wrote a dialogue between three cons and a screw in a prison library. It was about the frustration of 'Steve', one of the cons, over the light bulb in his cell, which should be 60 watt, but he would change it for a 100 watt bulb whenever he could get one. This led to constant conflict between him and his landing screw. It was ironic, cynical, and very real. I gave the script to David, hidden in a painting, when he came to visit, and he produced and directed it in a small lunchtime theatre in the West End. It was well reviewed in the national press, although the governor told me he wasn't amused; despite it being nothing more than a look at the ridiculous.

David put another ad in the *Statesman* for me, and after a couple of months I got a letter from a lady called Val. She met David before visiting me. She had a ten-year-old daughter from an earlier marriage, and was then teaching English at a London comprehensive school. Her first letter to me was put to the governor by the censor's office, and he suppressed it without telling me. A couple of weeks later, Val wrote to the governor asking if I had received her letter and he replied, saying 'no' – it was against the rules. She challenged his right to interfere with her mail. Val believed in the freedom of expression, and when I heard about all this I knew Val and I were going to be good friends. The governor conceded and Val began writing to me.

I had been on the island for almost twelve years.

Prisons all over the country at that time were melting-pots; sentences were getting longer and more guys were getting them on corrupt evidence, leading to a deeper discontent. The new prisons, like Albany, had to be seen, through the 'evil eye' of the press, as being successful and, if they weren't, the management would be at fault. So there were no 'big sticks' in the punishment unit after the previous experience of the Parkhurst bust-up. I wasn't going to get anywhere challenging my conviction. I'd 'confessed' – end of story. Missing documents – gone forever.

Then, one Friday, coming in from the factory for the midday break and unlocked at 1.30 p.m. to file back to work, I knew I wasn't going to play the game anymore. I'd had enough, just like that. When the screw came to check me out, he sent for the chief and I told him how I felt and what I thought of the system and why there was nothing they could do to me anymore. I had a bath and went to bed. The next morning an escort of screws took me to the segregation cells, and then in front of the governor on a discipline charge. 'How do you plead?' said the governor.

'Insanity – I'll function, but I'll do my own thing.'

Like I said before, prisons were melting-pots at that time, and throughout the country several of these high security places were bring wrecked by cons with serious grievances so the spotlight was on prisons. Had I been in Wandsworth, no doubt I would have experienced some major fracture. I believed that no one had the moral right to treat prisoners the way they were treated, there is too much double dealing in the system for anyone to be on the moral high ground, and many of the things I did in prison were directed at challenging the moral ground.

'Don't do this again,' said the governor. He cautioned me, and sent me back to the wing, and on Monday morning gave me a job carrying the tool bag for a civilian plumber who worked on maintenance. He was a nice old boy, always giving me Mars Bars. I was downgraded to Category B and, over the next couple of months I wrote another play all about the verbal and my time in the death cell. It went out the same way as the first one, and the following year David produced and directed it in the theatre upstairs at the Royal Court in the West End. I was told that most of the audience were coppers. I petitioned the Home Office for permission to attend the final night – and they gave me permission the week after it closed. The governor was not pleased about the play, or the publicity, but considered it prudent to ignore it, rather than encourage more publicity, because the play was getting attention and good reviews.

Val brought her daughter, Marion, to see me and our friendship began to develop into a relationship. I thought it was time to get a divorce from Maria, who apparently was now married for the third time. Bernie Symonds, my lawyer, hired a private detective to locate her but she wouldn't accept the writ – don't ask me why. I was taken to the divorce court in London; it was painless, and over in five minutes. Although that's an understatement, as to renege on a commitment never feels good and marriage is a relationship that creates links that won't wipe out, whatever.

Shortly after this I was told I was to be transferred to Coldingley, a Grade C, recently built, industrial prison, just outside of London. The idea, there, is to get cons into the habit of regular work. I couldn't see the logic of it. I didn't have a release date and didn't have the temperament to be another brick. I would have preferred to stay in Albany where I could take a few liberties and be tolerated. However, an assistant governor in charge of A wing told me that I would get a little money to spend in Coldingley, and a two-hour open visit every two weeks, and I could also buy a letter a day. If I didn't take the offer, they would throw away the key. Coldingley was just a few miles south-west of London, easy for visits, and Val and I were interested in each other – and I wouldn't have to go via Wandsworth.

I was in Coldingley for three months before being ghosted to Gartree, in the Midlands.

There were three maximum security prisons in the country at that time, and all having internal problems. They were claustrophobic and restrictive, and when I arrived at Gartree there was only one functional wing. The others had been wrecked in a recent disturbance and were undergoing repairs. There were a few guys there who had been framed for serious offences, like the 'Birmingham Six', convicted for an IRA pub bombing who first the police and then some screws beat the s**t out of when they were arrested, six average Irishmen returning to Belfast on the ferry after attending a reunion, on the day following the pub bombing. Some years later their innocence was established and all the coppers responsible for framing them got was promotion.

I was given a five-hour-a-day task, in a unit with four other cons, making bolts. The unit operated under two civilian instructors who were seriously not interested in making waves. They showed me what to do, and I sat down on a bench for the next two weeks, doing nothing, looking into the future. There was no provocative aggression, no abuse, no pressure, and my head was on crutches, looking for ways to deal with this. My only real link with the outside world was Val, without whom the system was set on burying me.

Val and I had been corresponding regularly now for over a year, and she visited me every other weekend. I was located on the top landing of the cell block in Gartree, and from my window I could see a field beyond the wire, with a hedgerow bordering the road. On the Saturday afternoon Val was due, I would get a glimpse of her blue Beetle car passing a hole in the hedge. She brought Marion and her friend Abby to visit me just after Christmas, and we sat around a table in the visiting room eating Christmas cake and wearing paper hats.

Before this, after a few weeks in Gartree, the assistant governor running the cell block offered me the task of keeping the wing cooker clean. It was an ordinary domestic electric cooker, used occasionally to heat a tin of beans and, most days, all it needed was dusting, which meant the rest of the day was mine to paint pictures. I wasn't getting special treatment, that's just the way Gartree was at that period. Anything for a quiet life, and not having a bunch of discontented Category A prisoners tearing the place up. Bad publicity was not good for the control image, and led to politicians asking questions. A psychologist was brought into the prison – not for the cons, for the screws.

That reminds me, I haven't told you how we used to make alcoholic brews for Saturday night parties; where a group of us would sit around in one of the cells drinking this often potent brew, smoking dope and occasionally splitting a couple of LSDs; listening to good music and telling stories. In its fashion it was an exclusive group, in another time.

Back at Gartree, there was a two hour art class in the evening once a week, with a young tutor called Reg Cartwright, not long out of college. He painted in a style we called 'modern English'. He was a great guy, and would bring in canvasses he was working on for various magazines and we would discuss them and he'd show us how he developed his pictures. Reg only did one term, then moved on into book illustration, and the last I heard he was doing good. (Next time I'm in one of the major book shops I'll find one of his books.)

He came in with a painting, one day, of a brick house he was working on, and he showed me how he painted the bricks. I started painting street scenes with lots of bricks in, so I decided to paint streets and buildings in and around the Elephant and Castle, where I used to knock around in my mid-teens. I now feel that the late '40s and early '50s were my 'period', as we all have a special period in our lives. I'd paint them as they were then, bricks and houses and bomb sites, in bright and warm colours. In the London Council Photographic Archives they have photos of every London street, back to the early days of photography, and Val would go there and get copies that I could use as models for my paintings.

Then one day, I had an informal interview with Brian Howden, the man in control of 'lifers' at the Home Office. There were 300–400 people serving life, and the number was growing as the length of time a lifer served was growing. He was on a tour of inspection, and I met him on the staircase with the governor. He had been a deputy some years earlier and I knew his face. He asked me how I was and why I couldn't cope with Coldingley, and I told him that, for me, it was negative, nothing to offer and that it didn't make any sense. I was doing time for a bunch of crooked coppers, what more did the system want from me? 'What do you want to do with your life?' he asked. 'You will be up for parole next year, and you won't get parole from here.'

'Well, I'll apply to go to art college.'

'Get yourself some qualifications and see how you go.' he said, leaving me with the impression that he wasn't just another condescending hostile.

Nine months later, with a grade A in Art 'A' Level, I applied for a place at Camberwell College of Art and was offered an interview. I wasn't allowed to attend the college, so that was the end of that. I'd try again. Val was being brilliant, and becoming as unpopular with the Home Office as I was. Our relationship grew and I was reviewed again for parole.

The parole system had come into existence late in the sixties, and functioned on two levels, local and national. First the local board, mainly personnel from the prison, who sent their recommendations to the national board who, in turn, in the case of lifers, sent their recommendations to the Lifers' Department at the Home Office where the Home Secretary made the final decision. This process took anything up to eighteen months; the average was around nine. The pattern was that a lifer would be given a release date one year hence, and during that year he would be allowed out to work in a normal job, pretty much the same as the hostel scheme at Pentonville.

It was something I hadn't thought about, and this was now my third parole review. I saw the whole procedure as yet another rip-off for me. Another insult. Since murderers were expected to show remorse for their killings when under parole review, and give the impression they won't do it again, but where did that leave me, who wasn't guilty of murder? And I knew where my assessors were coming from, and I also knew that that was the only route out.

Back in Gartree, the landing screws used one of the cells as an office where they kept an occurrence book to record who was friendly with who and what mood various cons were in. They also kept a mini-file of each con's records. I can't remember who nicked the files, but Charlie Kray gave me mine one day and said he only had it for an hour, so I had to skip through a lot of it. My advice to you is never read garbage that others write about you. There were observations and recommendations in this file coming from another planet, written by the same people who would be writing parole reports – totally out of touch.

I was having a problem with a varicose vein, and was transferred to Wormwood Scrubs Prison in London for treatment. I would be there for about a month, and had been there about a week when I was taken to the governor's office. I was told that, on my return to Gartree, I would be transferred to Leyhill open prison in the West Country – and reviewed again for parole after being there for a year.

From Wormwood Scrubs to Gartree to Wandsworth to Leyhill took a month.

The prison bus went on a Wednesday. It was in fact an ordinary coach, hired each week for the occasion, and it did the rounds from London to various prisons in the West Country. I knew nothing of Leyhill, and knew no one who had ever been there. As I got on the bus to leave Wandsworth, unhandcuffed for the first and last time, all I could tell you was that it didn't have a fence around it, and it was where the middle and upper classes did their time; doctors, solicitors, magistrates, county councillors, estate agents and all the ranks of coppers from constable to commander from Scotland Yard, and I would meet them all there.

The clothes I wore on this trip were my own, those that I had been wearing when I was nicked in Corsham. They may have been

a little out of date, but not for me. The quality was rich, the style
was right and they felt comfortable and good. Styles and fashions
and street life had stopped for me eighteen years earlier, everything had changed – women were driving cars – it was somehow
different. There were a few guys on the coach, maybe half a dozen,
going to Bristol prison, a few miles from Leyhill. They were cuffed
together in front and I sat alone in the back, looking at the countryside – sweeping green fields and miles of motorway that hadn't
been there before – and feeling rather strange. And by the time
the coach came off the country road into the driveway of Leyhill,
I was the only one left on board – and the place really *didn't* have
a fence!

At the reception unit I changed into prison overalls and I was
signed in. Then, a screw led me across the yard into a long corridor
that fed into wards, and in one of these wards I was shown a cubicle
containing a bed and a small cupboard and was told it was where
I would sleep. He then handed me over to the con who was the
ward orderly and suggested he show me around the place.

Leyhill was built in the Second World War – early 1940 – as a field
hospital for the US navy. A bunch of single storey units around a
circular drive, with a cluster of eight wards in the centre, two rows
of four, linked by a wide central cover corridor. Double swing doors
opposite each other opened into another short corridor with three
treatment rooms on the left, two ore and a wash and shower room
on the right. Then a second set of doors leading into the main ward,
a long rom with fifteen curtained cubicles on each side, no bars on
the windows, no locks on the doors, and a cooker to brew on.

The ward orderly's name was Dick Reid, a lifer with six weeks
to do before going to a working hostel in Bristol, and then out on
parole. We had known each other in Parkhurst years earlier. He had
been sentenced to fourteen years PD at that time, had appealed and
was given life, and now he was finishing. I always felt he was a bit of
a rough and ready loner, and wherever here was, he didn't belong.
He had been in Leyhill for eighteen months, and worked on the
arboretum, a small forest of trees from different parts of the world
that was part of the private estate leased by the Home Office for the
prison department.

We wandered around and chatted, Dick pointing out the various units and what they were used for, and we walked over a wooden bridge and into the arboretum. Had I been alone, I would have felt completely lost. The silence was different, and the squawk of a protesting blackbird reminded me of the one I would hear in the mornings when I was in the death cell – sharp and angry – one sound, one thought leads to another; not all of them welcome. Dick and I would meet up again in this spot two years on, with a pale moon giving just a glimmer of light and a heavy plastic bag full of goodies …

There was a roll-call three times a day, morning, noon and evening – 'stand-by-your-bed' style. There was a screw for each wing who had other jobs and who you only saw at roll-calls. Dick was the only con I knew in the place. He had gone from Parkhurst to Wakefield Prison in Yorkshire, and stayed there until he was moved to Leyhill. There weren't many lifers in the place, and apart from me, all had come from Wakefield. Dick knew them all, and most of them were in their early and mid-twenties, first offenders, for stabbing someone. The average time in Leyhill was eighteen months for a lifer, in lifer's language it was a phasing-out period.

I left Dick, to walk around on my own; to look at the football field, the tennis court and the bowling green and feel the sense of space. I turned back into the corridor and, within a few yards, I was lost. I didn't know what door to turn in or what ward to look for. When you haven't walked alone in an open field for almost a lifetime, the whole scene becomes an experience.

The following day, I went through the normal routine of being seen by the governor and just about everybody else, and given the job of keeping my ward clean. It was a nothing job, since there was always someone being given sedentary labour by the prison doctor and then their task would be to assist the ward cleaner, so we sat around all day playing cards and drinking tea and getting bored, and four months passed before I became assistant to a civilian carpenter who worked on maintenance.

In many ways the place had a lingering air of the old boys' club about it. There was a camp council elected every year in an organised poll. The current chairman was an ex-headmaster –

a paedophile, and keen rugby player – and every Saturday morning at ten, there was a council meeting to discuss affairs and make decisions; all taken very seriously. The chairman would meet once a week with the governor – the control behind the crown. Somewhere in the distant past, the council had written a constitution laying out the conditions of the various clubs within the place.

The clubs, in turn, each had a chairman and a secretary and treasurer, just like Manchester United. There were about a dozen clubs – from rugby to drama, from debating to music and what-have-you. You paid a small fee from your prison earnings to be a member, and each member would be allowed out into the community for club functions. Four times a year – debating the Bristol University students' union; or watching plays in the city theatres, or opera and ballet at the Hippodrome; and orchestral concerts in the Guildhall. I joined them all, and would exploit them all at every opportunity.

You had to be in Leyhill for a couple of months to get on the outside activities list, and it took me that long to integrate and get into the way of things and gain enough confidence to make the most of what was on offer. The few lifers in the place, in various wards, were mostly low-profile, and keen to get early parole and pass through unnoticed, so they would only join the football and rugby teams, or the 'rehab club' – to join this one you had to be serving a long sentence, and lifers had to be in Leyhill for six months before they could participate fully and be allowed out into the community on their own to do organised voluntary work.

The rehab club held a two hours' social meeting every Wednesday evening in the visiting rooms by the Gate Lodge, with a regular group of students from Bristol University who would come to Leyhill in a minibus, to chat and drink tea, and be friendly and adventurous enough to stretch the rules and stay within the boundaries. Over a period, we did all that and I became good friends with several, a bit at a time.

You see what I mean, the place was a 'country club' for the rich and famous. Cabinet ministers and nobility had done their time there, and governing bodies have a knack of taking care of their own; from the courts to Leyhill without ever seeing the inside of a prison cell, the old pals act had created a prison of few hardships.

Dick left, and I moved into his room and spent the major part of the days painting pictures and scheming. There were about forty rooms in the wards altogether. There was a waiting list, and the rooms were given to the cons who had served the longest time – which put me automatically on top of the list. I did about a month in the cubicle, and several in Dick's old room before becoming the carpenter's assistant, and so a lot of the time I was able to make picture frames.

Visiting was easier now for Val, a ninety minute drive down the motorway on a Saturday afternoon and served tea and biscuits. Val and I became closer. Then, in the New Year, she got a job as head of English in a new comprehensive school that was about to open in Bristol. She bought a house beside the park in the old village of Keynsham, thirty minutes' drive from Leyhill and fifteen minutes from work. I applied, and was offered, a place at Bristol Poly to do a three year art course but I was not allowed to take it up, so I got up a few noses, and took liberties, and played the game when I had to.

The only legitimate way I was getting out of prison was via the parole board, and the rights or wrongs of the conviction were not part of the criteria. I was convicted of murder, but hadn't killed anyone; nevertheless, admissions of guilt along with signs of remorse greatly influenced the people who made decisions – which rather handicaps the innocent. Recent history has shown that the innocent tend to serve longer than the guilty.

I had been in Leyhill for just over eighteen months when I was told I had been refused for parole and I would be reviewed again in another year. (Val and I had been vaguely hopeful, and were now disappointed.) It was unusual for lifers in Leyhill to be laid over for a second review, and I knew we were not flavour of the month with the Home Office. Val had a long-standing close friend, who had a friend who was a private secretary – very close to the Home Secretary – and he told Val's friend that the parole board had approved my release but the Home Secretary had turned it down. There was a report in my file on Val, which said she had spent the night with Fred the locksmith, who had recently been released, hence rendering our relationship suspect and Val's character iffy. I had asked Val to see Fred for me shortly after he got out of jail, and it appears he was under surveillance, we subsequently learned, by the recently formed 'Criminal Intelligence Team'. The head of this newly formed unit was Brian Moore, once the partner of Frank Williams. He was with Williams on both the occasions I was arrested and travelled with me to Tooting Police Station. He was one of the two guys who dropped out and let another take his place, to give false evidence of a conversation that had never happened.

Val had visited Fred shortly after finishing work and left after a couple of hours. Whether or not she'd been observed leaving, we'll never know. She certainly never spent the night there, and the inference from the intelligence report has more to say about whoever wrote it than what it implied about Val.

Val was now in the West Country, and making friends with a guy named Don Eatherden and his family. Don and his wife, Anita, had lived in Herne Hill in south London, just around the corner from the pet shop I worked in when I left school. Don and I were about the same age, and we had both grown up in the same culture. He believed in forming his own opinions of people and not getting bogged down in official garbage. He worked for the probation service in the area that Val now lived in. He was officially my case officer, and the only probation officer I had ever met who lived in the real world, although my knowledge of probation officers is very limited as I've only met a few. Don and his wife also ran a small art gallery just outside Bath, and I had a couple of exhibitions there. Don came to see me one day in Leyhill and we gradually became very good friends. In the years that followed I never once went to his office – my conviction was a fraud and I wouldn't report to anyone.

Across the entrance drive to Leyhill was a barrier for in and outgoing traffic, and on either side of this, a long single-storied building. The one on the right was the gate lodge and the officers' social club, while the opposite one was the visiting room, tables, chairs and a small kitchen. This area was out of bounds unless you had a reason to be there. It was to the visiting room on a Wednesday evening that the regular group of students came from Bristol University. They were all members of the Haddock Club at the Students' Union who did a weekly round of community services. I had joined the rehab club after a couple of weeks, and walked down to the visiting room with a couple of other cons, not knowing quite what to expect.

There were six girls, aged eighteen–twenty, and two guys about the same age. Their minibus arrived around 6.30 p.m., and would leave again about 8.30 p.m., and there were no guards around to ruin the atmosphere. It was all very strange, these young people from another age, coming into a prison as if the place was a social club. I was more than twice their age, though I didn't really feel I was from an older generation. I guess we were all, in our own ways, experiencing something different.

They broke up into sets of twos and threes and sat down at the tables, and any cons who were members of the rehab club would wander in. There never seemed to be more than ten cons interested, as most spent the evenings watching the telly. I sat down at a vacant table with a new friend named Graham, a twenty-one-year-old lifer who had stabbed and killed another boy when he was sixteen. He was very subdued and reserved, and quite a good painter of horses and western scenes. The three girls sitting on the next table were as hesitant about talking as we were, but kept looking our way and smiling. One of them was dressed like an Indian squaw that you would expect to see in an old Hollywood western, but without a feather. She reminded me of Minnie Ha-Ha from *Hiawatha*, which she thought was very funny when we finally got chatting. Then, over the coming months we all got to know each other.

Most Wednesday evenings we talked about the different clubs within the prison, and what we could do to make them function more usefully, and what events the students could organise outside that cons from Leyhill could attend, linked through the various clubs. Over several months I got a music club going and an art club, mostly made up of lifers, who never attended the weekly meetings required by the constitution to qualify for a related event in a concert hall. The weekly meetings would last five minutes and would go through the motions, and I was elected chairman of these clubs and then the debating society, because the chairman always went out.

Each club had to arrange its own activities, so I would arrange a trip to the theatre and buy a row of seats which each member paid towards – and always book one too many. An assistant governor would drive ten of us on these trips in the prison minibus, and I would give him a ticket for one end of the row, and sit at the other end next to the empty seat. Val would buy a ticket and when the lights went down, sit beside me and I would hope it went unnoticed. When we went to the opera or the ballet at Saturday matinee, some of the students from the Wednesday group would join us and they would arrange invitations to students' art shows at the Students Union, and things were happening. We were stretching the rules, and sometimes breaking them, and I was making enemies in the administration and I didn't really care.

Every evening I'd spend a couple of hours with a pal listening to music and getting stoned. Looking back, I know there was too much resentment hidden in me to be submissive to any of my keepers and everything between us was on the surface. The place had a new deputy governor who had been a screw in Liverpool, and to me, he was bad news. He didn't like the freedom of Leyhill, and believed cons should stand to attention and be locked up. I would not have put him in charge of a toilet roll.

Anyway, you go with what you've got. There were only about a dozen screws altogether and most of them were happy with the way things were, as the conditions were easy and the pressures few. But even in heaven there will always be a couple of malcontents wanting to impress the boss. You recognise them, and give them a miss. I remember one named Thomas, in his early twenties, always looking for problems. He took a sunbed away from me one day, when I was laying on it outside my room window. I had recovered it from a rubbish tip belonging to the screws' housing estate on the far side of Leyhill's perimeter. Soon afterwards, I walked down to the duty office in the central corridor where the screws spent most of their time and Thomas was there with a couple of others. I told Thomas he could keep the bed, but if he wanted to make an issue of it, then I'd make an issue of having his car fixed by the con in the prison garage – very much against the rules. I caught the grin on the other screws' faces, and knew they had set him up. I heard no more about it.

I fancy the 'macho' ones amongst the screws all thought I was a bit crazy, because I walked around the place with a smile on my face and never seemed upset. Another time, I was trying to talk a senior screw into taking a group out to help with an old peoples' Christmas party that the students were organising in Bristol and he told me his job was security – to keep prisoners in prison. In a prison with no fences!

On another occasion, this same screw had to write his opinion of me for the local parole board who, in turn, forward their recommendations to the main parole board. I got stoned for that occasion, as I needed that to help control my resentment. There was no love lost between me and this guy, and within a few minutes he was mouthing off, 'If I had my way, I would never let you out.'

'You don't even know what I'm in prison for,' I replied. This screw was a pal of the deputy governor.

I was friendly at that time with a lifer named Ronnie Cooper. He had served most of his time in Wakefield with an old friend of mine, so we had things in common. We enjoyed the same music and smoked the same dope. I've no real idea what he had been convicted of, or if he had any previous form. We were in Leyhill at the same time, so we spent some of it together. His room was the centre one of three, overlooking the sports field in ward eight.

I was in ward six at the end of the long corridor, 40ft below ward eight. The two wards were separated by the circular road, and from 9 p.m., after the final roll call, everyone was voluntarily confined to their wards. Most evenings I spent a few hours in Ron's room, listening to his music. Ron had a link with a mutual friend on the outside, and parcels would occasionally get dropped for collection in the middle of the night. Ron was a fine carpenter and worked with a screw on the estate house which was used for office training. He had an isolation attitude to the world we were in. He wouldn't get involved in anything. He went to work, had his meals, and stayed in his room, where he played his music and smoked his dope, when he had any. He had a fantasy of getting a boat, with built-in panels to stash his cannabis trade, and sailing around the world. He was in Leyhill for eighteen months before getting parole and moving to the working scheme in Bristol Prison. (When lifers got parole, they were told a year in advance, and the last six months were spent on the working scheme in Bristol.)

Val and I had written to each other daily for several years. She never missed an opportunity to visit me, or to protest to all and sundry about the corruption of my conviction. When we were told that I wouldn't be considered for release for another year, we were really feeling the pressure on our relationship. There were people in the system opposed to it, and probably hoped it couldn't survive another long period. Val was attractive, loved cats and hated injustice, and like the rest of us was completely normal!

'What does such an intelligent lady see in you?' asked the assistant governor in Gartree, once, when I was hustling him for an extra visit.

'I've got a big c★★k'

'Isn't that redundant?' he replied, and gave me an extra visit.

I had been in Leyhill for almost two years and I knew what times the moon came up and when the place was in shadow at night, and I learned to see in the dark.

It was the normal practice for a lifer to be allowed out on the 'rehab scheme' after six months in Leyhill. I was there for two years before it was offered to me. I was to help out on jobs for an old lady who lived in a village called Charfield, a mile from the prison., but all she really wanted was a bit of company. Someone to chat to and watch the wrestling on the television with, and she would shout and holler at them all. Her age was catching up with her and we got on fine.

There were ten houses in the village, scattered over half a mile of country road. About 400 yards from the old lady lived a couple with two kids, named Dave and Pat Williams. Dave was the head of maths in the comprehensive school where Val was the head of English. They were colleagues, and had been to visit me in Leyhill. So, during the course of the day as the old lady and I got to know each other, we talked of the Williams', as the old lady knew them both. 'How do you feel about me going over the road to say hello?' I asked her.

'Of course, that's all right,' she said.

'OK, I'll do that next week.' I knew that as long as I let the old lady know where I was the conditions of my day with her weren't broken – stretched a little – but not broken, and for several weeks after that I would go over to Dave Williams' for an hour and Val would phone.

But I was under review again. As a rule, incoming mail was uncensored, which was just as well because the screw doing any censoring was an overweight slob with an out-of-joint mind, who I wouldn't allow to intimidate me. I would leave the workshop about ten in the morning to collect my mail and always with a legitimate excuse, because my appearance every day would get up his nose. It was a Wednesday when he handed me a brown, already-opened envelope – a letter from David Halliwell, who I'd not been in touch with for a while.

David said he had answered his front door a couple of days earlier to an American, who said he was a friend of Bill Owens who had been in Albany with me a few years earlier. Billy was listed as a hippie, international, dope-dealer and he wanted my address. David gave it to this American guy, and that was that, I heard nothing more. The odd thing about the letter was the postmark, several days earlier.

On the Saturday morning I went down to the garage to board the minibus that should deliver me to the old lady, where I was told I wasn't on the list for going out. 'Why not?' I asked.

'Go to the office, they will know,' said the driver. So I went to the office, and they didn't seem to know: 'Come back at two when the senior officer comes on duty.' I went back at 2.30, and he told me he didn't know either.

Val came to see me on the Sunday afternoon. She told me that Dave Williams had phoned her on Thursday night and told her that the deputy governor, with the senior officer, had been to their house in the village to question them about my visits to them. They had first been to see the old lady, who told them that I would sometimes visit the Williams', but she had not told them of the connection between us. So the senior officer and the deputy governor were heavy-handed, asking the Williams' if I had intimidated them or used their phone, or threatened them in any way. David was alarmed by their questioning and attitude, and anxious for me, so he didn't inform them of his relationship with Val and me, and told them nothing.

I was pissed off.

Both the deputy and senior officer were about to have time off, and it was several days before the senior officer was back in his office. 'So why was I taken off last Saturday's list?' I asked the senior screw who was sitting at his desk in the duty room.

'You have been going to people's houses in the village,' he replied.

'I've been to the Williams' house in the village, so what? I've not broken any rules.'

'We'll find out about that,' he replied, 'and you can't go out again until we hear back from the Home Office.' I knew by his stance that he and the deputy were over-the-top and looking for problems.

'The Williams' are friends of mine, and Dave Williams is a colleague of Val's, they teach at the same school, and you were out of order giving them the third degree. You were in their house and you have no authority there.'

'You didn't tell us they are friends of yours,' he replied, looking surprised.

'I don't have to tell you who my friends are, and I have a feeling you are trying to do me some harm.' The following day I saw the assistant governor who was the case worker for lifers. He had returned from a long weekend. He said the deputy governor had sent a report to the Home Office and was awaiting a reply. 'What's the big deal on this? Why is nobody talking to me if you think there is a problem?' I asked.

'I haven't been here for a few days, I'll catch up.'

I went back to the duty office to confront the senior screw. I was calm enough, but angry. I couldn't confront the deputy governor as I didn't have enough control, and instinct warned me that he was looking for a reason to put me back into a closed prison and that it was personal. 'You're trying to make something sinister out of nothing,' I said to the senior screw. 'It's obvious who my enemies are. I need protecting from you and I think I'll not be going out again until I'm released, and you can put that in your report and the reason why.'

A few weeks later I was called to the governor's office where I met the current head of the lifers' department at the Home Office – I've forgotten his name. The governor was behind his desk, and 'top dog' was sitting to the side, and he told me who he was. 'I have bad news for you,' he said. 'You have been turned down for parole, and won't be reviewed again for another two years.'

I'd been hit in the head so many times over the past sixteen years, I could do no more than look at him and take a deep breath. 'That doesn't make any sense.'

'I'm sorry,' he said, 'this decision is above my head and I want to tell you personally, and get your reaction.'

'It doesn't make any sense.' My words were coming slowly, almost to myself. 'I've been here for three years, nobody does that long in this place.'

'I'm sorry, do you want to go to another prison?'

I shook my head. What I needed was some space to take this in. 'No,' I said, 'my partner has moved this way. We've bought a house and the kid's at school. No, I need to take this in, a move would be too much of a disruption. I don't believe this.' They sat there looking at me. 'I've been recommended twice before by the parole board for release and the Home Office has overruled – why?' 'Top dog' was giving me his full attention. What I was saying he could confirm, and he wasn't denying.

'You have enemies,' he said, taking his time. 'If you want to see me any time I visit Leyhill that will be OK.'

'Thanks. I've been refused permission three times to take up college places, twice I've been recommended for parole, now I've got to wait another two years for something to happen, and I'm forced to waste my life in prison because a couple of crooked coppers fabricated evidence that a five-year-old wouldn't believe. I'm not doing so good. It helps me, then I don't have to live other people's lies, and it's how I feel that is important to me. I'm not going out anymore until I'm released and I'm not participating in any further parole reviews, and can I have a phone call to my Probation Officer?' I was too deflated to be angry, and not alert enough to be able to express some of the things that needed saying. I knew this man wasn't among my enemies.

Don Eatherden, my probation officer, came to see me that evening with Val, and we had a couple of hours in the visiting room discussing the prospects. Don had dropped in to see me a few times when passing, and we liked each other. He cut through all the b*****ks and we were friends. I always said I wanted nothing to do with probation officers – inquisitive people who made demands. But somehow, Don was different. He was a nice guy and always came to me like a friend, which he was. Val and I became friends with his family and would often go to their home. Our friendship lasted till he died of leukaemia some years later, long after all supervision of me was lifted. He was disappointed that I wasn't getting out.

I think I became even more spaced out after that, and the next two years, as I try to think of them now, are hard to recall. They blend in with Leyhill as a whole and have no distinction. I spent most of my time in my room painting, listening to music and rolling another joint. Ron dropped off a lump of resin big enough to last a year, and I switched off and became more laid back. Val and I made arrangements so that we could meet and spend time together, when the moon was in the right spot, and clouds covered the sky and the fields were in shadow.

I would go to the dining room to eat and to the workshop to make picture frames and spend a few hours – being there – and over all, becoming part of the fixtures.

One day, walking down the corridor I saw two cons coming towards me. They had been around a week or two, and I knew who they were although we were never formally introduced. They were part of a larger group of recent CID members, convicted of corruption at Scotland Yard. They came to Leyhill straight from the Old Bailey. One was ex-Detective Commander Virgo – early sixties, skinny as a rasher and beady-eyed. The other, ex-Detective Bill Moody, was in his late forties with the stance of a thug and known for whacking suspects, planting evidence, and taking bribes. An all-round nasty guy, who thought he was invincible.

I had originally heard of these two from Jimmy Humphreys on the sports field at Gartree a few years earlier. Humphreys was doing eight years for GBH. He had whacked a guy for screwing his wife, and was very p****d off because Virgo and Moody couldn't give him any help. Apparently the CID who nicked Humphreys were at loggerheads with Moody and his crowd, and didn't like Humphreys because their fingers weren't in the Humphreys' pie – internal affairs. Humphreys had gained the title of 'King of Soho Porn' because he ran a small chain of dirty book shops in Soho. Virgo was the head of the vice squad, and Humphreys was paying Virgo two thousand a month for protection. So, Humphreys had the hump and was in the process of appeal. He had kept diaries of all his meetings and payments to Virgo and Moody and tape recordings of conversations, and was doing a deal on his appeal. Virgo and Moody and several others were in the shit. Their only interest to me was curiosity.

As they approached, Virgo kept his head down but Moody looked at me and smiled. 'How you doing?' I said, full of brotherly love, and stopped. Virgo kept his head down and walked out, but Moody stayed.

'I'm surprised you're still here,' he said.

'So am I. Tell me something, did you know Frank Williams when he was on the flying squad?'

'Yeah, I've worked with him.'

'What about his old partner, a dark-haired guy, used to wear a brown suit?'

'Brian Moore, he's now head of Criminal Intelligence.'

'Is that right?' I said, walking on, and that's how I discovered who the guy was who nicked me with Williams. Moore never gave evidence, another guy took his place.

Then, in May 1980 I was told to report to the admin office where a magistrate on the local parole board wanted to see me. Because I wouldn't participate in a current parole review, I can't remember much about it now, except for telling the guy that parole decisions would be made whether I participated or not, and that it was no disrespect to him and I wasn't being bloody-minded; and these reviews take an average of nine months and then a release date is set for a year later. My conviction was not for killing someone – it was the result of an oral admission the police decided to make for me, eighteen years ago, and nothing has changed.

August – three months later

The schools were on holiday. Val was at home, and she had her mum down with her for a week. It was Thursday, and her mum was staying till Monday.

Around midmorning a screw from the discipline office came to the workshop and told me that an assistant governor (AG) wanted to see me in his office. This AG was late twenties, a graduate with all the indications of remaining normal. One of his responsibilities was for the dozen or so lifers in the place and we had a mutual respect for each other. 'It's your lucky day,' he said, as I entered his office.

'You are to be released as soon as it's administratively possible.' He smiled at me.

'Oh!' It had to happen, but I wasn't yet expecting it and felt no excitement. 'What exactly does "administratively possible" mean?'

'Well, I hope it means what it says,' he smiled again. 'We have been notified, and the licence has to be signed and sent to us from the Home Office but as soon as we receive it, you can go.'

'How long do you reckon that will take?'

'Hopefully not long. You get five days home leave as of now, and I'll get onto admin and see if we can arrange it for tomorrow, it's too late for today.'

'Yeah, OK.' My head was in overdrive, and hadn't been functioning correctly for a while. 'I think maybe we ought to wait until next week.' I didn't explain to him that Val's mum was with her till Monday, and we wouldn't want her around. 'I need some space, and a few days won't matter.'

'All right,' he said, giving me his full concentration. He didn't know about Val's mum and seemed puzzled by my reaction. He must have thought I was really laid back. 'Come and see me this afternoon and we'll sort something out.'

Val collected me at 8.00 a.m. on Tuesday morning. Marion had gone to stay with her friends in the next village, so time was our own. Then, on Wednesday, we arranged to get married in Bath, a few miles down the road, at 2.00 p.m. on 1 September – three weeks away, and the day the school opened to start a new year. The schools open on the first day for staff only, and then only in the morning so Val would be free by noon. We had no idea whether or not my release would be through by then, but we would find out. Val dropped me back at Leyhill at 5.00 p.m. on Friday and, at 9.30 on Monday morning, I was at the duty office in administration asking if my release was through. It could only come with the post. I would go from there to the assistant governor's office and ask him to call his contact at the Home Office. He never got fed up with me like everybody else did.

It was now Friday morning. I was getting married on Monday and nothing was happening. I went to the workshop to see Ben, the civilian carpenter whose bag I sometimes carried, and I made a cup of tea. I had been with Ben for almost four years and we had a good relationship. At 9.30 a.m. I was about to set off on the morning round of enquiries when two screws came from the discipline office and said they had to take me to my room for a strip search. It was the governor's long weekend, and 'my friend' the deputy was running the place. I couldn't remember the last time my room was searched. I didn't have any dialogue with these two, although I could tell one of them wasn't completely comfortable as they took the room apart. They were doing what they had been told to do, and only the governor of the day could give that order. 'You OK now?' I said to the two screws, as they left the room and headed off down the corridor. I followed them a little way and picked up my small piece of resin. Me, and my room, were always clean unless I was smoking a joint, and then the room was locked. To be careless would have been a disaster. But I was convinced the whole scene would do me less harm being stoned, than it would sober, and by the time I got to the administration office I was philosophical.

As I turned into the office corridor I saw the chief officer coming out of the governor's office at the other end. He saw me – I'd caught him by surprise – he hesitated, and did a double-take. 'Is my release through?' I called down the corridor.

'Wait there,' he said, disappearing back into the governor's office. And I knew it was, by his reaction; and I fancied he had ducked back into the office to check out whether or not I'd been searched, and to find out what the next move was to be, because they could have sat on it over the weekend and been answerable to no one while the deputy was at the helm. 'Come with me,' said the chief, re-emerging. 'From now on two officers will be with you at all times. You are to empty your room, go to the reception and change into your own clothes, and be back here in an hour. Use the phone. You can be picked up any time after that.'

Val was washing the kitchen floor, and would be along when she was done – we had all the time in the world.

Afterword by Val Thatcher

The advert in *The New Statesman* in 1974 read something like: '231468, lifer and aspiring dramatist and artist, George Thatcher, seeks new outlets through correspondence and visits.'

My partner had died suddenly two years previously, and I was feeling very sorry for myself. So, on an impulse, I decided to answer. I got a reply from the playwright, David Halliwell, who had befriended George several years before and who was filtering the letters for him. We arranged to meet in a pub in Wimbledon near where I lived. By now, I was feeling rather nervous and wondering what I had got myself into. David had said he would be wearing a green carnation, so I would know him, but despite the lack of the carnation and the noise and darkness of the pub, I recognised him. He told me a bit about George, including the fact that he had always claimed his innocence, and also told me that someone in prison was not allowed to correspond with people he had not known before his conviction, so I would have to write as if I knew him. This first glimpse of the prison world interested me, because I wondered how someone was supposed to lead a different and positive life if he was only allowed to associate with people he had known before he was imprisoned.

So, I wrote to George, at Albany Prison on the Isle of Wight – and received no reply. By now I was angry with the system because, in forbidding George's communication with the outside world, the prison service was also forbidding me communication with him and I could not see any reason why they could do that. I wrote to the prison governor to this effect and he called George in. Apparently George had never received my letter, but the governor agreed to allow our correspondence, and George was impressed enough by my persistence to write back to me.

We wrote for some weeks. Our early letters were about the lives we were leading. I was a teacher in London, on my own with a ten-year-old daughter. George wrote about his early life, his father's death during the war, growing up in Marlow and then moving to London and being bombed out. His teenage years were spent in Kennington in south London after the war, and he was one of the 'lads' – Ronnie Biggs was another.

He sounded a very normal person, and his letters showed a sensitivity which I hadn't been expecting. Then I plucked up the courage to visit him, on 7 July 1974. Crossing the ferry to the Isle of Wight I felt as if I was crossing to another land. I had not been to the island since a childhood holiday many years before, but this trip had a different purpose, and I had a premonition that I was doing something irrevocable. I took the ferry across and then a taxi to the prison.

In 1974, security was much laxer than it is today but, as a visitor to a prisoner, I had an immediate sense of being treated by the prison personnel as if I were on the 'other side', that of the prisoners. I found this difficult, as I had been brought up to believe that prisons were full of criminals who were 'bad' people. Instinctively, I felt I was on the side of officialdom, not the other side.

I went into the little visiting room with the other visitors and sat down. The prisoners filed in, all dressed alike in striped blue shirts and jeans. George had told me where to sit and I had sent him a photo of me, so he saw me straightaway. I remember the first thing he said to me was, 'Well, you're better looking than your photo anyway!' He is a tall, good-looking man, and he put me at my ease immediately, sensing my nervousness. We were allowed two hours, which went by very quickly and we found a lot to talk about – my life as a teacher and single parent, and his conviction. Going back home, I had a lot to think about and a lot of readjustments to make. I was still sceptical that George could have been wrongly convicted and sentenced to death. I thought that that sort of thing just didn't happen. Yet, he seemed such a genuine person and I liked him.

We continued to write; and I visited the island several times, until George was sent to a prison on the mainland, in Surrey. Gradually, we grew closer and closer as we got to know and trust each other, and I realised that his future and eventual release was very important to us both. George had already been turned down for parole several times, but I became convinced that parole was going to be the only way in which he could get out of prison.

Police corruption was not something most people believed in, even in the seventies, and the police had fabricated the only evidence that had been brought against him. Over the remaining six years of his imprisonment, I and others tried hard to get both individuals and organisations interested in George's case – Lord Longford, Laurie Taylor, the Burnbake Trust, PROP (Police Reform Organising Project), the Howard League, Arthur Koestler, Malcolm Muggeridge. I approached lawyers, including Rock Tansey and Geoffrey Robertson, now a QC; journalists such as Angela Singer, Malcolm Dean and Bel Mooney; and broadcasters like Gerry Northam.

David Halliwell directed a play that George had written about his time in the condemned cell, *The Only Way Out*, and it was produced at the Royal Court Theatre in Sloane Square.

I handed Roy Jenkins, who was then Home Secretary, a letter which pleaded for George's release, and he spoke to NACRO (National Association for the Care and Resettlement of Offenders). Granada TV started to film a programme about George, including showing one of his co-accused confessing to the murder of which George had been convicted, but it was suddenly, and unaccountably, halted.

I met and talked to two of his co-defendants, Phil Kelly and Johnny Hilton, who was again in prison, and I met other people who had belonged to the criminal world, which was gradually becoming less strange and less the 'other' side to me. But, again and again, George was given a knockback for parole and we were both getting more and more frustrated by a system that seemed to allow no room for change, and which was punishing me as well as George.

After three years, he was moved to an open prison and occasionally allowed out, with an escorted group. But once again he was turned down for parole. We had to find a way to be together.

The only time I remembered ever having broken the law was when I was told off by a policeman for cycling on the pavement when I was nine years old. But, after a lot of persuasion and a lot of misgivings, I agreed to meet George at night. He would climb out and cross the fields in the darkness, avoiding the patrols which went round at easily predictable times – although we once had to hide in a ditch when they came round unexpectedly. There was never a time when I wasn't afraid; we both had too much to lose. He would lift me over the dry stone wall between the road and the fields and we would double back to the Nissen hut which was his room. I would stay with him for an hour or two, and then we would repeat the performance in reverse. If I was in his room when the guards came round to check on him, I would hide in a chest he had built 'for storage' at the end of his bed, lying there terrified and still. Once, we were taken by surprise and he had to lie on top of me, as I tried hard not to breathe.

Occasionally, I would stay there the whole weekend. A trusted friend would drive me to within a mile of the prison and pick me up again. We knew we had to be careful as there was too much at stake for both of us.

Then George was turned down for parole again. This was very unusual after someone had been in an open prison for some time. We were losing our nerve about meeting up as we had been doing, and were both in despair about what we could do. Suddenly, and soon afterwards, out of the blue, the governor of the prison phoned me up and asked me to come in and meet him. This was unheard of as I had always been treated by all prison staff as if, by association, I was guilty in some way.

I went into the governor's office full of trepidation. There was another man in the room, whose name the governor did not tell me. He was a member of the parole board, and he told me that at their last meeting George should not have been turned down, but that there was one member of the board who had argued very strongly against George's release. If George put in for parole again immediately (normally lifers had to wait at least a year before being considered again), then parole would be granted.

George, who had been turned down so often, was sceptical. He had no trust in the system or in anyone's word. We knew, too, that any parole hearing would take nearly a year before the result was sent down the line. In addition, lifers who were granted a release date were always given one a year in advance, to give them time to accustom themselves to the outside world. So, even if he were to be granted parole, it would not be for something like two more years. But he did eventually agree to try one last time.

The only alternative we could see was for him to escape, but that would have meant that we would have to be apart for a long time before I would be in a position to join him. I had a daughter, who was still growing up. My post would have been opened, and my phone would have been tapped in order for the authorities to try and find out George's whereabouts. For him, too, escape would have been a very risky business.

However, to our astonishment, the answer came through in a few weeks and it was 'yes'. Not only 'yes' but George was to be released 'as soon as was administratively convenient'. He was allowed to my home for a weekend visit and, during that time, we booked our wedding. We got married on 1 September 1980, and tried not to let anyone know, as we were anxious to avoid a fuss, but all the friends who had supported us both through our time of waiting turned up to the registry office. They came back to our house, and we had a party that lasted well into the night.

So our life together began. In 1994, we moved to Ireland and bought a dilapidated house which George restored for us. We now live in the wilds of County Kerry, where we can see the mountains over the valley and hear the ravens croaking overhead in the garden. We have finally managed to find peace and contentment.